This book is

- You've read all the "self-help" books you can handle, but nothing ever seems to change.

- You feel like you deserve so much more in life, but don't know why you don't have it.

- You wonder why everyone else seems to have it so easy and why life seems so much tougher for you.

- You feel you don't deserve your current situation; negative things just seem to keep happening to you.

- You feel generally stuck in life and not sure how to move forward.

- You feel like a spectator in your own life.

- You don't celebrate what you already have and you don't take ownership of the negative things you know you are responsible for.

- You believe luck and fairness exist.

- You want techniques, strategies and real world advice to take control of your life RIGHT NOW, not theory and platitudes.

You will learn:

- How to determine what you deserve. **Chapter 15**
- Why you don't deserve more than you already have. **Chapter 2**
- How deserve is about serving others and adding value. (to deserve is to serve) **Chapter 3**
- How to differentiate between desire and deserve. **Chapter 20**
- The factors that create your internal blueprint for what you feel you deserve. **Chapter 14**
- The difference between planners and settlers. **Chapter 1**
- Why luck is never a factor. **Chapter 13**
- The power of Gewüsst Wie. **Chapter 11**
- How to use the Circles of Truth. **Chapter 15**
- How Selfmore is the new selfless. **Chapter 3**
- Why Apple is more valuable than Google. **Chapter 1**
- How to un-deserve the things you don't want. **Chapter 19**
- ...and much more.

Praise for
YOU DESERVE IT

Greg W.
Great self-help books just seem to make sense and this is one of them. It requires reader's honesty and with that it motivates you to take control of your situation and empowers you to make a lot of positive changes to your life. If you're unsatisfied with a part of your life at the moment, read this book and take action to live the life you want to live.

Charlie S.
I have often viewed self-help books with a certain belligerence, but You Deserve It is written in such a way that I felt compelled to challenge some of my indoctrinations. If this book resonates with you the way it has with me you'll take action and you'll change your life. What have you got to lose?

Michael A.
You Deserve It will fundamentally alter the way in which you view your life and the consequences of your own actions. This book taught me that I am a product of my own decisions and past actions. Whilst many realise this at a superficial level have any of us ever truly internalised that fact? Or more importantly altered the way in which we live our lives to better control the outcomes we seek and the environment in which we live? Many of us have all the tools and skills we need to be successful, what we lack is the mindset of success. I believe this book is the answer so many of us seek.

To Marian

You deserve it!

James

Take responsibility. Take action. Change your life.

YOU DESERVE IT

James Newell

© James Newell 2016

The right of James Newell to be identified as the author of this work has been asserted in accordance with the Copyright, Designs and Patents Act 1988.

This book is subject to international copyright and may not be copied in any way without the prior written permission of the publishers.

www.youdeservethisbook.com

*For my wife Alice, and for my children.
I hope to make you as proud of me as I am of you.*

To my mother and my brother, thank you for everything.

Instead of regret, there will be understanding.

Instead of forgetfulness, there will be knowledge and acknowledgement.

Instead of guilt or shame, there will be acceptance and learning.

Instead of hoping, there will be appropriate action.

Instead of blame, there will be responsibility.

Accept what is gone.

Appreciate what remains.

Look forward to what's coming.

YOU DESERVE IT

Contents

Warning 1
Disclaimer 2
Introduction 4
My story 6
1 – Let it bleed 19
2 – Looking at the stars from the gutter. 38
3 – McDonald's 55
4 – Modelling 73
5 – Casualty/Causality 84
6 – Surprise! 98
7 - Conviction 110
8 – The girl at the bar 120
9 – You are right 131
10 – It's not fair 145
11 – Gewüsst Wie 159
12 – Ennui 180
13 – Lucky tattoo 193
14 – Let it be 205
15 – Circles of Truth 223
16 – Be afraid: a case study 244
17 – FOMO: a case study 258
18 – Funnelling 269
19 – Unsubscribe 280
20 – Confusion 292
Conclusion 302

Your questions answered 307
Glossary 309
The Five Principles 321
Acknowledgements 323
About the Author 324

Warning

This is not a get rich quick book, nor is it a paint by numbers, step by step guide to getting everything you want in life. If only it were that simple.

This is a book which looks deep into the concept of "deserving" things, in a bid to identify how to harness this concept in your own life.

We will look at the principles of YOU DESERVE IT and the techniques and exercises which will spur you on, but at no point will you not be responsible for your own progress. As you will learn, being responsible will be a defining part of your success.

The subject matter can be brutal at times. It's meant to be. I am reporting back on the harsh realities of life and of how it operates. Whilst I didn't make the rules, I understand from first-hand experience that they must be obeyed if you are to succeed, however harsh or "unfair" it appears.

Using my life experiences as the main example, I will demonstrate how it's possible to go from everything you have to everything you want. It took me commitment, hard work, persistence and a lot of guesswork to get to where I am.

You too will have to put in commitment, hard work and persistence; this book aims to remove the guesswork.

The following pages will serve as a guide on your journey to everything you want. It's definitely not easy, but it's definitely worth it.

Enjoy the journey.

youdeservethisbook.com

Disclaimer

The term "YOU DESERVE IT" is emotive. It can be positive, but it can also be damaging. As such, a disclaimer is needed to set the record straight before any conclusions are jumped to. The book, James' story and the intention are positive. It's about learning what you deserve, what you don't deserve and how to deserve more of what you want from life. It's not about blaming, shaming or pointing fingers. There is one thing to make truly clear to all readers of this book:

Some things in life, such as illness, accidents and the death of loved ones are truly not deserved.

If you have anything truly terrible happen to you, such as the above, then you truly don't deserve it. I lost a parent to suicide and nearly died in the tsunami; neither situation I could influence, thus neither situation I deserved to be in.

You can't deserve something you can't influence.

What you do deserve is your reaction to the situation, your decision about what to do about it. If I had turned to drink and drugs to cope with my life events I would have deserved the result of my actions as an alcoholic / drug user. I could point the blame for my addictions at my life events but it wouldn't have been the tsunami's fault, nor my father's. The responsibility would lay with me. And that's the point.

It's not what happens to you, it's what you do about it.

There is always a choice to be made. If you don't like something you can change it, if you can't change it you can change the way you think about it.

As you will learn, there is no such thing as "luck" or "fairness", just a series of events to which we seek to attach meaning. Taking responsibility for your actions towards that which you can influence

youdeservethisbook.com

and taking responsibility for how you react to the things you can't influence are at the centre of YOU DESERVE IT.

youdeservethisbook.com

Introduction

Welcome!

Have you ever felt as though you deserve more from life? Do you feel as though life "owes" you and can't understand why despite your best efforts you just can't seem to break through?

Have bad things happened to you, or even good things and you wondered how you ever deserved them?

Why do some people seem to deserve it all and others never seem to get a "break"? Isn't it time you got what you deserved?

These were the questions I asked myself when I began my journey. The answers changed my life, and I hope they change yours too. YOU DESERVE IT began with the single aim – to decode how to deserve everything you want. To truly understand how to deserve.

This book is for you.

This book is for all of us.

It's an exploration into what it means to "deserve", a word mired with so much emotion, so much bias and opinion. A word which in reality is simple, logical and emotionless.

A word which is based on outward serving and adding value rather than inward "what's in it for me" entitlement based thinking.

A word which until now, you have likely misused.

I'd spent 10 years of my life feeling I deserved more, convinced I couldn't work any harder, bemused and trapped by a glass wall that stood between me and everything I wanted, everything I felt I deserved. "What more can I do to succeed? What am I missing?" That one word was the missing piece.

Felt. I felt I deserved more but in reality I didn't. I deserved everything I had, no more, no less.

The feeling had been with me since childhood. Always striving, always working, always pushing, but never getting there. Feelings are biased and based on perception. That was the issue. As harsh as it was to admit, I didn't deserve any of the things I felt I did. I just desired them.

youdeservethisbook.com

YOU DESERVE IT is not concerned with feelings, emotions, sob stories or anything other than factual cause and effect of reality. That realisation was the first step on the road to deserving everything I wanted. Stripping away the perceptions, the feelings, the biases and focussing on the facts – THAT was what I'd missed and why I was so deeply unhappy in my work life and why I felt so directionless and unclear on what to do.

This book evolved over two years through extensive reading and research, painful soul searching and challenging everything I thought to be true. The pain was worth the gain. I am no longer an unfulfilled and confused corporate employee, I'm a happy and passionate coach, speaker and author, living with purpose, mentoring clients and spreading positive messages through my blog www.everydayshouldbefun.com.

I have everything I deserve and know how to deserve the things I want. It's definitely not been easy, but it was definitely worth it. Now I want to help others achieve the same.

If you don't know what to do to get what you want, if you think you deserve things which you don't have, then this book will be the turning point you need.

After all, isn't it time you got what you deserved?

youdeservethisbook.com

My story

I consider myself an extremely determined and lucky person, a true survivor of life. I think that way because I have triumphed over some major setbacks, any one of which could have drastically changed the course of my life for the worse.

Of course *luck* plays only a small part, it's mostly down to my own efforts that I have triumphed over my setbacks, but believe me it has not been easy. Believing I could not only overcome the things that have crossed my path, but to go on to deserve everything I dreamed of nearly broke me and pushed me to my limits. I was convinced that even though I didn't cause the terrible situations in which I found myself, I would be fully responsible for how I reacted to them. However "unfair" it felt, I would need to stay positive, keep going and keep pushing. It meant I didn't quit.

I am acutely aware that I have one life and each day a little more of it ebbs away. I could sit on the sidelines and complain about what wasn't right, or make the best of what I could and not squander what I had. I have not been able to succeed alone; the support of family, friends, colleagues and professional help in the form of counselling and medication have all combined to get me through.

Here in brief are some of the events which have brought me to where I am in my life right now. They will reassure you that I am no stranger to working hard to deserve the things I have and that even devastating events can be overcome.

*Remember, it's not what happens to you,
it's what you do about it.*

Parental suicide

One of the most painful experiences of my life was in 2002 when I discovered that my estranged father had committed suicide.

We had suffered years of mental abuse and bullying prior to this. It's not just physical abuse that destroys families and childhoods. The non-physical can be even more difficult to detect and contend with, as it's invisible. When times were good, it almost seemed as though we'd imagined the bad times, they left no visible mark, but the memories remain etched in my memory to this day.

Being subjected to drunken, violent rages, numerous suicide attempts and living on edge and in constant fear had finally driven my mother to leave the family home, and we wanted to leave too. My mother, brother and I simply ran away from home.

We packed up everything we had into our Audi 100CD (I still remember the number plate) and we drove away from the pain and uncertainty we had suffered, towards a bright and unwritten future.

At the time I don't think any of us realised the strength it took to do so or the significance of the event, we were simply looking to escape a life which had become so miserable and abusive.

My brother and I had reached an age where we noticed that our home life differed from those of our peers. It wasn't normal to overhear your parents' late night arguments which kept you awake nearly every night. It wasn't normal for my father to consume countless cans of beer and drink himself into a stupor nearly every night (this drunken stupor is what often triggered the arguments and the abuse). It wasn't normal that my mum waited on my father hand and foot and was thanked with insults, violence and threatening behaviour. It wasn't normal that as a 14-year-old boy I didn't truly feel safe in my own home, the one place where we should all feel safe and protected.

My brother and I were the catalyst to help my mum leave. She knew she didn't deserve the situation, nobody deserved what we had. She was waiting for us to turn 18 and leave home before breaking up our family, to this day she feels guilt for everything that happened. She had nothing to feel guilty for. She, like us, was a victim and was looking to remedy the situation we found ourselves in.

We packed everything we could into our car and ran away from home, it was August 24th 1997, a day I will never forget. It was the start of our new life. It wasn't instantly easy or better, the house we first rented had heating issues and no cooker which made winter difficult, we had neighbours who rowed and argued into the night, often coming to blows. And yet compared to where we had come from, I felt perfectly safe.

I have numerous memories of the fear and the bad times; my father once even threatened to "burn us in our beds" and another time to go for a drive and deliberately crash the car to kill us all. At a time when I was in my early teens, contending with GCSE exam work, the uncertainties of home made school a refuge. I could pretend to be normal from 8:45 to 3:45 Monday to Friday. These are my childhood memories.

I often slept fully clothed, ready to run, ready to deal with whatever horror I might wake up to. I was too young to even understand the terrible situations we had to endure; this adolescent naivety actually helped to insulate me, it kept me sane. Typing some of the detail doesn't scratch the surface of how home life felt and how things were. Only those who witness such things can understand the terror. Home should be a comfortable and relaxing place, a refuge from the world. For us, it was anything but. Thankfully this is all a distant memory now. As a father now myself, I am aware of the importance of a stable and secure family home, children deserve no less.

At the time of his actual suicide, I had not seen my father for five years following us leaving home and the subsequent divorce. It's sad to say, but at that time it was actually welcome news and closure to a turbulent time in my life. I finally felt safe. There was no risk of him arriving at our door, or at my workplace, and doing something terrible. When I received the news of his death, which happened whilst I was at work, I was actually elated. This is something which my colleagues could scarcely understand. I was not upset to have lost a parent; I was elated to finally be free of any further suffering.

Although my father was already dead to me, the finality of suicide, the social stigma attached to it, the terrible memories I have and my own fears of repeating his errors have played an enormous part in my life, and still do.

Once my anger at his actions eventually began to subside, which took about five years through counselling, I began to understand more that he was a man who suffered with the same depression, low mood and anxiety with which I had suffered. The difference was, he drank to cope with it, didn't take medication or seek help and ultimately this led to his demise.

Having grown up to such terrible parenting on his part has made me determined not to repeat history and has helped to highlight exactly how not to be a father and a husband. I fully understand that I need to take responsibility for my life and happiness. It's all up to me. I am responsible.

This has led to me giving up alcohol, maintaining a prescription to a course of SSRI medication, hundreds of hours of counselling sessions and continuing to learn as much as possible about how to get the best from what has been a devastating and life changing situation.

I'm not the first person to come from a "broken home". I'm not the first person to lose a parent, nor to lose them to suicide and sadly I won't be the last. My hope is that by truly understanding why he did what he did and the events which led to this point, I will be able to deal better with my own dark moments and not repeat his tragic story.

The 2004 Asian Tsunami

With an inheritance in my pocket and the deep desire to waste the money as swiftly as possible, I decided to travel for six months or so to get some time alone to clear my head and make sense of recent events. I was still only 21 at the time.

It was 2004 and in December I found myself on Phi Phi Island in Thailand, soon to be one of the worst hit islands in the largest natural disaster the world had seen in recent times. I had no idea of course; to me it was paradise on earth, a refuge, a pool of tranquillity in the turbulence of my life. I felt at home for the first time in a long time. I even allowed myself to feel happy.

Sadly, things took a dramatic turn at 10:36am on Boxing Day as I slept in my beach level bungalow. One of the largest natural disasters in living memory unfolded and yet again I found myself in a terrible situation that I had in no way influenced.

This is part of my story which I emailed to friends soon after my rescue:

> On Christmas day night I went for a few drinks to celebrate and was having a great time. It got to about 1am and the people I was with wanted to stay up and drink throughout the night and watch the sun rise; although this sounded great I was completely exhausted, broke and way too drunk so made my excuses and went back to the bungalow we had rented for the next month.
>
> I fell asleep fully clothed on top of my sheets the moment my head hit the pillow.
>
> The next morning I woke to the sound of screaming – at first I thought it was people just being loud and messing

about – but then I realised this was screaming like I'd never heard before.

Dazed, confused and still a little drunk I opened the front door to see people running past my bungalow and there was some water trickling in on the floor as though there was a flood.

It was very windy and felt like a bad storm was coming but I couldn't make sense of it. I shook my friend's leg to wake him and as I did so there was a large explosion and everything went black. Instantly I knew I was in water – there was no question of it – so what little breath I had in my lungs – I held on to.

I began to instinctively feel around for pockets of air as I was at the ceiling of the bungalow floating in the water. Struggling to find any air I panicked and began to thrash around, aware that I would die very soon if nothing changed.

Thrashing around when drowning exhausts you and speeds up the process so it wasn't long before I took my first breath of water, I could feel the debris as I swallowed knowing that one or two more breaths like this would be fatal.

After some more thrashing and struggling, I took one more breath and was certain I would die – thoughts of my mum and brother not knowing what happened to me filled my head.

Then all at once, the panic began to subside and I felt extremely peaceful – almost ready to die – the best way I can describe it is you know when you need to eat or drink or use the bathroom, I needed to die and it was the most natural feeling in the world. At this point I'd been underwater for the best part of 2–2.5 mins.

The next thing I knew, I had fresh air on my face and I was gasping for breath.

As it happens, the multitude of debris and sheer force of the water had caused my bungalow to collapse under the pressure which had in turn sent me shooting upwards to safety. Had this not happened, I would have been trapped in my bungalow, underwater and I would have drowned.

After my return home the large haematoma on my thigh and nerve damage on my lower back were traced back to being hit by this debris as I made my ascent. At the time I felt nothing. As I looked around I felt like the world was ending – nothing but rushing water, destruction, wind, bodies, debris, screaming and the unmistakable fear that I was in mortal danger.

Beneath me I could feel things rushing past and hitting me, I became aware I was rushing through the water and held out my hand for anything to stop me being dragged to the sea. I grabbed on to a tree and as if by magic a sheet of metal hit the tree and bent around it which effectively formed a shield for my legs against the multitude of objects rushing by.

Eventually the water subsided and I climbed down from the tree to take in the devastation – no buildings were standing and there were bodies and screaming people as far as the eye could see (over 1000 people died on the island I was on).

Still trying to work out just what was happening and if the world was actually ending (I genuinely thought the world was ending, such was the scene I faced) someone shouted, "It's coming again."

Although I didn't know what a tsunami was, or what was happening, I instinctively knew that if I stayed where I was I would almost certainly die.

Half naked, cut to shreds and totally shocked I ran barefoot past the piles of wood, glass, bodies and luggage to reach a hilly area only 100 metres or so from where I stood. From there I launched myself into the stinging nettles and undergrowth, pulling myself to safety just as the second wave swept in.

I had survived.

This is the cut-down, edited version of what was truly a waking nightmare. There was so much happening and so much to take in that my memory of the event now feels almost as though it happened to another person.

12 | YOU DESERVE IT

This picture is from early 2005 when I returned to Phi Phi. This is my best guess at where my bungalow should have been; along with hundreds of other bungalows, mine was simply washed away. Note the bungalows just metres behind me which didn't wash away – people would most likely have drowned in them when fully submerged for two minutes plus, and not had the lucky escape I did when my bungalow collapsed and sent me upwards into the fresh air. At the time someone commented that survival relied on seconds and centimetres. I was nearly out of both but managed to escape with my life.

If you want to get a real idea of the destruction of the tsunami then the film The Impossible is extremely realistic and the first few minutes of destruction echo almost perfectly my own experience.

I've had extensive counselling to keep the panic attacks and night terrors at bay, but still have to manage my anxiety and fear on a daily basis.

Having nearly died and seen how easy it can be to die, I have a renewed appreciation for the fragility of life which will stay with me forever. By focussing on how lucky I am to survive, rather than how unlucky I may have been to actually be there, I have put a positive angle on what was a truly devastating situation.

I had the polo shirt I was wearing that day framed, it hangs on my wall to remind me how precious life truly is and how close I came to losing mine.

14 | YOU DESERVE IT

I also have the shoes I found on the day which protected my feet. I don't know who these shoes belonged to, there was so much debris strewn about that I needed to protect my bare feet and was able to use these, although I'm haunted by thoughts about the fate of their owners.

Depression and Generalised Anxiety Disorder (GAD)

Long before my father killed himself or I found myself nearly drowning on Phi Phi Island, I have always struggled with low mood and a constant feeling of emptiness. This was mostly met with "why are you miserable" or "what's wrong" which of course I didn't know the answers to and only made things more frustrating…

It was only after returning from Thailand that I sought professional counselling and medication for what is ultimately an illness, but which is sadly perceived negatively by society as a form of weakness or inability to cope. I'm not ashamed to say that I have, and suffer with, depression and generalised anxiety. I have spent days and days in bed, avoiding people, not going out, not eating, not washing, not really doing anything and totally withdrawing from life in my bid to cope with the feelings I have until they pass.

When you suffer depression you develop strategies to help you cope. Mine is avoidance. When my mood drops I withdraw from all contact with people and all activities, entering a strange existence of inactivity until the feelings pass. This is my way of "dealing" with it and minimising the damage. It can take anything from a few hours to a few days, or more, but it's the most effective way for me to overcome the feelings and has become known to my family and friends.

Depression can come for no apparent reason and leave for no apparent reason, if only you could "just cheer up". I used to drink alcohol to help "relax" and distance myself from these feelings but as I am now a father myself I have decided to quit alcohol altogether and concentrate on handling these difficult situations and emotions without the aid of anything temporary such as alcohol.

My late father used alcohol to "relax" and I think this aggravated his own feelings of frustration and depression rather than helping him to cope with them. I still suffer to this day with depression and GAD (Generalised Anxiety Disorder) but drastically less so. I am sure it will never truly pass and like a long term incurable illness I simply need to find the best way to manage it. It's a sobering thought to even type those words, as until now I've never truly considered that I may _always_ feel low at points and have to manage myself out of it.

These experiences do not make me special, unique or worthy of your sympathy. They have simply put me in a position to help others deal with their own issues and to share my experiences and my strategies for coping with the worst life can present. They have brought me (finally) to my destiny in life; to write this book, to become a coach and a speaker and to spread inspiration to as many people as I can. It's through my pain that I found my purpose and for that I am grateful.

Cars

After my return from travelling I found myself back working with cars. I had always worked with cars as although I had no idea what I wanted to do with my life as far as a career was concerned, I enjoyed cars and working with them was my first attempt at finding happiness.

Working now in a sales position for a prestigious car company, I threw myself into the role and decided to get on with creating the (financially) successful future I had always wanted for myself. Bonuses, promotions, the appreciation of clients and superiors, a company car, the ability to work from home and not missing a single target followed. On paper things were going very well indeed.

I deserved it all, I worked harder than I ever thought possible in those early years. The year prior to creating YOU DESERVE IT, I was responsible for selling some £40million-plus worth of vehicles.

I was deeply unhappy; even though I was "successful", had favourable job conditions and despite having a new company car every few months. It didn't feel enough.

I felt terribly ungrateful for quite some time, surely I "should" be happy, what did I have to complain about? I only had one thing to complain about and that was my unhappiness. I was unhappy because I was unfulfilled. My work was going well, I was good at my job, but I'd reached a glass ceiling, I'd reached an impasse.

At this point I questioned myself. Do I coast along in this comfortable life not feeling 100% happy (or even 50% sometimes) but with a high degree of stability and comfort, or do I pursue my dreams and realise everything I ever wanted (whilst "risking" everything I have worked for)?

Creating the YOU DESERVE IT concept, writing this book and becoming a coach, speaker and author turned out to be all I had ever wanted, it just took me 10 years to find it.

Every Day Should Be Fun (.com)

In 2013, I finally committed to maintaining a blog, having threatened to do so for many years (much to my wife's delight, she had tried to convince me for years to stop talking about blogging and to actually get blogging.)

youdeservethisbook.com

As I'd had such a turbulent life I was grateful for the "self-help" industry as a source of inspiration and motivation when all around me seemed to be falling apart. I have consumed more videos, books and audio CDs than I care to remember. I owe a large part of being where I am today to the optimism they brought to my world. At my lowest points and darkest times, they are the reason I am still here at all and have not succumbed to drink, drugs or even suicide. Self-help reminds me that we can always choose better, there are always options; you just have to keep going.

You only fail when you quit.

Understanding that it's not what happens to you, it's what you do about it and understanding that you can overcome anything in your path are the guiding principles that have finally allowed me to find the happiness I so desperately sought for so long.

As a means of "paying it forward" I created Every Day Should Be Fun to collate all of the inspiring things I found and have used in my own life. My hope was to help others, but truthfully the blog was for me. It's my personal resource should I ever find myself in need of a lift. I share inspiring websites, resources, people, quotes, videos, anything I can find and I share it as often as I can. I was fortunate to find motivational literature so early on and I want to share it with others who are also struggling with the rough and tumble of life.

So that's a little about me.

I have faced some difficult times; you may wonder how I survived the things I have. (I certainly do.) Despite the difficult times, I've stayed focussed on finding my purpose, pursuing my dreams and I have found success, happiness and fulfilment. I've not divulged some of the most vulnerable details of my life to gain pity or your admiration, but knowing more about my history allows you to understand more about who I am and why I created this book.

I'm not a sanitised "self-help" guru who will insist on positive thinking and affirmations. I'm a regular person who has faced some challenges and overcome them. As a result I have a unique insight on what it takes to deserve the life you want, and it's my aim to share this with you.

youdeservethisbook.com

But we're not here to talk about me.

We're here to get you deserving more and following **your** dreams.

Let us begin.

youdeservethisbook.com

1 – Let it bleed

You deserve everything in your life right now.

- Why always me?
- Why doesn't it always work out?
- What do I need to do to change?
- What did I do to deserve this?

In this chapter, we'll look at why you deserve to be where you are in your life right now. We'll also explore the fact that we're responsible for the worlds we create, both good and bad. We'll consider the difference between planning and settling, the importance of action, the importance of having a "why" and the etymology of the word "deserve".

Are you sitting comfortably? Well, I wasn't and I didn't know why.

On paper, life was extremely good; a loving family and a comfortable job, but as I had been in the job for so long, constantly overachieving and constantly ahead of where I needed to be, it left me bored and unchallenged.

With years of accumulated experience and contacts, I was able to constantly meet and exceed my sales targets. The amount of time and brain power required to meet targets reduced as I looked to systemise, delegate and sharpen my working practices.

To reach this level of efficiency and performance, I had even divided my entire job into 19 definitive situations and then ensured I was as efficient and prepared as possible in each area.

To anyone else this would be an amazing situation to be in, the surety of future income, the freedom and lack of pressure to enjoy the present moment, the new cars; surely this was nirvana? Why wasn't I happy? What was wrong with me?

There was nowhere to go within the company, no progression; I was trapped in my cage (albeit a gilded cage) for the foreseeable future. There was no challenge.

I looked at my colleagues, some of whom were 60–70 years of age, as cautionary tales of what could happen to me if I settled for this existence. At 31 years of age, the thought of another 30 years of my current life, however seemingly comfortable and perfect, scared me to death.

> *"Don't live the same year 75 times and call it a life."*
> **Robin Sharma**

I felt guilty to be so ungrateful. Certainly my friends thought I was crazy for wanting to upset things at work in the pursuit of "happiness" – they didn't see why I wasn't already happy.

At the time, due to feeling so trapped, I didn't even consider myself a success. I realise now I was suffering "Imposter Syndrome" which we'll cover later.

When you succeed in something you don't enjoy or have little interest in, it's a hollow victory. I used to enjoy the work and found it challenging, but once you do anything for 10 years you begin to become bored and unchallenged. The challenges are replaced with routine and the fun is replaced with boredom.

Looking back, I was very successful and in a very comfortable and privileged position. Except I was unhappy. Deeply unhappy. Without happiness, not much else matters. Without happiness, it's not really success.

The new cars (I received a new company car every five–six months), the money (I'd doubled my salary from the previous position I held), the freedom to plan my diary and visit customers when I chose, it all sounded great. I had worked very hard for a long time to be in this position, it was not luck or any special favour that brought me here; I was enjoying the fruits of my labour.

I used to "joke" to friends that on paper I had the best job in the world, but that I was dying inside and nobody knew my pain. Looking back, I suppose I was dying inside.

With no "reason" to be unhappy I was forcing myself to continue the charade of "happy successful man" to please onlookers who would deem me otherwise ungrateful if I bared my true feelings. I was living for the approval of others (and societal norms) at the cost of my peace of mind.

Why was I so unhappy and feeling so unfulfilled and empty? This feeling of guilt, of not being able to control my life and steer it towards my true happiness permeated my thoughts for years, until the fateful day when I realised I *deserved* to be in my current predicament.

youdeservethisbook.com

I realised that good or bad, my actions (and as I would discover my inaction) meant that I deserved everything in my life.

I'd gone through life feeling so powerless, which was the root of my unhappiness, the feeling of not being in control and of drifting along.

I realise now that I was in control all along, I was always responsible and able to guide my life, it just didn't feel that way. I deserved everything in my life; from the money to my loving wife and children and everything else that was going well. I deserved it all.

That was fine. Deserving positive things is an easy prospect; I even began to allow myself to enjoy the fruits of the hard work I had put in.

It was deserving to be unhappy that struck me.

I had spent so much time focussing on being a provider for my family, a good employee and pleasing everyone else that I was left behind and forgotten in my seemingly perfect life.

The day I realised I deserved to be unhappy everything changed. It was an awakening – of sorts.

The truth was, deep down in my heart of hearts I already knew all this. The difference now was that I could feel myself gearing up to take action. I couldn't stomach another year of drifting; however seemingly great my life was, I needed a new challenge and to follow my heart.

I looked at my colleagues and was terrified to follow their paths. Although they appeared to be happy with their careers, this was not how my life was supposed to pan out for me. I felt like an outsider, an imposter, a fish completely out of water. I used to joke that I "sold my soul to the devil" for my amazing company cars and "easy" life. It was no joke at all, it felt very real indeed.

I think we all know deep down that we create our lives. From the clothes you wear to the partner you choose, your home, your job, your finances and everything else. It's all you, you decided it, YOU DESERVE IT.

It's decisions, not conditions, that shape our lives.

The difficulty comes with "owning" our actions. Owning our world and being responsible for it all, good and bad. Being responsible is perceived as a scary prospect, we associate responsibility with blame, additional work, hardship, negativity. Seldom is responsibility related

youdeservethisbook.com

to in positive terms, but being responsible *can* be a truly enjoyable thing.

The word "responsible" derives from being *able* to choose your *response*. If you're not responsible, not able to choose your response, then you will be at the mercy of circumstances and may find yourself unhappy as a result. This is where I found myself. I took responsibility for my work, being a good father and a provider but in doing so I found myself in a job I no longer enjoyed, "trapped" in a prison of my own creation with no idea how to escape. I hadn't taken responsibility for my own happiness. In hindsight, this is no surprise.

I'd grown up in a household where "scarcity" was the word of the day; we weren't truly poor but we certainly struggled. I witnessed many arguments about money, saw friends have things I didn't. I was at an age where I didn't understand why I didn't have these nice things, but I was aware that if I acquired money I could right a lot of these wrongs.

I grew up, as most people do from poorer backgrounds, determined to make enough money that money would no longer be a problem. This was my primary objective; I saw money as the panacea for life's problems. I worked so hard and was so determined to make money that I put everything else to the side.

This included the one area of my life I didn't take responsibility for – my happiness. I thought happiness was a by-product of money. I did nothing to focus upon achieving happiness itself – and I suffered.

Without accepting responsibility (being able to choose your response) you are leaving things to chance and circumstance. I discovered, as you will, that *inaction is a form of action*. Through not focussing directly on happiness and taking positive action towards it, I was unlikely to achieve it.

I foolishly thought happiness was a destination, a feeling and situation obtained on that amazing place "The Someday Isle": "Someday I'll be happy," and, "Someday it will all work out," I used to say to myself in my quieter moments.

My lack of happiness was nothing to do with my circumstances (conditions) and everything to do with my actions (decisions) – or lack thereof.

I deserved the success I'd had, years of dedication and hard work preceded me. Through the process of writing this book and exploring my life I had even begun to enjoy the success I had. I deserved my relationship, years of happy memories attested.

I didn't deserve happiness; I'd done nothing except *desire* it. As I learnt, it takes focus, desire and action to achieve what you truly want.

> **We often know what we don't want,**
> **but don't know what we do want.**

So what (now)? I was looking, but I wasn't seeing.

I had spent years in a trance-like state pursuing money, success, certainty, and then complained I was unhappy, expecting happiness to just appear. The only way to change would be to act and to *deserve* happiness.

It made no difference that so many other areas of my life were going well and that I "should" be happy. Happiness, or any goal you seek, is seldom the by-product. It takes desire, focus and action to meet your goals. Anything achieved without this combination is often unfulfilling.

Now, consider your current situation. Your job or business for example; whether you enjoy or hate what you do each day – you chose to do it. You may have been forcing yourself to do it for money or other reasons but given your circumstances you still chose to do it – and as such YOU DESERVE IT.

If you dislike your job you could choose to be unemployed or work for less money, doing something less stressful or more fulfilling to be potentially happier – but you don't.

But why? Fear of failure? Fear of the unknown? Or are you so comfortable where you are that even unhappiness can't spur you to move? I recognise limited options make limited choices. But they are choices nonetheless.

When you truly understand – and I mean truly understand and not just "know" – when you truly understand that it's your decisions which shape your world, not your circumstances, then you'll make different decisions.

I'd chosen my job. I'd chosen to stay (despite being so bored and unhappy) and it had got more comfortable as time passed, very comfortable in fact, but I was still unhappy. By ignoring happiness and focussing on "success" which to me was simply lots of money, I was literally choosing not to be happy.

youdeservethisbook.com

We can only focus on a limited number of things in our short lifetimes; if you choose not to focus on something then you are almost certain to never achieve it.

I'd not chosen to be happy – so I wasn't. (Surprise!)

I'd chosen steadiness and practicality, believing this would indirectly deliver happiness. Happiness is seldom the by-product and often the journey itself. Happiness is all about what you do day to day, why you do it and who you do it with.

> "Circumstances don't make the man – they reveal him."
> **Epictetus**

The Settling

Did you choose your job? Or your partner? Or your house? Or your clothes? Or your car? Or your holidays, education, friends and so forth.

Yes. You chose them because you believed it was the maximum you could achieve given the circumstances. The important part here is "given the circumstances". If you let circumstances shape your reality, this is called settling.

Now, settling is great when you know you can do no more and are performing at your best, but this is seldom the case. You were faced with choices, made the best decision you could and settled on the result. The settling is generally a negative; conditions, rather than decisions, have guided you.

"The Settling" is not making decisions based on your goals and letting circumstances dictate your options along the way instead.

Planning ahead / considering in advance what you want and how to get it is the opposite of The Settling. When you don't settle, when you plan ahead, consider what you want and set out to achieve it, this is when you have the greatest chance of deserving what you want.

This sounds so painfully simple – because it is. If it's so simple, why are you reading a book about deserving more? And why did I write

youdeservethisbook.com

it? You need to understand and internalise the difference between settling and planning to get the best from it.

If you're making decisions based on the prevailing circumstances you are settling. If you're making decisions based on objectives, then you are planning.

- Planning leads you to deserve what you want.
- Settling leads you to deserve what you get.

I hadn't set out to plan for happiness – so I didn't deserve happiness. I'd settled for less by pursuing the other areas I deemed more important, circumstances had decided for me.

Wherever you are in your life, you deserve everything you have because you either planned for it or settled for it. The things you planned for and have taken action towards are generally the positives, the things you want. The things you settled for are generally unwanted. (But they are nonetheless deserved.) The unwanted things are deserved based on your actions (or inaction). Whether you want them or not, action makes it so.

So what does it mean to "deserve"? Let's examine the word itself.

deserve
/dɪˈzəːv/

verb

do something or have or show qualities worthy of (a reaction which rewards or punishes as appropriate)

It's interesting to note that the origin of deserve focusses on what you can do for others rather than what you do for yourself.

youdeservethisbook.com

deserve

Middle English: from Old French *deservir*, from Latin *deservire* 'serve well or zealously'.

It has nothing to do with the sense of entitlement that seems to prevail in modern society; we all feel we deserve so much, but aren't prepared to put the planning and work in to get it first.

It's about giving, then getting. The adage "givers gain" rings true, the value you add reflects the value you receive.

If you have everything you want then it's likely you planned to achieve it and have added sufficient value to others. If you didn't actually plan for it, you have unknowingly taken appropriate action to achieve it.

If you don't have everything you want, or everything you feel you deserve, then you are not adding sufficient value to earn (deserve) the outcomes you want.

Let's consider a real world example. Look at large companies such as Google and Apple, both of which add tremendous value to our daily lives. This tremendous value and the number of people who benefit reflect in the large monetary values of these companies.

The more you serve, the more you deserve.

Google is an integral part of life in the 21st century. It's used to help countless millions of people across the world find, store and share information each day. Google's core value is that of searching for information and if you're like most people, you will use it several times a day for a myriad of reasons. Google serves its users, saves them time and adds value to them. As it adds so much value, to so many people, so often, it's one of the largest companies on earth.

youdeservethisbook.com

At the time of writing Google had a market capitalisation of $395 billion. At the time of writing, Apple had a market capitalisation of $465 billion and was the largest company on earth (Source: http://money.cnn.com/2014/02/07/investing/google-exxon-market-value/)

Think about the number of Apple products not only available – iPhone, iPad, iPod, iMac, iTunes, Apple Watch – but the number of times a day the users of these products benefit from them. Then extrapolate that across the world.

I would argue that Apple is the largest company in the world (based on monetary value) because it serves more people on a more regular basis than any other company.

Looking at my story, and perhaps your story too, I was adding value to others and thus deserving my material success but I wasn't adding value to myself so I didn't deserve happiness, I just *thought* I deserved it. I felt entitled to happiness without specifically considering and pursuing what would make me happy.

Serving yourself can seem selfish or self-important but this couldn't be farther from the truth. Serving yourself simply means living deliberately, validating and pursuing your goals. It's about respecting yourself and ensuring others respect you.

"We teach people how to treat us."
Dr. Phil's Life Law #8

Serving yourself leads to fulfilment, happiness and deserving your outcomes. To not serve yourself (as I didn't) leads to unhappiness, guilt, fear, indecision and more.

Serving others / serving yourself

Those who deserve more add more value not only to others, but to themselves. They value their time, look after themselves and have higher levels of self-esteem than those who simply feel they deserve more than they have, but aren't prepared to work for it.

Serving yourself is about deliberately considering what you want and setting out to achieve it. It's predicated on the notion you can achieve anything you set your mind to. If you feel you deserve more than you have, you need to validate and respect this, by setting out to achieve it (serving yourself).

youdeservethisbook.com

When I realised my actions, not my circumstances, dictated my outcomes, I began to take action. The first step was my goal – what did I actually want?

All too often we know what we don't want, but don't know what we do want. I wanted to have fulfilling work, to add value and to inspire others. I also wanted to be a role model to my children. As it stood, I wasn't making any progress towards these ideals as I simply hadn't focussed upon them or taken appropriate action. I merely *desired* the outcome.

After years of keeping my true ambitions concealed and suppressed, safely tucked away from any prospect of failure (or success) I finally admitted to myself that I wanted to become a coach, speaker and author. I wanted to pursue my purpose; I couldn't sit on the sidelines anymore. My first action was to finally admit to myself that this is what I wanted. I had suppressed this feeling for a long time, fearing others' response to my plans as it was such an unusual path to follow.

I needed to confront my feelings, to validate them and to serve myself. Why should I be embarrassed to be me?

"Admit", like responsible, is another seemingly guilt ridden word that can actually be truly liberating. "Admitting" to myself meant taking responsibility. With my goals coming into focus I was able to begin the process of moving from "The Settling" to "The Planning" and to finally deserving what I wanted.

Throughout my life, I'd consumed countless books, videos and talks looking for inspiration and motivation. I was thankful for the positive impact they'd had upon my life and wanted to help make similar impact on the lives of others. I'd had numerous episodes of depression and low mood, from which "self-help" literature had rescued me. In a stronger place now, I wanted to offer this "rescue" to others, to serve them through my passion for self-improvement.

Rather than focus on being a provider, a father, a model employee, I decided to focus on what would make me happy. I decided to serve myself.

In now pursuing my own happiness, being a great role model for my children and being a provider were the by-products and I was a lot happier to boot.

I felt more responsible and far more in control of my destiny. As a self-confessed control freak this pleased me greatly. Whatever it is you want in your life, to deserve it you have to have a plan.

Chance will seldom lead you where you want to be.

My plan would not move forward without enlisting outside help which I found in the form of my coach. Tim helped me by first connecting me to my "why". Your "why", if you weren't already aware, is your purpose, your reason for doing everything you do – your modus operandi.

"He who has a why to live can bear almost any how."
Nietzsche

Most people have no "why" because they've never taken the time to look into it or don't understand its power. Society is so ingrained in the 9–5 culture that few stop to ask why they do what they do. If you ask most people why they work and do what they do, the answer is most often money rather than following a set goal or passion.

This is a by-product of "The Settling". Letting circumstances and life take over leaves little room for pursuing, or even considering your dreams. John Lennon was *almost* right; life is what happens when we're busy *not* making plans.

As an outsider, Tim was able to ask unbiased and seemingly obvious questions. I couldn't fool him as I'd fooled myself, he was the catalyst for change. We looked at all parts of my life in a bid to deconstruct them and truly understand what made me, me and what would make my life fulfilling and challenging enough to make me happy.

"The unexamined life is not worth living."
Socrates

This was a painful time. I had to challenge everything I thought and perceived, as clearly what I was doing was not getting me where I wanted to be. Through the framework of where I was versus where I wanted to be, I questioned everything I could. I felt guilty for my previous lack of awareness, ashamed of my lack of progress and bitter at the lost time.

youdeservethisbook.com

These strong negative emotions soon subsided under the power of optimism and *control*. I wasn't where I wanted to be, but now I was finally doing something constructive about it. It felt great.

It took hours and hours of questions, soul searching and thought, but I made the breakthrough I'd felt like I needed (and deserved) for so long.

It transpired that the reason I had not let the tsunami, the suicide of my father and my difficult childhood overwhelm me was that I felt I didn't deserve it. The pain of feeling like the victim of so many terrible circumstances had left me more determined than ever to succeed. I certainly wasn't a quitter and I'd made a "success" of myself despite the setbacks. I felt I deserved more than I had, in terms of being capable of deserving more than I had. This feeling kept driving me forward.

It would have been easy for me to give up on life, becoming "the settled" and allowing circumstances to dictate my path. It would have been easy to turn to drugs and alcohol, letting my life drift because I'd experienced so many traumas so early on. I could have abdicated responsibility for what had happened; blamed everyone, played the victim, but I knew that was a one-way street.

If I'd "settled" I would have been travelling farther away than ever from my goal of being happy. Although I didn't give up, I found myself trapped between "The Settling" and "The Planning". I didn't want circumstances to dictate my life but didn't know what to do or what I truly wanted and was therefore unable to plan or take action.

After all, none of what had happened to me was deserved, none of it was my fault. I was a classic victim. I'm grateful I didn't give up. This was my fighting spirit and it's saved my life.

My predisposition to not take no for an answer and my belief that I could overcome any obstacle, which I inherited from my mother, told me I had one life to live and no matter how great or terrible it was, it was up to me to make the most of it. My why was quite simply "I deserve it". Although it's early in this book to define my why, the journey had taken me some 31 years.

Having a why is no cure-all; it's not an end in itself.

Having a why can help you define your destination, and with a destination you can begin to plan your journey.

youdeservethisbook.com

Having decided this one thing, I soon began to notice "deserve" all around me.

"YOU DESERVE IT," I'd overhear, "You don't deserve that," or, "But I deserve it."

It started me on a quest to define my own why of "I deserve it" and then explain and discuss this concept as my way to add value with an original message as a motivational coach/speaker/author. This was to become the basis of my career and future work.

As soon as I decided on what I wanted, it became clearer how to shape my destiny. It would be easy to let you think this was an overnight process or something which took two or three hours to define. The reality was that at 31 years of age it had taken me 10-plus years of active soul searching, research, testing, failing, heartache and not giving up to reach this point.

I didn't give up. I couldn't give up. If only I'd met Tim earlier, I thought...

I realise now, I didn't deserve to meet him earlier. Everything in my life to that point had led me to him, everything that had happened had created the circumstances that led to our meeting, which led to my why, which led to this book.

Had I given up, had I "settled", the story of my life would have taken a different path indeed. I doubt I would have ever found happiness. Yet again my feeling of deserving more than I had kept me from quitting and now it was finally encouraging some progress.

For me, the concept of deserving everything in your life right now is a positive one. It's not about blame (I certainly hadn't deserved parental suicide or the tsunami), it's about how you handle life and your decisions, not conditions.

There are things in all of our lives which we truly don't deserve, but most things can be influenced by us to some degree and as such are deserved; the key is understanding the difference.

It's not what happens to you, it's what you do about it.

It's about being "response able", able to choose your response to the things you can't control. Being responsible can, for some, be a suffocating and heavy concept; for me it was empowering. If I was responsible I was able to effect change. YOU DESERVE IT does not recognise victims of circumstance.

Whether you have a terminal illness or whether you've won the lottery, it's your actions given those circumstances that deserve the outcomes you receive.

Parental suicide and the tsunami gave me a tough set of circumstances to begin with, no question. Had I been terminally ill or suffered other terrible circumstances would I feel "I deserved it"? Absolutely not, but my reaction to the circumstances would deserve the outcomes. And that's the point.

When faced with adversity you can blame circumstances, be a victim and be subject to the vagaries of "The Settling" or you can take responsibility for the situation and decide what to do for the best to get to where you want to be: "The Planning".

It may seem so harsh, so unfair, so clear cut. But as I would learn, these are the rules of YOU DESERVE IT. Like it or not, it's your actions which dictate what you deserve. Luck, misfortune, sob stories, feelings – these are meaningless in the context of YOU DESERVE IT.

Having decided to write this book, having decided to explore the concept of YOU DESERVE IT and having decided to finally pursue happiness I was awash with a warm feeling of accomplishment. It's this feeling of fulfilment that I want for you, my dear reader, and for my clients.

I want this for everyone I can spread the YOU DESERVE IT message to. When you decide what you want and set out to achieve it- your life is full of purpose. YOU DESERVE IT is about choice; whether you choose the path of your life or whether you let circumstances choose for you.

Action and lack of action can be just as potent as each other.

Acting to achieve something such as losing weight at the gym or gaining weight at fast food restaurants are the same. They're both action, they both have outcomes. One is planned for, one is settled for. Both are choices, one is obvious, the other is hidden. No one chooses to gain weight or be unhealthy, but your actions will deserve the outcome.

Now that I decided to choose happiness, to consider what would make me happy and to plan to achieve it, I would fully deserve the outcome. It was all on me.

youdeservethisbook.com

Are you are finding that life is full of "bad circumstances" and outcomes you don't feel you deserve? If you feel that life is so unfavourable, question which choices or lack of choices could have created this outcome for you.

Take responsibility. Be as unbiased as you can be. Consider causality; what are the possible causes? And more importantly, what can you do about it?

It was my own lack of choice that held me back from happiness. It was my choice to be a provider and model employee that led to my success at work. If your life is full of things you want and you are happy (truly happy) with your "lot" then I would wager this is no accident. You have likely put time, thought and energy into achieving the outcomes you have achieved.

If you are offended by the prospect that you deserve everything in your life, I ask that you remain objective for this chapter, and the rest of the book. YOU DESERVE IT is an act of causality and logic, not emotion and bias.

As we'll discover, fairness, like luck, doesn't exist.

causality
/kɔːˈzalɪti/

noun

1. the relationship between cause and effect.
2. the principle that everything has a cause.

If you plant apple seeds, you get an apple tree. If you didn't plant the apple seeds but have the apple tree anyway then you can choose to eat the apples, make strudel or prune the tree. The point here isn't that you are responsible for everything (because you can't be) but you can take responsibility and as such, shape your destiny. To deserve everything in your life that you want, you must first take responsibility for your actions and for defining what it is that you want.

It was intriguing that as I observed the world around me through the lens of YOU DESERVE IT, I began to realise that much of the world is driven by the notion that people want more than they currently have, they feel they deserve more than they have. They feel entitled to more than they currently deserve.

That's an important point. People want more than they have, they feel they deserve more than they have; this drives the world. Shiny new cars, hi-tech new phones, new appliances, special treats, gifts, exotic holidays, jewellery – these are all purchased with the notion that they are deserved (as well as desired). If we didn't feel we deserved them we wouldn't pursue them.

10 things to remember

1. You deserve everything in your life right now as your actions (or inaction) have brought you to this point.
2. If there is something you have no influence over, you don't deserve it. Instead you deserve the results of your response to the situation.
3. To deserve more, you have to take responsibility for the things you already deserve.
4. Inaction is a form of action.
5. Deserve derives from Deservir which means to "serve zealously".
6. Settling leads you to deserve the life you get.
7. Planning leads you to deserve the life you want.
8. It's not what happens to you, it's what you do about it.
9. It's natural to feel you deserve more than you have.
10. YOU DESERVE IT does not recognise victims or sob stories. No emotion, just fact.

youdeservethisbook.com

Exercise – Bad Times

Acknowledging and accepting the bad in life is the only way to be responsible for them. Once you are responsible for something, you are in a position to change it. Pick something bad that has happened to you, or something you regret doing. Remember it in vivid, painful detail – relive the pain of the event as much as you can. Accept the event and consign it to history. Once consigned to history jot down at least three things the bad experience has taught you or how you could avoid it next time around. Take the wisdom and goodness from the event and discard the rest. You win some, you learn some.

Example

I often recall my turbulent childhood, past failures and missed opportunities and my path to becoming a speaker. Rather than feeling guilt or shame for "failing" I look to extract the wisdom and the lessons from the situation to propel me forward.

Possible examples include:

- A job you didn't get
- A knock back from a potential partner
- Failing a test
- Missing a deadline

Guidance

Limit yourself to one hour – if you find it difficult then a finite time frame helps to get you through. Seek to understand that bad situations exist to teach us, not to haunt us. When things go wrong it's an opportunity to learn, to try better next time and to improve. This exercise uses the Japanese management principle of Kaizen – continuous improvement. If you let something bad happen to you and you don't seek to learn from it then it's a tragedy. If you seek to learn from your failures then they can form the basis of your triumph.

Ask yourself:

- What was so bad about this situation?
- Why did it happen? Could I have prevented it?
- What has this situation taught me?
- How would I approach this situation if it happened again?

Tip

Try something you are embarrassed about – these are often the events where you have the most control. Things you regret carry a great deal of pain which is ideal – the more painful the experience, the stronger the lesson.

What you'll need

Pen, paper, painful experiences

Duration

1 hour

When completed, ask yourself:

Having examined and confronted the painful memory is it more or less painful now? Have you been able to extract goodness and change from the situation?

youdeservethisbook.com

2 – Looking at the stars from the gutter.

> Right now, you don't deserve more than you have.

- What more do you want from life?
- Why don't you already have it?
- What do you need to do to get it?

In this chapter we'll look at why you don't deserve more than you have, however you may feel about it. We'll look at how to set about deserving more through planning, being responsible and taking action, however small, to get started.

We'll look at how inaction is a form of action – and how this affects what you deserve. We'll consider the biological process of homeostasis, the nautical concept of "Course Made Good" and continue to dissect my own YOU DESERVE IT journey.

There are a few defining moments in my life. My birth (of course!), my marriage (of course! – she'll be reading this!), the birth of my children, the tsunami – and the day I realised I didn't deserve more than I already had.

When I realised I didn't deserve more than I had, even though I didn't agree, I could appreciate this was reality. After all, I didn't have the things I wanted and thought I deserved. This was where I found myself and where I suspect you find yourself, reading this. It's logical, it makes sense, but it's difficult to digest. Very difficult.

Once you make this discovery, as I did, you are taking responsibility for your situation. When you take responsibility for something, you can set about changing it. Throughout researching this book, those I have discussed this concept with go from initial objection to understanding to empowerment and I'm planning the same for you.

2 – Looking at the stars from the gutter. | 39

In a way it's about hope. Hope is not far away from luck in my estimation – neither take any input, neither can be relied upon or controlled.

Feeling you deserve more is a form of hope, that somehow the universe will readjust, realign and realise how great you are and settle the outstanding tab and the imbalance by giving you all the things you feel you deserve.

By hoping (and not taking action) we are shielded from potential failure. We can blame luck and chance for our lack of progress but the reality is that we are responsible. Without taking responsibility for our circumstances, we remain "the settled" – we let circumstances decide for us.

- When were you last late for work but then found £20 on the way?
- Have you ever lost your job only to find a better paid one elsewhere?
- Have you ever hoped for things to get better – and they just have?

I suspect not. The universe owes us nothing. If we want it, we have to make it happen.

Action is the key. Without action, nothing is possible. With action, nothing is impossible. Far from feeling scared to act, if you embrace action you will see things change for you. You will see results, change your outlook and gain momentum.

In the context of YOU DESERVE IT, if there are things you feel you deserve, which you don't have, you just need to take some action towards them. To deserve more, you simply have to do more and serve more.

On my journey I became acutely aware that action is the foundational key. I would also discover that appropriate action, rather than just any action, is required to achieve results.

You don't deserve more than you have right now because what you're doing can only get you to this point and no further. To deserve more you need to change what you're doing.

To not take any additional or new action in my life, I was unlikely to deserve more than I had. I was stuck. Of course I naturally wanted

youdeservethisbook.com

more and hoped for more, but nothing changed because I didn't change. This, again, was hope.

To deserve more than I had, I had to assess what I was and wasn't doing at this point and then establish what I could do in the context of my goals. A YOU DESERVE IT audit, so to speak.

> "Insanity: doing the same thing over and over again and expecting different results."
> **Unknown, but attributed to Albert Einstein**

Along with accepting I didn't deserve any more than I had in my life, this thinking reinforced the things I *did* have and the fact that I deserved them. With this new perspective, I began to focus on the positives more than the negatives.

Focussing on the positives in your life and admitting you deserve them is practising gratitude. Practising gratitude is a healthy way to boost happiness and self-esteem. Being thankful for what you have focuses on the positives which can help to keep out the negatives.

I had spent so much time focussing on what I didn't have that I didn't appreciate what I did have. When I realised my family, my health, and the success I'd had at work were all deserved – it felt good. Forget that, it felt GREAT!

Grateful for what I had and filled with new confidence and self-belief, it was easier to understand that I deserved no more than I had right now. It took the sting out of not deserving, of "not being good enough". I simply hadn't yet done what I needed to do in order to deserve more. I deserved no more in my life, but likewise I deserved no less.

You may find it presumptuous for me to tell you that you deserve no more in your life, and you'd be justified, as it's a somewhat bold statement.

I suspect however, you *feel* you deserve more than you currently have. If you broke down into facts why you deserve more, you will find your argument may no longer stand; it is likely to be biased and emotional rather than unbiased and factual.

Remember, YOU DESERVE IT doesn't care about your feelings (sorry). It's the feeling of deserving more and then realising you don't deserve it that is making this a difficult chapter (and book) to read.

youdeservethisbook.com

Are you finding this difficult to read? Maybe you're even a little affronted? Good. This means we're making progress.

Every shiny new car advert, every exotic luxury holiday advert, food, drink, clothes adverts – they all attempt to tap into the fear of not having everything we feel we deserve.

The fear of feeling you deserve more but not yet having it; this is a form of FOMO – "Fear of Missing Out". It's the fear of not being "good enough" or not "having enough". It's a feeling of inadequacy, of being incomplete, of not being where you want to be.

Feeling you deserve more than you currently have drives much of the Western world.

If you didn't feel you deserved more than you had, you would buy less, act differently and the world would be boring and dull. We strive for more, for better, for what we feel we "deserve" in a never ending cycle. This is the Hedonic Treadmill at work.

> **The Hedonic Treadmill Theory is** the supposed tendency of humans to quickly return to a relatively stable level of happiness despite major changes.

An example:

You feel you deserve a shiny new Mercedes-Benz / BMW / Audi. Realising you don't actually yet deserve it, you take action and eventually save enough money to get the car of your dreams. Before long, driving your shiny new car, you spot a really lovely looking Porsche – if only you had that! You now strive to obtain the Porsche, feeling you deserve that instead.

As a man who changed cars every five or six months I can confirm that you are happy for a limited amount of time before you want, or feel you deserve, more again. (Usually about 1500 miles or when that "new car" smell fades.)

This is as true for cars as it is for houses, holidays, clothes et al. There is always that moment when the desire fades. Far from being fulfilled to have what you wanted, you're considering the next thing

youdeservethisbook.com

you want (and completely missing the gratitude of what you already have).

It's about pursuing happiness and fulfilment as some finite destination, pinning everything on outside factors. It's about not being responsible for your own happiness and expecting to find it in material pleasures.

When we are left feeling we deserve more, but not achieving it, we have come to a point where we can't or won't do what is necessary to achieve it. This is also a form of homeostasis.

homeostasis
/ˌhɒmɪə(ʊ)ˈsteɪsɪs, ˌhəʊm-/

noun

the tendency towards a relatively stable equilibrium between interdependent elements, especially as maintained by physiological processes.

Physiologically we are designed to exist within certain tolerances (blood sugar level, pulse and so forth). In the same regard, externally we seek to attain and retain similar equilibrium.

When the environment changes, we seek equilibrium and stability as quickly as possible; this explains why some things "lose their sparkle" or your desires change over time, you are returning to a "static equilibrium".

This also explains why, when I had the unlimited use of my dream car – a Ferrari 430 Spider – for my wedding, I actually became bored with it on the first day.

I collected the car from a friend in Wales, drove back to England and ran last minute wedding errands. The speed, the heat, the noise, the stares – it was everything I'd imagined and more. As the day wore on and as I grew tired; these very same things made driving the car seem like a lot of hassle, rather than a lot of fun. As I tried to explain this to my wife she couldn't quite understand it. I genuinely had driven the car that much that the thought of driving it again didn't appeal to me.

I had spent weeks fantasising about driving the car, researching it and watching videos in anticipation – only to find it didn't make me as happy as I thought it would.

2 – Looking at the stars from the gutter. | 43

For cars in particular, I was so used to a new car so often that the time required for my own homeostasis had become far shorter. I had a dream car on my driveway but was bored, yet again I felt ungrateful and dissatisfied. I couldn't understand why I felt this way.

I'd got something I'd wanted, I dreamt about it, talked about it, read about it and it simply wasn't enough – I was left wanting, confused and feeling ungrateful. I had become used to the car so quickly and the excitement of it faded so quickly that homeostasis (Ferrariostasis) was achieved within hours.

The difference is that while many people feel they deserve more – few act to make it so. This is the basis for the book. Making the distinction between desire and deserve, between action and hope is the only way to get what you truly want. Failure to act means failure to set out to actually deserve more; leaving you with hope, daydreams and a feeling that the world is "unfair".

On the other side, action leads you to feel in control, reveals opportunities and helps you to advance.

*"I know the world isn't fair,
but why isn't it ever unfair in my favour?"*
Bill Waterson

If, like me, you've experienced this "unfair" feeling time and time again, wondering how other people seem to be getting on in life whilst you stalled, then you didn't have the answer. The answer is action. The answer is action even if that means to not do something.

Inaction is a form of action.

To bring ideas to life takes action, so too the things you feel you deserve. I deserved no more than I had in my life because I needed to take more and different action to achieve different results.

The only way to stop moving backwards, or to start moving at all in the direction of your goals, is to understand and accept where you are right now. This is vitally important.

I didn't realise where I was, thought the world "owed" me due to my bad experiences and as such made negligible progress in the years which preceded this book.

youdeservethisbook.com

Think of this chapter, if not this book, as a form of intervention. In the same way those who overeat or drink too much emotionally justify their behaviour and need a third party to step in with a "dose of reality" – so too if you feel you deserve more than you have and are doing nothing about truly deserving it.

If you change nothing, nothing changes.

Being told you are fat – sucks. Being told you drink too much – sucks. Being told you don't deserve more than you have – sucks. But, once the shock subsides, you are left to question something that until this point you held to be true.

It's easy to be offended or to cast doubt and mockery on new ideas such as those in this book. It's easy because it yields no results. It's not taking responsibility. What's easy seldom delivers what you want.

I get it now. As a man who spent many a year "resisting" such "cold turkey" action and advice, and as a man who now realises that action is the key to YOU DESERVE IT, hopefully my words will resonate.

"Resistance is futile."
Borg saying (Star Trek)

It's one thing to agree you deserve everything you have in your life right now. It's another to take ownership of the bad things you deserve, that takes real courage, real awareness.

It's yet another leap to accept that all of the nice things you want in your life are unlikely to transpire unless you work towards them.

It allows you to reset, readjust and reassess – as I did. Rather than being depressing or daunting, being responsible and accepting your current reality is empowering, it gives you a firm starting position from which to plot your destination. I realised that I didn't have everything I wanted or felt I deserved. And yet I didn't know what more I could do to change my situation. I had been resisting.

youdeservethisbook.com

2 – Looking at the stars from the gutter. | 45

This is known in the maritime world as "course made good". Course made good (C.M.G.) takes the most efficient route from one point to another depending on the direction of the wind. It's also known as the "Leeway effect".

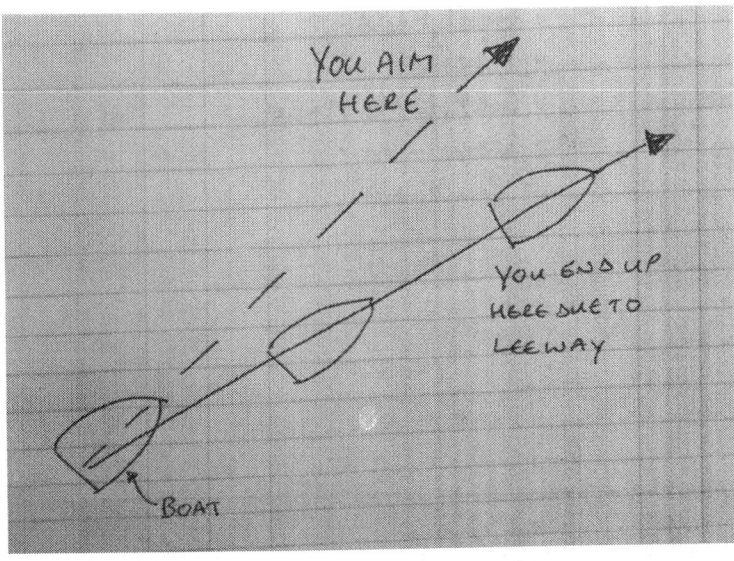

When setting out with a destination in mind (either in life or in a boat) other factors such as the wind, the tide, experience, skill and perception can affect your course. Along the way you need to adjust your actions to account for these factors and reach your intended destination.

I had set out without a definite goal, so it was clear to see why I would never reach my destination...

I had no idea where "there" was and by definition would never get to "there". How can you adjust course to an unknown destination?

youdeservethisbook.com

You can't. You will sail around in circles and be subject to the wind, tides and everything else. You'll become tired, lost and despondent – and you'd deserve to be there too.

Having established my goal, I was able to be more specific.

When I realised I deserved no more, my first question was simply, "What do I need to do to deserve what I want?"

This is the magical part. This is how you begin to deserve everything you could ever want. You start with the goal. In my case becoming a motivational coach, speaker and author.

What do you want? What is it that you want to achieve? What's your goal? Careful consideration is paramount. If you settle on the wrong goal or are not specific enough, you may waste time and risk heartache – as I had.

With your goal established in your mind, you can step back and ask yourself what you need to do to deserve the end game you have visualised.

This is planning – and as we established in the previous chapter, planning is not settling.

- **Planning** is adjusting course en route to a destination (Course Made Good).
- **Settling** is letting circumstances dictate the destination.

From my life experience to when I began this journey, it became clear that you need a roughly organised plan to achieve what you desire. When you plan, you deserve what you want. When you settle, you deserve what you get.

It's pretty basic. If you want something; make a plan to achieve it. But how many of us take the time to plan?

Even a rough plan is better than no plan.

A plan is a consideration of what you want, and how to set about getting it. Having a plan isn't fixed. You can change your plans as you correct course, but you must have a plan to begin with.

The plan reminds you of your destination and as such keeps you focussed and moving towards it. Plans keep you from settling.

We all know life doesn't just happen by accident. There are some instances of seeming luck or happenstance, but anything worth having takes work. It takes planning, consideration, persistence, effort, courage and much more.

If you agree this is obvious and need not be reiterated; let me ask you this:

- What are you doing to achieve your goals?
- Have you even defined your goals?

If, like me, you cringed when confronted with questions like this then you deserve to be reading this book. It's okay to not know your goals, but with no goals you are doomed to being a "Settler" – letting life decide what you deserve.

For too long I had no goals. I hadn't spent any time working out what I actually wanted. I had no idea where to begin.

"Plans", like "responsibility", seemed too weighed down with difficulty and potential failure.

For too long, I took "some" action. I would read, plan, or even just *think* about what I wanted; I felt I deserved things but didn't achieve them and was mystified as to why not. When you don't take responsibility for what you deserve you are playing the victim.

Victims don't deserve it.

This is such a common trap we can all fall into. You can spend time reading, researching, thinking, dreaming – you may even plan out your goal.

The Procrastination Illusion occurs when you think, plan, want, dream and research the things you want but take no appropriate action towards them. You remain theoretical in your approach, or take small inappropriate action which is unlikely to advance you and eventually it peters out.

Until you take action, appropriate action, you won't deserve anything more than you have.

That's the harsh reality. However you feel about it. You may feel as though you deserve progress, especially if you've spent a lot of time on the planning and researching phase, but without appropriate action there is no progress.

My goal here isn't to embarrass you or teach you to "suck eggs". Actually, yes it is. You need to truly understand what YOU DESERVE

youdeservethisbook.com

IT means. Without this understanding you are unlikely to make any progress and this book will be a waste of your time.

My goal in this book is to be the wakeup call you need, the wakeup call that I so desperately needed in my own life. The wakeup call that eventually came, but which came years later than I would have liked.

I was 31, married and with a son when I set out to find out why I didn't have everything I wanted and everything I thought I deserved. Within six months, I was writing this book, focussing on my goals and generally feeling confident and fulfilled, safe in the knowledge I was progressing and I had a plan.

No longer was I just a planner, a dreamer and a talker. I was taking appropriate action, setting deadlines, I was beginning to move towards my goals at last. I realised that, for me at least, happiness is progress.

This was a paradigm shift. I used to believe that happiness was the outcome, the destination, the shiny Porsche (or BMW / Mercedes).

It's the journey which is where the true happiness is to be found, not the destination (or the car).

If you put off happiness until XYZ event – you may never be happy as the goalposts will continually be moving. Relying on external events for happiness is a sure fire way to be disappointed, there's too much you can't control.

Small, incremental, daily progress holds the key to much of life – from creating a savings account to losing weight to learning a language; it's the "constant dripping" which "hollows the stone".

Few things worth having are achieved quickly or without consistent effort.

This book was written over the course of two years. I didn't just create it in an afternoon. Each chapter was brainstormed, researched, written, edited, edited again and then put together – then edited some more.

youdeservethisbook.com

2 – Looking at the stars from the gutter. | 49

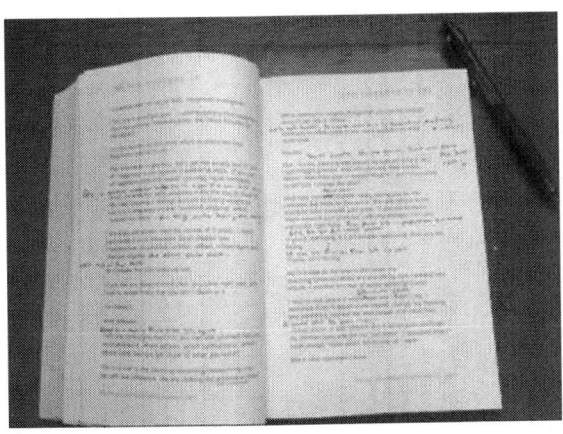

So consider this your wake up call. If you feel you deserve more than you have right now, you need to accept firstly that you don't deserve more – if you did deserve it, you'd have it already.

You don't deserve it. You *desire* it. VERY different.

Once you realise you desire it, you can ask yourself how you could deserve it. Which actions, which connections, which people could help you get closer to what you want?

This is similar to the planning / dreaming / researching trap but with one difference. We are looking for *actionable* steps. We're looking for tangible things that you can do straight away to get you in motion.

We're not looking to waste more time in theoretical daydreaming and research – the Procrastination Illusion. Once you've made some notes, take some guesses on what could work.

You act. You do something. However small. That will start the ball rolling.

Now, for me, planning was always considered to be a very rigid thought process and with planning often comes failure; what if the plan is wrong? What if I don't know what to do? Can I change the plan?

Step back and consider taking broader steps, caring less for the immediate outcome, but more for the action and potential precessional effects (We'll cover this with the honey bee example, Chapter 3).

The only failure is not trying to move towards your goals. If you are trying to move towards your goals but suffering setbacks then you are on the right track. The power lies in persistence – you keep going until you find what works.

If you're not trying, if it all remains theoretical, then you are failing. If you are trying, then you are doing well.

Trying isn't failing.

My first step on the road to this book, my coaching / speaking career and everything else I wanted was simple. I enrolled in a "fear of public speaking" course. I had no idea where it would specifically lead and I really didn't care. I somehow knew it would cause ripples; change my thinking and potentially connecting me with people who could help. (Coaches and speakers attend speaker clubs.)

It was starting the ball rolling. It was action, it was relevant and it would push me from my comfort zone and get me "out there". I reasoned that I could always "make good" my course as I went.

Worst case scenario? I tried. To try is not to fail.

I decided that I would need to understand some of the technicalities of speaking, get some practice and feedback and as an added bonus – meet likeminded people.

Until I attended that first one-day course, I had read about what I wanted, talked about what I wanted and dreamt about what I wanted. I felt I deserved to be a motivational coach, speaker, author and all round "great guy".

The reality at that stage?

I deserved none of it. I'd done nothing to deserve it, except want it. It hurt to admit it, but realising this and realising I needed to act was incredibly motivating.

When I stood up for the first time to speak, nerves jangling, heart racing – it was then that I felt I could deserve it all. It felt great. I was taking action, taking risk and doing something relevant and constructive towards my goal.

I was miles from my final destination and had taken but the first step on a journey of as-yet-undetermined length. But I was so incredibly happy.

youdeservethisbook.com

2 – Looking at the stars from the gutter. | **51**

If you get stuck with the thought of what to do or when to begin, pick something relevant to your goal and pursue it. Give it a try, get out there, and talk to people.

"People are the people who can help you."
Gary Vaynerchuk

Unless you want to be a doctor or a teacher (or similar profession) which both have well defined paths, then there are no paint by numbers approaches in life, you just need to get started, get painting.

It's about trial and error; none of the finest masterpieces were paint by numbers.

10 things to remember

- You don't deserve more than you have. If you did deserve it, you'd have it already.
- You might deserve no more than you have, but you deserve no less. Celebrate and be thankful for what you have.
- The universe owes us nothing; we have to make things happen.
- The Hedonic Treadmill keeps us trapped in a cycle of constantly wanting more.
- If you change nothing, nothing changes.
- "Course made good" is a nautical concept of setting a destination and adjusting course along the way.
- To deserve more you need a plan, although a rough plan is better than no plan.
- Taking time to define what you want is vital.
- Trying isn't failing.
- You can't negotiate with YOU DESERVE IT.

youdeservethisbook.com

Exercise – Fear

From asking someone out on a date to getting a health check-up, checking your finances, visiting the dentist, apologising, confronting someone who is mistreating you – do something that you are presently putting off because you fear it. You must be genuinely avoiding or fearing the task for this to work, but it must also not be detrimental to you – so fearing jumping off a cliff doesn't count.

Example
For me, checking bank balances and statements always gets my blood pumping as I have experience of being heavily in debt and overdrawn – even though now I'm not and there's nothing to fear.

Possible examples include:

- Check your bank balance.
- Ask for a pay rise.
- Ask for feedback from your peers.
- Book an activity such as zip lining or a skydive.
- Apologise to someone you have wronged.
- Speak up in public where you wouldn't do so usually, such as a staff meeting.

Guidance
Fear is often misaligned to the thing that is feared. Confronting fear and challenging yourself allows you to push forward in life and make progress. Once you have confronted something you fear, however small, you will not only be surprised by how better things are than you'd hoped, but you'll feel energised to confront other things and question why you didn't do it sooner.

When confronting your fear, ask yourself:

- Why was I / am I afraid of this?
- How could I reduce this fear?
- How could I be more prepared the next time this happens?
- How could I prevent this happening again?

youdeservethisbook.com

Tip
Try something small to begin with, checking your bank balance rather than ignoring it, or saying "no" rather than making excuses. Start small, be gentle, but be firm – you need to confront things which genuinely scare you.

What you'll need
Something you fear.

Duration
1 hour

When completed, ask yourself:
Now you have confronted something you have been putting off or fearing – was it better or worse than you imagined? If confronting it was less painful than you thought it would be – what else could you confront? What other fears could you smash?

3 – McDonald's (over 99 billion served)

To deserve more you have to serve more.

- What value are you adding now?
- How can you add more value to others?
- Who else can you help?

In this chapter, we'll look at how focussing on helping others helps us, we'll acknowledge that to deserve is to serve. We'll learn about the circle of YOU DESERVE IT and how this can help in your own life. We'll consider the importance of passion and law of diminishing returns; how "Selfmore" can turbo charge your results and we'll compare ourselves to the honey bee.

It's insightful that the word "deserve" derives from the French word "Deservir" which means to serve vigorously.

Deserve – a self-focussed word at best in modern society derives from helping others, adding value, serving others.

On my quest to decipher how to deserve everything I wanted in my life, this was a massive clue to unleashing my true potential.

It's a clue for us all. It's a reminder.

Deserve isn't a self-centred or selfish concept – it's based on serving others and subsequently being rewarded. If you feel you deserve something but don't have it yet – perhaps you need to focus on serving others more first.

You need to focus more outwards than inwards. You need to give before you can receive.

In hindsight, I realised that the origin of the word "deserve" held everything I needed to know about how to harness its power. Like many great discoveries on my journey, the simplest were the most profound. I was beginning to "crack the code".

> *"Life's most persistent and urgent question is*
> *"What are you doing for others?""*
> **Dr. Martin Luther King**

youdeservethisbook.com

To think or feel you deserve something is an inwardly focussed approach; using your judgement and perception, you decide what you think you deserve. You are biased – this is why you feel you deserve things but don't actually have them. The issue here is that what you deserve is decided by your actions and by others. It's not all up to you – and it's nothing to do with how you "feel" either.

It seems counter-intuitive, but shifting from yourself, from everything you want, to helping others to get what they want is a fundamental of the YOU DESERVE IT strategy.

Without serve, there is no deserve.

If you focus on helping others get what they want, you will get what you want. I call this the "Circle of YOU DESERVE IT".

If you don't have what you want in your life but feel YOU DESERVE IT and don't understand what's missing – this could be the answer. This could explain why you don't have the things you feel you deserve.

It was for me.

I wanted to add value to the world. To be known and respected, to be proud, to make my children proud, my wife proud. Above all else, I wanted to be fulfilled and "happy".

I just couldn't see how to get there. At this point I still saw happiness as a finite destination. Ironically I would never "get there" as "there" just didn't exist.

I'd spent so long thinking about what I wanted, what I deserved, what I didn't have that I went around in circles.

There are people everywhere – from home to work to holidays, shops and roads, cars, schools, planes – everywhere.

And yet so many of us interact with so few people on such a limited basis it's no surprise that I, you, we don't deserve more than we have. We're not serving enough people; we're not connecting, not adding value.

We are likely to have reached homeostasis; the limit of everything we can do or want to do. Our results will reflect this limitation.

If you interact with more people, if you "seek first to understand" as Steven Covey recommends – listening to the needs of others and understanding them better – then your world will change.

It's not about "me"; it's about "you".

youdeservethisbook.com

We're all too busy looking at what we can get for ourselves that we neglect to help others or at least give it a lower priority as we put ourselves first.

The magic of serving others is hard to understand at first. After all, if I don't have what I want, why should I spend my time helping you get what you want? Surely that won't help me?

It's helping others, being helped by others and being "of service" to one another that greases the wheels of the world. Much of life is "give and take" – but notice that "give" comes before "take".

When I realised I'd fallen victim to "me first!" mentality, I decided that life from here on in would be a contact sport.

> Greg: "This entire business revolves around the phone. Play the numbers. This is a contact sport. The more people you contact, the better you'll do. I mean a good broker makes over 700 calls a day."
> Seth: "What? What's the phone bill like here?"
> Greg: "This month was approaching $400,000."
> **Boiler Room (2000)**

By that, I mean making more contact with people to increase not only my practice at being a friendly, helpful person, but to also increase my chances of interacting with those who may be able to repay the favour and help me – it's about opportunities to be more Selfmore. (We'll learn about Selfmore in just a moment.)

Among my handful of close friends I felt like I was always the one who would help unconditionally (this was my incorrect perception – they would do the same for me) so I was familiar with what to do, I just needed to open this up to the world at large; from my colleagues to my customers to everyday people on the street.

This wasn't to say I planned to become subservient or a doormat. Far from it. I took the decision to help those I could if it was within my power and if they were in need of help.

It's foolish to mistake kindness for weakness.

Being "of service" can also mean just being polite and courteous. Driving is now for me a stress free experience as I seek to give way to as many motorists as I can. It may cost me five minutes on my journey, but the warm feeling of doing good, even in a small way is addictive. I let pedestrians cross in front of me, let motorists pull out from side roads, I give way to buses. I "serve" all of these people, it costs me a fraction of time but gives me an enormous sense of wellbeing and calm. Previously, I was "that guy". I'd speed up to *not* let you in, pretend I didn't see you, not give way and generally put myself first.

The net result? A feeling of stress and angry responses from others, as well as the increased risk of an accident, and for what? I was no better off for this behaviour but it felt so natural to put myself first.

"Be kind: everyone you meet is fighting their own battle."
Plato

Okay, so giving way to people in traffic and holding open doors won't get you where you need to be, per se, but it will help to shift from self-obsessed mentality to service mentality. This is also the shift from the "you don't deserve it" to the YOU DESERVE IT mentality.

I treat people now as though they are a guest in my home, rather than ignoring them or treating them with selfish contempt as I had previously. I realise now that life is not a zero sum game – there is no finite "pie" from which we all "take a piece", we can all prosper and grow together without taking from others.

Perhaps I'm not the norm here. Perhaps, given my personal history, I was more guarded and more selfish than most. Or perhaps this is the norm? Either way, it feels so harsh to write it down and admit to it.

I think we're all selfish to a degree; it's a primal survival instinct: to kill or be killed. We have to be this way sometimes; we just need to consider putting others first as a counter-intuitive means of making progress.

Be our guest! Be our guest!
Put our service to the test
Tie your napkin 'round your neck, Cherie
and we'll provide the rest
Soup du jour
Hot hors d'oeuvres

youdeservethisbook.com

Why, we only live to serve
Beauty and the Beast, "Be Our Guest" (1991)

There's a reason the phrase "it's not what you know, it's who you know" rings true. How many jobs, opportunities or anything have you managed to achieve in your life without "knowing someone" or having a "good word" being put in for you? If you're like me, it would be 80 / 20 "knowing someone" versus not "knowing someone". This is the "Circle of YOU DESERVE IT" at work.

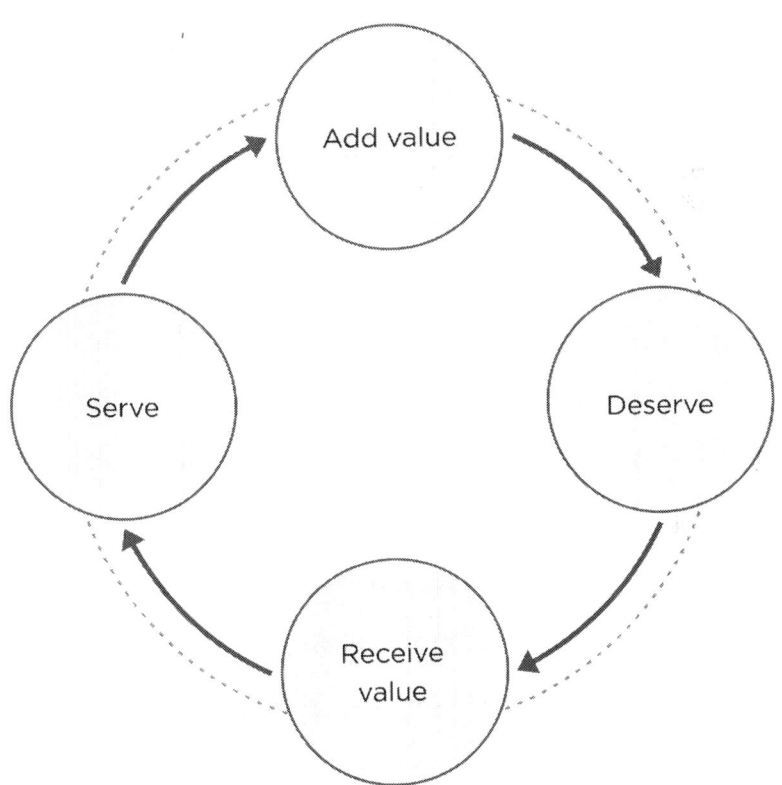

If you've previously added value for someone, be it small or large, size is irrelevant, if you've added value, proved yourself trustworthy, reliable and willing to help, then this has created a desire in the recipient to reciprocate.

youdeservethisbook.com

reciprocity

/ˌrɛsɪˈprɒsɪti/

noun

the practice of exchanging things with others for mutual benefit, especially privileges granted by one country or organization to another.

I discuss sales in a later chapter, but thanks to YOU DESERVE IT I realised that at work I was subconsciously putting my client's needs first, sometimes above my own or even to my detriment and <u>that</u> was the defining reason they were loyal to me and I enjoyed the success I'd had. I was serving them in over-drive.

I'd felt "undeserving" of my success as selling felt so natural – I didn't even consider it selling, I was just talking to people. As I expended little effort, and it felt easy, I felt I deserved little reward. I'd unknowingly tapped into the Circle of YOU DESERVE IT.

The amount of value you add may not reflect the amount of effort you put in.

To provide the most value to others, or to serve them more "vigorously" you need to be playing to your personal strengths. You need to be doing something you enjoy and are passionate about to add the most value. You can't be good at something you don't enjoy or are passionate about – or more accurately you can, but at some point you will plateau and your interest will wane. This is where I'd got to.

This is the law of diminishing intent; over time your interest and intentions can naturally wane.

youdeservethisbook.com

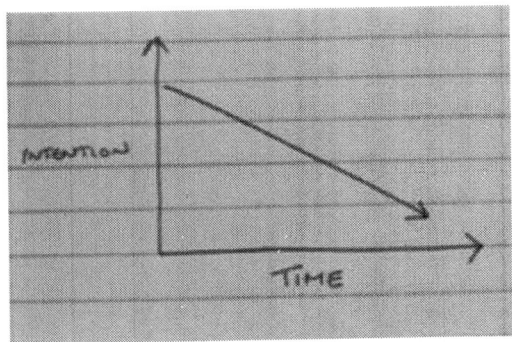

I had enjoyed my job, but after 10 years I knew my interest was waning. To be honest, after two years it had waned dramatically. Although I was good at what I did and enjoyed success, I knew I needed to find fulfilling work before maintaining my current enthusiasm level became too onerous to handle.

I was comfortable in life, but felt uncomfortable with my life. I knew I could do more, be more and serve more. I knew I could be greater than I was. I just couldn't understand how to get there – I was stuck.

It's amazing how my journey has unfurled. I'm writing these words right now as a result of not feeling happy and wanting to take action. Of feeling I deserved more from life, but not receiving it. I'm writing these words because I now deserve it and I understand how to deserve.

Once I'd switched my focus from inward to outward, from strangers to house guests, it was only logical that I try to find my passion so I could add the most value and thus deserve as much as I would ever be capable of. I'd seen the power of YOU DESERVE IT at my office, where my passion had vanished, and I still did well, so **with** passion I would be unstoppable!

Adding the most value would mean I would deserve the most I could get from life. Serving more relates to how much you add value and how many people you add value to. Ideally you want to maximise both, but not at the cost of your sanity or at the risk of being a doormat.

You want to help where you can, but with an eye to what you want and where you want to be. Remember, you're a "planner", not a "settler".

youdeservethisbook.com

Taking serving others to "the next level" will only accelerate its potency. By exceeding expectations and pre-empting the needs of others, it makes it clear that you want to help them get to where they need to be.

After much self-analysis during the process of writing this book, I realised this was my own secret tactic for success. I would pre-empt needs, do more than is required and be as relentless in this pursuit as possible. As a result I won the loyalty, respect and good favour of my customers, colleagues and friends.

Although claiming to not enjoy my job, I would start work early; ensure no stone was left unturned. I would seek out opportunities and coach some of my clients on how to increase sales and improve business practices. My goal was to serve them and never to sell them. Always.

Serving more can also mean caring, taking an interest. Showing others that you care about them and are interested in them (genuinely interested) builds and strengthens loyalty, trust and goodwill – all vital to deserving more.

If you feel someone cares about you, you care about them. This is reciprocity.

If you look around at those close to you, or in the public eye – those people who are "successful" are often those who connect and add value to as many people as they can.

Successful people do not reach the top alone. It takes many others to help them get there. For that reason, people are always their top priority. They put people before profit because they realise that without people there is no profit.

I can think of three people in my close circle who seem to always be on the phone / in meetings / connecting / conversing. The fact that these people stand ahead of their peers in terms of performance is no coincidence.

It's all about being selfless – or better yet "Selfmore". My concept of "Selfmore" helped me to make another paradigm shift. I went from selfish, just thinking about myself, to selfless, just thinking about others, to Selfmore which is a hybrid of the two and a classic "win, win".

youdeservethisbook.com

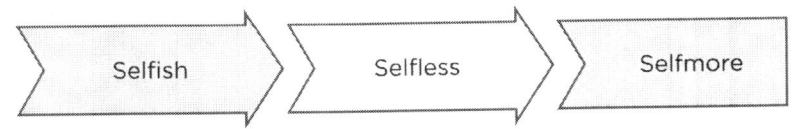

Selfmore is the act of helping others to achieve their goals but with an eye kept firmly upon achieving your own goals.

Far from feeling in competition with the world at large, that I needed to "compete" for my "piece of the pie" I began to feel more co-operative and supported.

Being "Selfmore" generates a void, a vacuum, a deficit. If you help others and ask nothing in return you are generating goodwill and loyalty. You are triggering reciprocity. Many of those you help feel in some way obligated to help you – and as you made the first move and helped them first, their reciprocation may be disproportionately greater than if you selfishly asked them for a favour instead.

It's give, then take, serve, and then deserve, you, then me.

This is a recognised part of social psychology. Reciprocity refers to responding to a positive action with another positive action.

> *"Appeal to others' self-interest,*
> *never their mercy or gratitude."*
> **Law 13 – The 48 Laws of Power**

If you deserve no more in your life than you have right now (Chapter 2) then you need to make new action and new connections to get to your goal.

A great place to start is to focus on being a valuable person. Be that at home, at work or amongst your friends. Which skills or abilities which you currently are not sharing with others could be used to add value?

Focussing on your worth (not net worth) as a measure of success is a form of "Selfmore" – focussing on being the best you can at what you do, and adding the most value along the way, will not only set you more aside from the selfish masses, bemused by why they don't deserve, but it will naturally open up avenues for you which you may never have considered.

There is no set path to YOU DESERVE IT.

That's logical, with so many unique people and paths in life – there is no "cure all". There are, however, principles. Principles which can help you to deserve more. The principle of seeking to serve before deserve is the most salient.

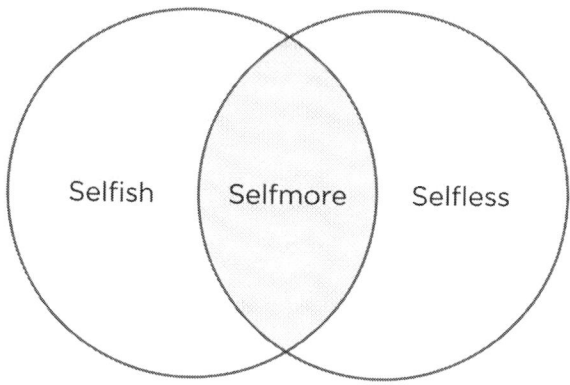

The Five Minute Favour

YOU DESERVE IT is about adding value to others and serving them.

This idea, from the book "Give and Take" by Adam Grant, is interesting as it is so simple.

Basically if you are able to help someone or are asked for a favour and it will take you five minutes to complete, then not only should you oblige, but you should do so as quickly as you can.

There are two benefits to this approach.

1. The first is that doing favours for others and helping them encourages you to consider others and to move to a more Selfmore state of mind which is where YOU DESERVE IT is maximised.
2. The second is that doing favours and helping others creates reciprocity. You add value, you become more valuable – and of course if you ever need a small favour you are likely to be helped.

Make it your goal for the next week that every day you do at least one five minute favour for someone.

Remember, givers gain.

youdeservethisbook.com

YOU DESERVE IT is not a processional idea. It's not always a straightforward sequence of events. Two plus two does not always equal four. If you're doing it right, whilst you're adding two plus two, someone you've selflessly (Selfmorely) helped introduces you to someone who can help you.

All of a sudden 2 + 2 = ∞

But how?

To reap this benefit you have to understand and have faith in the power of serving others and helping them selflessly (Selfmorely) whilst asking nothing directly in return.

Processional vs. Precessional – honey bees and pebbles

We've all been taught that achieving anything in life, particularly wealth, is a simple input/output, logical, processional affair. Output always follows input.

Study hard, get a job, work hard, get a promotion, save some money, buy a house and so forth. The system does work, but you need to understand the precessional effects can be just as, if not more, powerful.

Precessional effects are not linear. They are non-linear. The link from input to output is not necessarily direct or even obvious.

Let me explain. When you drop a pebble into water, the processional element is the splash of water. At the same time however, shockwaves, or ripples, resonate from the pebble being dropped – a precessional effect and not what you set out to achieve.

Precessional effects are essentially "side-effects" of taking action to achieve an outcome.

Another example would be the honey bee. The honey bee goes from flower to flower in its pursuit of collecting pollen to create nectar and honey. Its purpose is to collect the pollen and this is the simple cause / effect processional outcome. At the same time however, the honey bee is helping to pollinate the flowers it lands upon and helping them propagate.

This is the precessional effect at work; the bee is "adding value" to the plants to help them grow by pollinating the flowers, and in return there will be more plants to visit in future.

Selfmore comes from nature. Consider fruit: apples, pears, bananas – whichever. Fruit tastes great and is a desirable thing to eat.

The plant or tree which grows the fruit needs to spread its seeds to propagate, which is what it is there to do. Alone, the plant or tree can't spread seeds very far, so it creates tasty and juicy fruit which is eaten by animals, along with the seeds, which are then discarded or defecated at another location.

The key to the plant propagating and spreading seeds comes from Selfmore. It gives the animals something (the fruit) and in return the animals give the plant what it wants (relocate the seeds).

When I began to think of myself as a honey bee and the people I interacted with as the flowers – I questioned what goodness I could spread to them, how I could help "pollinate" their lives and thus add more value and help them.

At the point before I started this book, and my new path in life, I cared little for how I could help others outside of work (I carried little pollen). I put myself first, and as such served those around me less than I could have. As a result I deserved less than I could have.

It's a tough thing to write, but looking back I can say I am ashamed of my selfishness in some situations, but there was a clear lesson to be learned. As someone who was convinced he deserved more, I was intrigued to discover exactly where I was going wrong. This was a fundamental principle of YOU DESERVE IT which I hadn't yet grasped.

I needed to try focussing on others first.

In my work life I spent all day every day interacting, sharing information, adding value; as such I experienced success in that area of my life. I was the honey bee doing my duty and serving others. I dedicated myself to helping customers, finding opportunities and adding value wherever I could. All day, every day.

Outside of work, I did little or nothing to help "pollinate" the lives of those around me. I helped friends and family of course, but didn't dedicate myself to serving others in the same way I did at work.

As I added so much less value outside of work, I noticed I deserved so much less. I realise now, that's why I stayed stuck for so long in the same place not achieving the things I wanted. I'd reached my limits.

Perhaps this is the same for you? Are you looking to serve and add value to those in your life outside of work? When did you last help someone even if you knew they may never be able to repay the favour?

youdeservethisbook.com

Favours are the currency of YOU DESERVE IT. Earn them, invest them, spend them, and give them away.

My duty is to serve

In my professional capacity, it was my duty to serve. "Don't worry, I get paid to help you," I'd tell clients who worried they were wasting my time or being too demanding. I was being paid to sell, to serve, to look after these people. Outside of this in my life there was no duty to serve and this was limiting my results. At work, as "my duty" to serve, I was committed. I was dedicated – always asking how I could add more value, how I could do more.

> *"England expects every man to do his duty."*
> **Admiral Nelson**

What if you made serving others your duty? What if you focussed on adding value, being helpful and cooperative? Be this inside or outside of a work setting. What if you set aside pursuing what you wanted and deserved in the first instance? To focus on helping others first?

If you shift from selfish to selfless to "Selfmore", how could you trigger the precessional effects like the honey bee?

Which seemingly unconnected people and situations hold the key to your future? If only you'd give more of yourself and serve more? Who in your life right now could help you get everything you've ever wanted or felt you deserved – if only you'd help them get what they want first?

Serving more utilises an important element of the YOU DESERVE IT theory. You don't deserve more than you have in your life right now – if you did, you'd have it already.

We feel we deserve more; it's the hedonic treadmill at work, the constant march for improvement. The sense of entitlement to things is commonplace and exists as an emotional response linked to self-image, self-confidence and self-worth. It's natural.

By helping others and adding value to them "off your own back" without asking anything in return, you are subconsciously indicating that the recipient is worthy of deserving more than they currently have – as you try to deliver it to them. As the recipient feels entitled to more than they have, and you are helping provide them with more – it generates goodwill. This triggers feelings of reciprocity as you are helping and adding value with no ulterior motive.

These feelings of reciprocity and "owing" something encourage the recipient to find ways to help you and to be more responsive to your needs.

Win-win. And so the Circle of YOU DESERVE IT is complete. Genius.

Whatever your age, race, colour, job, location, net worth – we are all people trying to get to where we want to be, to get what we think we deserve (or could deserve) and to feel valued.

By showing those around you that you care about them and want to help them, even though there's potentially nothing in it for you, means you will, in turn, be helped to deserve what you want.

Of all my research, musings and theories on deserving – serving others more is truly the way to deserving more. To serve is the definition of YOU DESERVE IT after all.

youdeservethisbook.com

10 things to remember

1. To deserve more, you have to serve more.
2. The law of diminishing intent states that over time your interest and intentions wane.
3. Focussing on others rather than yourself is the essence of YOU DESERVE IT.
4. Life is not 100% processional; sometimes it's precessional – meaning that your actions trigger indirect results.
5. Reciprocity greases the wheels of deserving. You help others, they help you.
6. You must give before you can receive.
7. Life is not a zero sum game – we can all reach our goals and enjoy success.
8. "Selfmore" is helping others to get what they want, with an eye on what you are trying to achieve.
9. Serving others can simply mean taking a genuine interest in them.
10. Appeal to others' self interest, never to their mercy or gratitude.

youdeservethisbook.com

Exercise – Kindness Days

Kindness is a central part of YOU DESERVE IT. Adding value to others, serving them, is about highlighting their needs and then satisfying them. Selfmore encourages us to move from selfish to selfless to Selfmore – the only way to make this possible is through kindness. For the next three days experiment with kindness. Spend one day being completely selfless, the next being completely selfish and the final day being Selfmore.

Example

My favourite act of kindness is letting in as many people as possible when I am driving. Far from being a stressed out driver, racing everywhere, I let people in, drive within the speed limits and am showered with thanks from other motorists as a result.

Possible examples:

- Drive more courteously.
- Buy someone lunch.
- Send your partner a gift or flowers.

The selfish day is always a difficult one as none of us is truly selfish, but it's great to indulge yourself once in a while. Switch off your phone, ignore everything and everyone. Go for a walk, watch films, have a duvet day, eat ice cream – act on every whim to please yourself.

Possible examples:

- Turn off your phone.
- Ignore everything and everyone.
- Eat what you want.
- Spend the day lounging in bed watching films.

The Selfmore day provides you an opportunity to align your goals with others, seek collaboration, barter and trade off your skills and services – do something nice for someone but without the requirement they must do something nice in return.

youdeservethisbook.com

Possible examples:

- Create working partnerships with colleagues or clients.
- Trade skills with neighbours such as gardening or washing windows.
- Offer to help your partner with anything they choose.

Tip
Be selfless first, then selfish, then Selfmore, in that order for maximum contrast.

What you'll need
Imaginative ways to be kind and selfish.

Duration
3 days

When completed, ask yourself:
Doesn't it feel great to be kind? How can you stay as close to kindness as possible, even when you feel frustrated or are having a tough time yourself? Kindness is a powerful catalyst to change – it's also enjoyable.

4 – Modelling

Find someone who deserves what you want and emulate them.

- What is it that you want?
- Who has it already?
- What are they doing that you aren't?

In this chapter we'll look at how others achieve and how it's possible to emulate and be inspired by their actions. We'll ask, "What would Jesus do?" To help guide us, we'll ask better questions and we'll look at connecting the dots.

This chapter is about creating a plan and taking inspiration from those who have what you want; and what better place to start?

"What have I done to deserve this?"

A simple question we have all asked of ourselves at some point in time.

But. Have you ever looked at someone who has what you want and asked what *they* have done to deserve it?

If not, then perhaps you should… As mentioned in Chapter 3, YOU DESERVE IT is all about focussing on the external – how can you add value to others, not simply "what's in it for me?" This is no more important than when it comes to creating a plan of action.

You deserve no more than you have right now (Chapter 2) so to deserve more, or to deserve different things you must take more or different action.

As a sales person I knew nothing of the world of coaching, teaching and motivating, other than that which I'd consumed over the years to help deal with the early traumas I had encountered.

I needed a plan of action to be able to move forward, even a rough plan, to help guide me to my goals. Until this point I had drifted. I had no clear goals and nothing to focus on. I hadn't even defined what I wanted (I was trapped in the Procrastination Illusion) – it's no wonder that 10 years slipped by with no real progress.

Most things in life aren't "paint by numbers" so you need to take a different approach.

You can paint on the canvas and see what happens, but you're more likely to have an incoherent result rather than steadily progressing to a definitive goal. This is classic Planning vs. Settling.

I now use the technique of modelling on nearly everything in my life; it helps me understand how things work, how they interact with the world, how to use them and how to benefit from them. Rather than be unsure of why others appeared to succeed and I didn't, I began to question it.

The simple question: "What have they done to deserve it?" This can be used for both positive and negative outcomes equally.

No doubt something undesirable has entered your life and you've asked, "What have I done to deserve this?" It's the same principle. It's just focussing outward, rather than inward – a core part of YOU DESERVE IT.

I looked to the likes of Tony Robbins, Robin Sharma, ET the Hip Hop Preacher, Brendan Burchard and others. They represented the "end game" for me. These were people living the life I wanted, doing what I wanted to do. I studied what they were doing and how I could emulate their actions and recreate their success in my own life.

This is called "modelling" and is a tenet of NLP – Neuro Linguistic Programming. If you're not familiar with NLP, it's the study of success, and of literally "programming" your mind.

> Neuro-linguistic programming (NLP) is an approach to communication, personal development, and psychotherapy created by Richard Bandler and John Grinder in California, United States in the 1970s. Its creators claim a connection between the neurological processes ("Neuro"), language ("linguistic") and behavioural patterns learned through experience ("programming") and that these can be changed to achieve specific goals in life.
>
> Bandler and Grinder claim that NLP methodology can "model" the skills of exceptional people, then those skills can be acquired by anyone.
>
> Source: https://en.wikipedia.org/wiki/Neuro-linguistic_programming

Asking what others have done to deserve it is another way of "starting with the end in mind". I couldn't see how to get where I wanted to be, so it was hard for me to imagine what I needed to do. By looking to those who had already made the journey, the signposts and directions became clearer.

Thinking about what you want; the destination, finding others who have already reached the destination and studying the path they took to get there is a powerful tool.

One large caveat is that we are all different. Simply replicating the exact actions of others is not only impossible; it's also a disservice to you and your talents. Modelling, starting with the end in mind, whatever you want to call it – it's about finding what worked for others and translating that into what may work for you. It's about harnessing its power.

I say "may" work for you as there are no guarantees (as I discovered) but studying others and using that to inspire your own action sets off the precessional and processional shockwaves that will help advance you toward your goal (see Chapter 3).

It's about principles. Principles such as serving others more and seeking to add value first, which help accelerate results.

Finding the other principles, routines and attitudes of those who you want to emulate are pivotal to your success. There is no "one size fits all" approach. If success was guaranteed through pure imitation, life would be boring and modelling others would be a lot more commonplace.

It's about taking what's worked and adapting it.

So who to look at and what to model? For me, it was a case of dissecting the talks and books of those people I had consumed over the previous 10 years and then asking some open and constructive questions.

It's about asking better questions. Simple questions such as "why did I find this book useful?", "what made that talk resonate?" and "why do I instantly feel connected to XYZ person?".

By stepping back from self-focussed thinking and considering things which seemed so unconnected from the things I wanted seemed illogical at first, but soon made perfect sense. Above all else, the question to ask when studying or modelling the action of others is "how are they adding value" or "how are they serving me?"

youdeservethisbook.com

If you take one concept away from this book, it's that focussing on adding value to others and not focussing on yourself is the way to turbo-charge your results.

Studying those who already serve you and add value to you is logical to establish the "recipe" or "roadmap" they have used. When I began to study coaches (including my own coach who was helping me bring YOU DESERVE IT to life) I realised they all had one thing in common.

They were all genuinely concerned with helping, teaching, guiding, coaching others to do better. This genuineness shone through easily, characterised by an eager demeanour and an excitable and curious nature. They were passionate and this passion helped them maximise who and how they served and added value.

You know when someone genuinely wants to help you or is being honest with you; it's an unmistakeable feeling and something which can't be "faked".

I would urge that whatever it is you want to deserve in your life, you will find it far easier to make progress when you choose a path you genuinely care about that will allow you to genuinely help others and utilise your talents.

If you're not 100% passionate about what you are doing, or worse, only doing it for the money, not only does it show and can put people off (I studied some speakers to establish why I felt no connection with them; disingenuousness was always the route cause), but it means your potential to deserve everything you want in your life and the value you add to others will be limited. You may even experience diminishing results over time as I did.

If you're not 100% passionate, no matter how hard you try your results will be limited and interest will wane over time.

Let me be clear that there aren't always "a-ha!" moments – I must admit I didn't have confidence in the YOU DESERVE IT concept when I began working on it. I couldn't see how to write a book about what I perceived as a limited subject (and seemingly very simple), nor could I envisage charging others to hear me tell them they deserved everything they had in their lives – and that it was all their doing (!).

It took time, experimentation, but most of all faith that the pieces of the jigsaw puzzle would fit and the dots would connect.

youdeservethisbook.com

4 – Modelling

> *"You can't connect the dots looking forward; you can only connect them looking backward."*
> **Steve Jobs**

Modelling others allows you to see the whole jigsaw and the dots connected and then work backwards. It also helps you understand that no matter how skilled, successful, famous or rich someone is, at some point they stood where I was (and perhaps where you are) with an idea of what they wanted to achieve but a very limited idea of what to do to achieve it or even how to begin.

Taking action, large or small is the only way.

I wanted to be a speaker and so I joined the UK based Pony Express Speaker club (http://www.ponyexpressclub.com/). This one decision connected me with my coach and with others already making a living from speaking and coaching. This allowed me to see that it is not only possible to achieve what I wanted to achieve, but that there is no single set route and that we all have to start somewhere.

It was the feeling of being stuck in my job with no clear idea of how or when things could change that was the biggest impediment to my success. By interacting with those who had "made it" my viewpoint widened and my confidence was boosted: it was all possible.

To deserve more or to deserve different things, you have to take different action – or simply take some action – however small.

Studying what people did, how they did it, and how they served others was important to providing some clues relevant to where I wanted to be.

One action which never ceases to impress me is also the simplest. It can make you feel self-conscious or even a little silly the first time you try it – but go with me for a moment.

You may have come across the phrase "act as if" before, but have you ever truly considered what it means or better still given it a go? Act as if is all about changing your physiology. Literally changing the way you act and "pretending" or "acting" as though you were the person you wish to model.

WWJD

In the Christian faith there is an expression "What Would Jesus Do" which is used to help put many of the judgements, commandments, rules and considerations into a simple, actionable question. It works because it focuses on principles, not specifics.

Considering what someone else would do in a given situation (whether they're the son of God or not) can be a quick way to escape the self-obsessed mindset. It's a shift in perception.

Sometimes a shift in perception is all you need.

We can guess what we would do in any given situation, but may have never taken the time to stop and consider what someone else would do. Different thinking produces different viewpoints and different results.

Chances are, the person you are modelling would take different action to yourself (it's almost certain, as they have what you don't have). Different action = different results. Using this technique is a subtle way of changing things in your world, but without feeling too responsible for the outcome. It's a form of testing.

In this context, replacing Jesus with someone who has what you want and then considering what they would do in any given situation is a paradigm shift and can open up new possibilities. Pick someone who is where you want to be and has achieved what you want. Consider how they would act and try this yourself.

What Would I Do?

If there isn't someone you can model or you don't want to, then you can always consider your future self. If you had achieved everything you ever wanted, then what would your life look like? How would you speak or treat others? How great would it feel to finally have everything you've been striving for?

Filled with this warm sense of pride and accomplishment, would you feel like helping others or giving back in some way? Would you eat differently? Work differently? Take up new hobbies? Think in detail about what your life may look like and how you may act differently as a result.

Act as if and WWJD are both tools to help change your behaviour and to experiment with what works. I considered how I would be as a coach, speaker, author and motivator – even though I was still trapped in the job I no longer enjoyed, feeling as far away from my dreams as I could possibly be. I began to focus on how I would be as the coach, speaker and author I planned to be. I found I was more generous with my time and my money, more genuinely connected and interacted more with those around me, as well as feeling more content.

How about that. Without a single client, a published book or anything else that would "make me" a coach, I was able to tap into how it would feel to have achieved all I set out to. Instantly. It was motivating and enjoyable.

This also has two distinct benefits. Initially I had a lack of faith and confidence I could "make a go" of the YOU DESERVE IT book and coaching path. By tapping into the "finishing line" and considering how I would feel, act, behave and think if I were already established – it gave me a rush of confidence, well-being and faith that everything I wanted was possible – I just needed to get out there and make it happen.

I just needed to connect the dots. You can only connect the dots looking backward, so to imagine looking back from your end goal provides new insight.

The second benefit was the change in my behaviour when I tapped into this world. When I sat in a coffee shop to write, I would pretend I was already "James Newell; coach, speaker, author, founder of everydayshouldbefun.com and firm believer that it's not what happens to you in life – it's what you do about it."

I noticed myself smiling at the baristas more, being more patient, and being more present. I felt confident I could fill the pages I planned to and would achieve what I wanted. I moved instantly from anxiety about the future to confidence it would all turn out.

Nothing had changed, other than my perception. This is so important. I just changed how I viewed things.

When you change the way you look at things,
the things you look at change.

I felt inquisitive of those around me and how they may benefit from my book when it was published. I imagined helping others, being recognised for my skills and living an authentic life of passion.

youdeservethisbook.com

Okay, so having told you to focus on others to advance toward your goals, such self-focussed thinking may seem counter-intuitive – even contradictory. But.

It was these sessions of "daydreaming" "pretending" and "acting as if" that helped fuel this book, boost my confidence and above all make the progress I needed too. The difference was I was also taking action – not just daydreaming.

To deserve more you definitely need to serve more, but you also need to be in the right frame of mind and in a "good place". To get to this "good place" you "act as if" and "WWJD" as often as you need to.

By modelling others to give you a plan of action, acting as though you believe they would act, or acting as you would act if you had achieved all you wanted, you trigger new behaviours, new thoughts and generate more hope and faith.

You also build momentum. In the words of Les Brown – "It's possible".

10 things to remember

1. Find someone who has achieved what you want to use as your inspiration.
2. Ask "what have they done to deserve it?"
3. Ask better questions, be positive, and be open.
4. Focussing on how others have succeeded can help you succeed. Don't be envious, be curious.
5. Reframe your thoughts – ask "what would the future me do?"
6. Reframe your thoughts – "Act as if" you have already achieved what you want, how would you conduct yourself differently?
7. Emulating others' actions is the goal, straightforward copying is not.
8. It's easier to pursue and deserve things which you're 100% passionate about.
9. Different action will yield different results – get out there and try new things – the only failure is not trying.
10. When you feel stuck, focus outwards on serving others to keep going.

Exercise – Creating

Using Lego, wooden blocks, twigs, sand or any building material, set out to create something. It could be anything but create a structure – a house, a tower, a sculpture – anything of form.

Create it from your mind without a thought to planning, keep going until you have a structure that stands without falling over and is of a decent size, you will know when you are done. Once you have completed it and think nothing more can be added, add more. Improve upon the design in some way either by adding more building materials or by removing some to make the design cleaner.

Example

I love sandcastles. I love to build them, improve them, smash them down and start again. I am enjoying being fully in the moment, creating and thinking as I go.

Possible examples:

- Build a playing card house.
- Attempt to balance stones atop one another.
- Build a structure using books or CD cases.

Guidance

Yes, building a Lego house is not going to have much impact, but creating something and focussing on the creation helps you to build confidence in yourself as a "creator". Too often we are theoretical in life, waiting for the "perfect moment" to begin.

Building something ad hoc and from your own mind demonstrates that imperfect action gets the job done rather than waiting to take perfect action. Learning to create and then iterate are pivotal to overcoming "perfect moment" syndrome.

When building, ask yourself:

- Do you need to have a plan to begin or can you just begin?
- Could having a plan actually limit you versus creating freehand?

Tip
Use Lego if you can, it's easier, quicker and cleaner, use more tactile materials if you want more of a challenge. Don't make a plan, just begin.

What you'll need
A building material, an imagination and a camera.

Duration
1 hour

When completed, ask yourself:
Do you feel a sense of achievement – however small – from creating something from your imagination? Did you enjoy focussing on just this one thing and not multi-tasking?

youdeservethisbook.com

5 – Casualty/Causality

You either deserve it or you don't.

- If you have it and it's unwanted – why don't you feel YOU DESERVE IT?
- If you want it but don't have it – why don't you have it yet?

In this chapter we'll discover the Hope Bias, the impacts of deserving within your means and why Picasso was wrong. We'll look at asking better questions, consider why playing it safe is risky and consider the "unfairness" of it all.

We all know that you have to do things to get an outcome – it's simple, logical sense. Its cause and effect, input then output.

So why, at age 31, was I frustrated that I wasn't "happy" or doing work that fulfilled me? If I knew outcomes derived from actions, why didn't I take the actions to create the outcomes? It was a bitter pill to swallow. I'd fallen victim to trying to negotiate with YOU DESERVE IT.

As we'll learn, YOU DESERVE IT does not negotiate. As such I remained where I was.

I'd had a tough life and some challenges to face. As much as I didn't actively play the victim and let things get the better of me, I finally realised I'd been subconsciously feeling I was "owed". A lot.

The gambler's fallacy gripped me; with so much "bad luck" and so many "bad experiences", surely the *next* roll of the dice would yield a double six, after all... I deserved it.

This is known as the "Just World Theory", that for every bad thing, something good happens to counter it. It took me a long time to realise this was how I approached life. A very long time.

> **The gambler's fallacy,** also known as the Monte Carlo fallacy or the fallacy of the maturity of chances, is the mistaken belief that, if something happens more frequently than normal during some period, it will happen less frequently in the future, or that, if something happens less frequently than normal during some period, it will happen more frequently in the future (presumably as a means of balancing nature). In situations where what is being observed is truly

random (i.e. independent trials of a random process), this belief, though appealing to the human mind, is false. This fallacy can arise in many practical situations although it is most strongly associated with gambling where such mistakes are common among players.
Source: https://en.wikipedia.org/wiki/Gambler%27s_fallacy

The just-world theory is the cognitive bias (or assumption) that a person's actions are inherently inclined to bring morally fair and fitting consequences to that person, to the end of all noble actions being eventually rewarded and all evil actions eventually punished. In other words, the just-world hypothesis is the tendency to attribute consequences to – or expect consequences as the result of – a universal force that restores moral balance.
Source: https://en.wikipedia.org/wiki/Just-world_hypothesis

I would boast about being a "lucky" person, and to some extent I was (I even had it tattooed on my back). I had survived the 2004 Asian tsunami for starters, but I was hoping this "luck" would deliver everything I wanted from life and be the key to all I wanted. Sadly this was not the case.

Hope is not a strategy, but if you are feeling unsure of what to do and that you are "owed" or "special" in some way (as I did) then it's a great way to spend a decade making negligible progress towards your dreams, trapped in the productivity illusion. <Sigh>

Hope is important. It keeps us from quitting, keeps us motivated and in pursuit, but hope is no substitute for action. Its hope AND action which get results.

YOU DESERVE IT is a logical state of affairs – you do X and you get Y. It might take some time, some trial and error, some self-discovery, but in the end your actions will advance you towards your goal.

Hoping is not taking action.

Feeling "lucky", hard done by or "owed" is not taking action; without action there is no progress. And so my "lost decade" of negligible progress had only served to frustrate me and in my quieter moments, embarrass me.

youdeservethisbook.com

I was unaware of what I was doing at the time. Unaware that I wouldn't achieve half of what I wanted unless I changed my ways. Hope consumed me, hope held me back, but crucially, hope didn't let me give up. It was a double-edged sword.

The only weapon I had which served me was the burning feeling that I did deserve to achieve everything I wanted. I realised that I didn't quit. Ever. I kept going, no matter what.

This is an important part of success and achievement. Continuing to try, to adapt, to act, until you get to where you want. (Remember Course Made Good.)

Yes, I'd spent 10 years not making progress and drifting, but I hadn't given up.

> *"It doesn't matter how slowly you go,*
> *as long as you don't stop."*
> **Confucius**

I enjoyed competition and I pushed myself hard to achieve because I felt I deserved so much more than I had, I felt I was owed it.

It turned out my results were limited by my limited thinking.

The thought I was "owed" and should receive more not through action but through simply "deserving it" had kept me in neutral for far too long. I was literally "waiting for my ship to come in".

It was time to explore what YOU DESERVE IT actually meant as I clearly had a lot to learn. It was the next logical step; it just took me far longer than I ever hoped to reach it.

But this was what I deserved. My actions had brought me to this point.

Believing we deserve things with no logical reason or through no specific action keeps us away from making progress and in the realm of hope.

Hope is addictive. It's pleasant enough and can be useful, but it's not a strategy. Hope requires no action, no responsibility and after a while you feel even more worthy of the end result as you have "spent so much time on it". I call this the "Hope Bias".

The Hope Bias is the erroneous belief that by thinking about something for a long time, you will eventually deserve it as you've "invested so much time in it". This is despite taking minimal or no appropriate action towards truly deserving it.

This is why things such as the National Lottery (in the UK) and lotteries around the world work so well.

I have been playing the National Lottery myself for over 15 years. Each time I didn't win (and that would have been quite a few times now...) I felt more "likely" or more "entitled" to win the next time. After all, it has to be my turn to win at some point. Doesn't it?

Remember the "just world" theory that for every bad thing, something good happens to counter it. With that in mind I'd believe I had "more chance" if I just play again... Dangerous stuff.

Hope can keep you from action, from responsibility and from deserving what you want. It's anathema.

Through hope and lack of progress it dawned on me that inaction was a form of action. Choosing not to act – is action. By not choosing to pursue X, you are in fact choosing to pursue Y.

For example, you choose not to tend to your garden; the result is a scruffy garden full of weeds. Your inaction is "action towards the outcome". Though you don't actively want a garden full of weeds, your actions will cause you to deserve it.

I call this the hidden choice.

> ***The "Hidden Choice":*** *When you take no action or make no decision. Your inaction or indecision is actually a choice toward the outcome that the inaction and indecision brings. You may not seek or want this result, but you have "chosen" it and thus it's a "Hidden Choice".*
>
> *Examples:*
> *Not choosing to eat healthily is a "Hidden Choice" to eat unhealthily.*
> *Spending beyond your means is a "Hidden Choice" to accumulating debt.*

Seem unfair? It feels unfair but this is the way of the world. This is the way it works. This is reality. Not cleaning your car is choosing a dirty car; not exercising is choosing to be unhealthy and so on.

These may not feel like "choices" but they are. Realising you are responsible for your outcomes, you can change your approach and

youdeservethisbook.com

weed the garden or you can accept that by not doing anything the garden will be full of weeds and you will deserve them.

Seemingly innocuous examples, but the principles are life changing.

Deserving within your means was a concept I explored during this time. Society is rife with those of poor health and poor bank balances – the problems of obesity and debt.

Obesity and debt are examples of individuals having decided they "deserved" something – without deserving it.

Let me explain. These people reward themselves without taking action first, or as I see it – deserving out of their means.

The notion that you must serve before you deserve – you must add value before you can receive value is the reality. By deserving outside of your means you obtain something you don't deserve and cause issues such as financial debt or contempt of others.

To deserve outside your means is to put yourself and your wants first, which goes against the principles of YOU DESERVE IT. It's trying to deserve before you serve.

How many times have you been low on money or haven't exercised in a while and thought "I need something to cheer me up"?

Perhaps you feel "owed" or it's justified somehow. This was how I felt for too long. It's the "just world" theory again; when things don't go your way, you feel you deserve something good to reset the balance.

Often this "something" is a temporary fix which can actually set you back on your path to YOU DESERVE IT.

Let's say you've had a tough time at work – long hours, late nights. The gym has taken a back seat for a couple of months and as a result you feel a little lethargic. It's a late night again at the office and rather than eat the healthy salad you should and go for a walk – you have a coffee and a chocolate bar, followed by another. After all you've had a hard time – YOU DESERVE IT, right?

A little treat? How bad could it be? This is a Hidden Choice.

Let's go back to that shiny Porsche – there has to be some input, some action, some "serving" of others and adding value – something which leads you to deserve it.

If you simply took out a loan today and bought the Porsche – after all, you haven't had a treat in ages and things have been tough... not only would you have to retrospectively deserve it (make repayments) but at some point that shiny Porsche may no longer appear so shiny – and it's a sparkly new Lexus that catches your eye.

Remember the hedonic treadmill? Attempting to deserve before you serve will keep you firmly on the treadmill going nowhere. There will always be something "better" to catch your eye.

All of a sudden you have a Porsche you don't deserve and you're making eyes at a Lexus you definitely don't deserve. You're falling victim to deserving outside your means – and as a result you may find yourself with other issues such as debt to contend with. You deserve the debt as you created the situation, but your strong desire for the Porsche and the need for a treat (which you feel entitled to) are justifications to make you feel less responsible for the situation. You needed a treat and times have been tough lately – what else were you supposed to do?

Life is just so unfair.

To acquire what you want without deserving it first is inherently unfulfilling; just look at those members of society (and I would expect you know at least one) who have the latest everything, designer everything – and a mountain of personal debt.

Look at how happy they are…

Today, instant gratification is the standard, anything else is deemed too difficult, or worse, impossible. If you can't have it today, then you may feel let down or perhaps in some way a failure.

To deserve isn't difficult but it does take effort, timing, forethought and persistence.

In most cases you have to have a plan to deserve what you want and to readjust your course along the way. Seldom will your actions allow you to "stumble across" everything you desire – this is hoping, and I assure you that hoping isn't helping.

When I sat down in the cold light of day to consider what I wanted and what action I'd taken I was astounded at how clouded my judgement had been.

I was familiar with the phrase "what have I *done* to deserve this" but I wasn't considering *what I could do to* deserve this.

With this question, the future tense provides a positive and constructive angle, the past tense is often overlooked; we seldom dissect why we deserved the good things.

I didn't have a plan or even a rough idea. All I had was hope and a lot of wasted time and a growing despair of what to do. I also had a "sob story" of why all the bad things I had dealt with should combine and entitle me to some "good luck".

This was a milestone on my journey – possibly the most important one:

> *Assessing where you are right now,*
> *where you want to be and*
> *considering how to get there*
> **is the only way to make progress.**

I know, I know, I'm not a rocket scientist either but it makes sense.

The reason I didn't (and perhaps you haven't) done this properly comes back to honesty, fear and being responsible.

For me it was the honesty to admit that I wanted a lot of things from life, hadn't taken any real structured action towards them, didn't have them and as such felt "owed" in some strange way.

I felt "owed" because I'd spent so much time wishing and hoping that I had little energy to take action and felt more deserving of them. This is the Hope Bias. When you realise you don't deserve any more than you have in your life right now (Chapter 2) all hope fades away.

When you are honest with yourself and others about where you are and what you're doing – you can change it and make a plan of action.

When I took responsibility for my actions, I was able to choose my response. Once that happened things began to move forward.

Ask a better question

When I asked "how could I deserve" rather than "why don't I have" I got better answers. When I asked "what have I done" rather than "why don't I have" I got better answers. When I asked "what could I do right now" I got excited.

Knowing I was not a coach, speaker, or author I had to find my starting point.

> *"Action is the foundational key to success."*
> **Pablo Picasso**

This is one of my all-time favourite quotes, but if I could make one change I think it needs the word "structured" to be inserted. (Sorry Pablo.)

youdeservethisbook.com

> *"Structured action is the foundational key to success."*
> **James Newell**

That's better.

I had taken various actions over the preceding 10 years; most were irrelevant to my goals. I even considered "hoping" an action, reading books as action, watching videos an action. I was completely lost in the Hope bias and the Procrastination Illusion. I had taken action, but it was indiscriminate action; only structured considered action will advance you towards your goals. I now considered what *appropriate* action I could take to help advance me toward my goals.

What could I do right now to build momentum towards my goals?

My immediate thought was to join a speakers' club. It was not guaranteed to help, but would allow me to meet others and to speak. I thought that I was scared of public speaking, needed to improve my techniques and get technical help – these would be vital in my future career.

Appropriate action is better than just action, but any action is better than hope.

My lack of action was because "I didn't know what to do" – a thinly veiled excuse and subconscious form of abdicating responsibility to avoid failure. At that point I didn't realise I was responsible for everything in my life.

If I never tried I could never fail – but I could never succeed either and day to day life was starting to suck my happiness and my soul from me. Despite the seemingly perfectness of my situation.

I'm not alone here.

I believe most people you meet are "playing not to lose" rather than "playing to win". Those who play not to lose risk little and as such get rewarded little. They live in fear of losing what little they have rather than pursuing their full potential.

It takes no planning, no courage and no ambition to sit still, be conservative and make no waves. If you realise inaction is a choice, playing it safe is a choice – a choice that will keep you from your dreams – would you still take them?

I didn't.

youdeservethisbook.com

When I realised I was "playing not to lose" and in my eyes "losing" anyway as I was so unhappy – it seemed a no-brainer.

After all, what do you have to lose? Money? Respect of peers? Wasted time?

I was wasting time hoping, suspecting my peers didn't respect my lack of action – and you can always make money somehow.

Ironically being so risk averse had limited me in such a way that I felt I had nothing to lose – especially now time was marching on. (Reaching 30 and becoming a father were both significant turning points for me.)

Those who play to win are long term thinkers; they have a plan, even a basic one, and don't feel they are "owed" anything. They feel they deserve more than they have but are setting out to get it, they don't feel automatically entitled to it. They are Planners, not Settlers. They are responsible. They are alive.

And this is a good point – they are alive.

Doing the same job for years with no prospect of career advancement, however comfortable the job had become, had left me feeling like a spectator in life – not truly alive.

Playing it safe is risky.

A profound statement, but my frustration had crescendoed.
I was making no progress, aside from hoping for more and it had left me disappointed, exhausted and lost.

This, sadly, was what I "deserved". I took no appropriate action, no risk and had no real plan – my results mirrored this.

If you don't have everything you feel you deserve (and reading this book tells me you don't…) then <u>NOW</u> is the time to think clearly and objectively about where you are.

What do you want?
What do you need to do to get it?
What have you done so far?
What could you do?
Or simply ask yourself – "Why don't I deserve it?"

WYCTWYLATTTYLAC

When you change the way you look at things, the things you look at change.

youdeservethisbook.com

You need to act to get a result. So knowing that, why didn't I take action? Why had I not achieved everything I felt I deserved? For a long time I simply didn't understand how it all worked and didn't know why.

Why have you not achieved everything you want (yet)?

Knowing <u>and</u> understanding are the answer. We know about causality and progression, but you need to understand it. The understanding is the key. When you understand you are just hoping for what you want, you will understand you are not going to achieve it. When you understand you are taking no action toward what you want, you understand you don't deserve it.

Think of a friend who wants a new job but doesn't take any proper action; they don't update their CV or sign on with the relevant agencies, they browse a few highly paid positions online, but that's about it. They really dislike their current job but want something better. So they continue their "search" when they're not out with friends or watching TV.

We can agree they don't deserve to get that better job and they are unlikely to make any progress until they take structured action towards it.

It's no different for you.

The difference is your perspective.

As an outsider you can spot the issues, as an insider you are naturally biased.

This is why my coach was such a powerful influence; he brought fresh thinking and feedback to me. I was so biased and blinded I couldn't see where I was going wrong.

To stop hoping and start acting, and to realise where you are – you need to look at things differently.

This book seemed obvious when I set out to write it. The YOU DESERVE IT concept IS obvious – but most of us are hoping for things or feeling "owed" due to the "unfairness" of life and making little or no progress.

We feel things should go our way "just because" or "because I've had a hard time" or simply because we feel "I deserve it".

Sadly YOU DESERVE IT just doesn't work like that.

Tough life? YOU DESERVE IT doesn't care.

youdeservethisbook.com

Not sure what to do? YOU DESERVE IT doesn't care.

Can't be bothered? YOU DESERVE IT doesn't care.

Think of YOU DESERVE IT as the Simon Cowell of life. Just because you have a sob story and the audience love you – if you can't sing for toffee then you don't deserve to win. And you won't. YOU DESERVE IT doesn't care.

It only cares about one thing, causality: that you have done what you need to do to deserve the outcome.

This is such a pertinent point.

I wasted years of my life subconsciously feeling "owed" as though the terrible things I'd overcome gave me some kind of "credit" which would be repaid. If 10 years, 3650 days, have taught me anything, it's that life isn't about being fair. It's not about negotiating with YOU DESERVE IT or having a sob story.

It's about putting a constructive effort in to achieve the outcome. It's about serving others, adding value, following your passion. It's about doing the best you can, where you are, with what you have. If you don't know what to do, then you first have to start asking better questions.

If you plant apple seeds, you get an apple tree. You don't get anything else – no matter how much you do or don't want the apple tree.

The question is: what seeds are you planting?

10 things to remember

1. You can't negotiate with YOU DESERVE IT. It's a cruel hard thing – it doesn't have emotion or reason.
2. Be wary of the "just world theory" which fools you into thinking that bad things are "rebalanced" by good things.
3. Hope is not a strategy.
4. Limited thinking yields limited results.
5. The Hope Bias is the incorrect belief that hope alone will get you what you want, without action.
6. Playing it safe is risky.
7. Deserve within your means. You must serve before you can deserve.
8. Structured action is the foundational key to success.
9. When you change the way you look at things, the things you look at change.
10. Play to win, don't play to not lose.

youdeservethisbook.com

Exercise – Desire

Consider what you want. What is your ideal day? Where would you live? How would you spend your time? Who would you spend your time with? If you had £100m in the bank what would you do with your time? If money were no object what car would you drive, what business would you run, where would you travel?

Seek to define in great detail the things and experiences you want. For each then consider the next step you could take to achieving them.

Example

I am always asking myself how I'd live if money was no object. By removing the obligation of money you get closer to what you would actually want to spend your time on. If money were no issue I would write, read, speak and connect with others. I have been able to create a career around this thought and am fulfilled in my career as a result.

In your own life, ask yourself:

- What do I enjoy doing?
- What would I do for free?
- What activities do I undertake where time seems to fly?
- What and who makes me happy?
- What are my passions, my skills, my strengths?

Guidance

Defining what you want is the first step to pursuing it. Taking the time to consider exactly what you want (which you may never have done before now) is the first vital step you must take.

Wanting to be "rich" or "successful" are not goals – they are dreams. Wanting "£1m in the next 12 months" or to have one million customers are goals. Goals have deadlines, deadlines inspire action.

Ask yourself first what you want, and then what you can do about getting it.

youdeservethisbook.com

Tip
Don't self-edit. Whatever you want put it down – there are no limits on what you can want to do or achieve.

What you'll need
Pen and Paper.

Duration
1 hour

When completed, ask yourself:
Now you have a clearer idea of what you want from life, how could you take next steps towards some of the things you want?

youdeservethisbook.com

6 – Surprise!

You can deserve things you don't want.

- What don't you like about your life?
- Why is it a part of your life?
- How can you remove it?

In this chapter we'll look at how you can fully deserve things you don't want, the importance of inaction and action, the power of taking responsibility and how things have to deserve you as much as you have to deserve them.

Take a deep breath, get comfortable.

Actually, DON'T take a deep breath. Breathe slowly and rhythmically, it's better for you. Shallow breathing can lead to poorer oxygen supply; deep, rhythmic breathing increases oxygen supply and relaxes you at the same time.

Science shows rhythmic breathing promotes higher body oxygenation demonstrated through a higher CP score. The CP (Controlled Pause) test determines how long you can go without taking a breath which is an indication of oxygenation. The fewer, deeper breaths you take, the more oxygen you intake. I digress...

This is going to be a difficult chapter.

YOU DESERVE IT has dual meaning; it can be both good and bad. You can deserve the good things in your life; you can deserve the bad things too. The issue is that we want and feel we deserve the good things, but are dismayed and annoyed by the negative things we deserve.

Working hard and adding value? You deserve success and money. Thanks very much!

Not exercising and eating poorly? You deserve to be unhealthy. But why? I only ate a *couple* of donuts this week, plus I've had a lot on at work and can't find time for the gym...

No-one wants to deserve the bad things in life.
But you can deserve them nonetheless.

youdeservethisbook.com

To deserve the bad things (the things you don't want) comes back to responsibility. Being able to choose your response. If you aren't responsible for the negative things you deserve, then you aren't able to change your response. You aren't able to change the situations and you are being a victim of circumstance. You feel "owed" or unfairly treated and as such circumstances decide your fate (remember "The Settling"). It's this victim mentality; this feeling "owed" that kept me unhappy and making no progress for 10 years.

To accelerate your progress and save yourself the time wasted and anguish I encountered – you simply need to "own" your actions, be honest and move on.

Yes, it's not nice.

Like checking your bank balance when you know it will be overdrawn; it takes courage, but the moments of guilt and disappointment from facing reality are far more palatable than 10 years (or more) of kidding yourself. I can attest.

Deserving bad things, the things you don't want in life often comes from inaction.

As we've learnt, inaction is a form of action. Inaction comes from a lack of being "response-able" for the situation. You don't want to confront the reality. You might be fearful of "reality" or have no idea how to handle it. Avoiding it seems so much easier. Whilst playing the victim or feeling "owed" it's easy to not make decisions or take action which is avoiding responsibility.

But inaction is action.

Indecision is decision.

By not working out, you choose to be unfit.

By spending more than you earn, you choose to be poor, or worse, in debt.

It's crazy! Who would choose to be fat or poor?

You do. I do. We all do. They are Hidden Choices.

But we ignore it because we don't want to be responsible for it, hoping it will all just blow over and go away. We know our actions have outcomes; but we won't admit we're choosing to deserve the bad things because that means taking responsibility.

But we are responsible. I was choosing not to progress or to find my happiness. I was choosing to stay still. It didn't feel like it at the time of course, I wanted to deserve more, I wanted to move forwards – but my actions prevented it. If I wanted to make progress and move forward I should have acted differently. I was confusing desire with deserve – perhaps you are too?

When it comes to deserving the bad things, this is what is happening. When you don't "deserve" to be unfit, what you're saying is you don't "want" to be unfit. Two VERY different things.

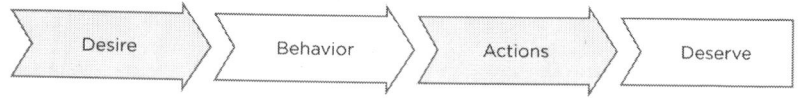

Deserve is all about what you do and what you get. It has little to do with what you actually want. What you want drives your behaviours and your behaviour drives your action and your actions decide what you deserve.

When you think of the negative things in your life and, with a calming deep breath, accept for a moment that you perhaps do deserve (at least some) of them, then you are finally in a position of power.

You can finally take action. As an important side note (and common sense advisory):

Some things in life will <u>absolutely</u> not be deserved.

The disclaimer at the beginning of the book did not exist in my first draft. After initial reader reviews, I had to clarify that you don't deserve **everything** in your life, because you can't. The deciding factor is what you can influence.

So what can't you deserve?

Terminal illness is one, accidents which aren't your fault, another, stock market crashes, housing prices, epidemics and so on. If you exercise clarity and common sense you will come to realise you are in control of deserving more than you realise (but you are not in control of everything – nor can you be).

For those things you absolutely cannot control such as the death of a loved one or a terminal illness, you can at least control your response to them (response-able) as it's not what happens to you, it's what you do about it.

I can only use my own life as the example here. If one of your parents committed suicide, if you battled with depression, if you nearly drowned in the tsunami – how would you react? I'm pleased to say that I've managed to turn these tragedies around, but it's nearly broken me and is taking everything I've got to keep moving forward positively. No one said this would be easy, but if you want it bad enough, you do what it takes.

If I gave up, played the victim and let life take over (become "the settled") who knows what could have happened? If you take ownership of the bad things in your life, deserved or not, then the fun begins.

If you agree you did deserve it, you can begin to ask "what did I do to deserve it?" You can dissect your behaviour / actions / results and look to make changes to alter the outcome. (Remember decisions, not conditions, shape your life.) Until this point you will not change and you will not deserve anything different.

This is where I was for so long. Being responsible is an empowering and exciting thing. It just gets a bad reputation as being something heavy, guilt ridden and boring.

responsibility
/rɪˌspɒnsɪˈbɪlɪti/

noun

1. the state or fact of having a duty to deal with something or of having control over someone.
   "women bear children and take responsibility for childcare"
   synonyms: authority, control, power, leadership, management, influence, duty
   "we train those staff who show an aptitude for managerial responsibility"
2. the state or fact of being accountable or to blame for something.
   "the group has claimed responsibility for a string of murders"
   synonyms: blame, fault, guilt, culpability, blameworthiness, liability
   "the organization denied responsibility for the bomb attack at the airport"

This is how my story progressed and how this book came to be.
I took responsibility for everything.
Unhappy in my job – I deserved it.
Not making progress – I deserved it.

youdeservethisbook.com

Not sure what to do next – I deserved it.

Talk about give myself a hard time! But tough love gets results. Being honest with myself was a form of "serving" myself (see Chapter 3). I was finally giving myself the courtesy, respect and service my clients had enjoyed for years.

I was serving myself. It was then that things really started to take shape. I listed everything I disliked and wanted to change; from job, to health, to personal life, everything. For the first time ever, I was in charge, I was responsible and ready to design the life I wanted.

Now I understood how to begin to deserve it.

There were many revelations on my YOU DESERVE IT journey but making peace with deserving the things I didn't want was the most profound. My feelings of being "owed" or feeling unfairly treated vanished overnight. As did much of my unhappiness.

I was left with optimism.

Optimism is hope based on confidence; confidence often comes from action. It was a tough day when I finally considered my life "warts and all" but the pain was short lived. The pain was well worth the gain and what followed was incredibly exciting.

Understanding why you deserve the bad things can help you deserve the good (the things you want). Once you change your actions in an attempt to stop deserving the things you don't want, it's confidence boosting. It encourages you to take more action and more "risk" towards the things you do want. It's playing to win instead of playing to not lose.

Seeing results and making progress, however small, reinforces the exciting prospect of being responsible for everything and thus being able to change it. My first action was to minimise and eradicate the negative things I currently deserved.

Yes I was unhappy in my job, but I was choosing to be there whilst I sorted out where else I wanted to be. I was choosing to be there and as such I could leave tomorrow if I really wanted. I wasn't actually "trapped" and that realisation made my situation all the more palatable.

It was choice, not obligation that actually kept me there. I was always responsible, always in control.

Through this thinking, I actually realised how great my job was and although that didn't deter me from following my heart and pursuing my YOU DESERVE IT journey, it made life less difficult and my feelings of ungratefulness dissipated.

I realised you can be grateful for what you have and still pursue more.

Besides this, being "grateful" was less of an issue now. I worked hard to get to where I was – I deserved it. Feeling I deserved it rather than feeling grateful for it as though it was simply given to me was a far more fulfilling experience.

I'd always felt "grateful" to have success in my role – as though it could be taken away at any moment, as though I was here as a favour and it could all end overnight. Nonsense. I deserved all of the success I was enjoying and it felt so great to finally acknowledge it.

At this point, I really felt like I was getting somewhere towards my goals and best of all I knew I deserved to be where I was. Being responsible wasn't so bad after all.

All actions have consequences.

Many things in your life right now don't deserve your attention, less so, your action. (Deserving things doesn't just apply to you and I – it's a universal concept.) Understanding what does deserve your attention and focussing on it will accelerate your results. You have to deserve things, but, in turn, things have to deserve you.

This is the idea of focussing on strengths rather than trying to fix weaknesses. It's also playing to win, rather than playing to not lose (see Chapter 5).

If I lined up 10 people in a room and told you nine of them love you but one of them doesn't – what do you focus on? The one person who doesn't love you? Or the nine who do?

Life isn't a zero sum game. For you to succeed, no one needs to fail.

I used to think like this; it's the path away from your success. In this metaphor, that one person who doesn't love you may never love you and you could waste a lifetime trying to convince them otherwise. Focussing on the negative minority adds nothing positive to your life. They don't deserve your attention. Surely in this example it's better to focus on the nine people who do love you, to focus on the positive.

youdeservethisbook.com

I digress, but the point is, when you study your actions in any given situation, it reveals what you focus on and thus what you stand to deserve. Are you giving television 15 hours a week of your time? Does it deserve your time? Will this behaviour serve you?

I suspect not.

You have a right to be served in the same way you have the right (the duty) to serve others.

> "We all have 24 hours in a day – your success depends on how you use the 24."
>
> **ET The Hip Hop Preacher**

So what deserves your time? The things that will bring you long term value and happiness. The things that will get you closer to your goals.

> **Family** – *actually having conversations and spending quality time with them.*
>
> **Health** – *running, walking, water, fruit, vegetables – it's clichéd because it works – but it's just easier to do nothing and eat biscuits…*
>
> **Passion** – *hobbies, sport, travel. Even if you don't have a passion, spend time trying to find one.*

When you realise that time is infinitely more valuable than money (and if you shop around for your car insurance I suggest you pay attention) then you start wanting a good return on your investment. Return on investment, or rather return on time is a powerful consideration.

A consideration you may never have made before – as I hadn't.

And yet our time is so infinitely more precious than anything else we have.

If you spend two hours watching television what will you get?

If you spend two hours jogging what will you get?

I'm not saying give up TV, relaxation or other pleasures, I'm saying consider the return on your time invested. Are you investing as wisely as you could be?

Do these things deserve your time?

youdeservethisbook.com

Are you aware of how much time you spend watching TV and eating biscuits?

Your time is the one thing you can invest to reach your goals. If you spend it on the wrong things, you are hindering your chances and have less time to invest on the things that matter.

Life is not a zero-sum game, but time is.

The question I ask myself now is "Can I afford to spend my time on this?" (Remember – ask a better question – see Chapter 5.) As we'll explore later, I gave up the news and feeling I needed to work or be contactable 24/7. As a result I felt more relaxed and present, without affecting my performance at work or any other part of my life.

I was being responsible. I felt in control.

If I can remove something from my life such as checking the news, which I spent an enormous amount of time on – then why did I decide to check it and spend so much time on it in the first place?

How did it come to be?

The answer came to me in "The Four Hour Work Week" by Timothy Ferriss. In it, he touches on the concept of "results by volume" As a society we work 9–5 and feel compelled to fill the hours. We are led to believe in this framework, that more = better. So, spending hours and hours on something must be beneficial – right?

As it turned out, no.

I was spending hours checking the news and the return on my time invested was simply that I felt anxious and that we live in an apocalyptic unsafe world.

Did the news deserve my time? No.

Was the news helping me reach my goals? No.

The light wasn't worth the candle.

It was the first thing to go.

It was painful to begin with, but I am now "news free" and enjoy not worrying about things which do not impact me directly. I realised that even if I spent the time I would have spent checking the news, sitting still in a dark room – I would be better off and markedly led anxious.

Being responsible in this way, for something seemingly innocuous, was hugely motivating. I'd proven to myself that I could change my path to seek a better outcome – and I felt so much less like the world was at an apocalyptic war, rape and violence strewn place.

Had I continued to check the news on the industrial scale I was, these words may never have been written and I would not be on my current path. Watching the news was, in a way, choosing to not pursue my goals. It didn't feel like it at the time though.

Remember that inaction is a form of action. If I'm not choosing to move towards something, I'm choosing to move away from it. It's another Hidden Choice.

Even small changes can affect your overall results. That's why it's so important to be deliberate about as much as is possible in your life. You can only be deliberate when you ask better questions and take a more structured approach.

It's time to start living on purpose; it's time to stop deserving the things you don't want.

youdeservethisbook.com

10 things to remember

1. You can deserve bad things even if you don't want them.
2. Inaction is a form of action.
3. Indecision is a form of decision.
4. You can only deserve things over which you have some influence – terminal illness, natural disasters and the like are not deserved.
5. Responsibility is being able to choose your response.
6. Taking responsibility for everything is the key.
7. You have to deserve things, but things have to deserve you.
8. Every small action and decision affects your overall result.
9. Live on purpose. Be a planner, not a settler.
10. Consider return on time before undertaking an activity.

youdeservethisbook.com

Exercise – Viewpoint

This is about changing your perception and your viewpoint. Read books, watch programmes and listen to music or talks which are completely at odds with what you like or what you believe in.

If you enjoy classical music, listen to Metallica (and vice versa), if you are interested in reading only fiction books, switch to non-fiction, if you believe in a certain religion, read texts from a different religion entirely, the list is endless. The goal is to learn more about something that you don't agree with.

Example

For me, this is all about reading. I read a book a week (or more) and exclusively non-fiction books. I love to learn and to experiment; I have no time for "stories" and entertainment. (or so I thought) For this challenge I began reading fiction books. Whilst I'm not a convert, I have a greater appreciation for the use of description and imagination they provide, as well as the feeling of escapism.

Having dismissed fiction as a "waste of time" I am now aware of its appeal and understand why it's so popular – it's still not for me, but at least I gave it a try.

Ask yourself:

- What don't I like or agree with?
- Do I have any concrete reasons for feeling this way?
- How can I challenge or prove these feelings?

Guidance

Pick something you truly do not like or agree with and seek to understand it as best you can (even though you may not feel comfortable doing so). The world is what you make of it; your perception is your reality.

Once you realise that perception and viewpoint play such an important role you can healthily question it, which can reduce your personal "blind spots" and errors of judgement, rather than doggedly keeping to the same thoughts and beliefs without question.

Tip
Remain as open minded as you can – you will feel your old thought processes fire up but quiet them as best you can. Be open to new ideas and as unbiased in your thinking as possible to allow yourself a new viewpoint.

What you'll need
Books, videos, music or anything which is contrary to your current tastes/beliefs.

Duration
1 day

When completed, ask yourself:
Are you more aware now that the world exists only in how it is perceived by us? Do you agree that technically there is no one "reality", rather many viewpoints on the same environment?

youdeservethisbook.com

7 - Conviction

I deserve it without action is delusion.

- What do you need to do to get what you want?
- Can you do it?
- If not, why not?

In this chapter we'll look at learned helplessness, the importance of self-belief, your Reticular Activating System, Hotchkiss's 7 Deadly Sins of Narcissism and how these can conspire to keep you from action.

A delusion is a "belief held strongly despite superior evidence to the contrary". It's a perceptual issue and one that I hope to put right for you in this chapter. Consider this your wakeup call.

It's never too late to get a wakeup call.

Believing you are entitled to something with no supporting evidence is delusional behaviour. I felt I did have evidence though; the depression, the suicide, the tsunami, it all felt so unfair and so undeserved that it made me believe at some point the "debt" would be repaid. Sadly (or not) this isn't how life - let alone YOU DESERVE IT – works.

I was experiencing "learned helplessness". Learned helplessness is a form of victim mentality. I was limiting my results because I didn't think I could change them, even though now I realise I could.

youdeservethisbook.com

learned helplessness

noun PSYCHIATRY

a condition in which a person suffers from a sense of powerlessness, arising from a traumatic event or persistent failure to succeed. It is thought to be one of the underlying causes of depression.

Learned helplessness had left me feeling frustrated (I knew I was capable of more) and kept me treading water in all areas of my life.

The worst part? I didn't even realise I was doing it. I felt like I was trying my best, giving my best, but there was always a barrier in the way. As we'll discover shortly – it's actually possible to have a fear of being *successful*.

Oh the irony.

My YOU DESERVE IT blueprint (which we'll cover later) involved years of "just getting by", "not having much" and being an unconscious victim of circumstance. There was always a reason I was not successful, but sadly the reason was never me. Now, 10+ years after the tsunami, 12+ years after the suicide and with no more financial issues, the excuses were starting to wear thin and my lack of progress became more aggravating.

The killer was that I had no idea of any of this: my blueprint, learned helplessness, self-sabotage. All I saw was my lack of progress.

I wonder what beliefs, expectations and blueprints you use in your own life, subconsciously or not, that have kept you standing still; or maybe even moving backward?

My own subconscious strategy, coupled with my belief that one day everything would turn out kept me hoping but not acting for far too long. It was the Hope Bias. This is why my YOU DESERVE IT journey was more of an awakening. For the first time I saw what I was doing and where I was going.

Like the dieter who is always starting tomorrow – I was perpetually putting off everything.

But why?

Fear of failure? Of course, we all fear failure.

Loss of money, reputation and the embarrassment of "failing"?

youdeservethisbook.com

I remember talking to my counsellor (after the tsunami) and she introduced me to the idea of being afraid to succeed. Absolute nonsense, I thought at the time…

But with success eluding me so many years on, perhaps there was more to it? You will have friends, colleagues, clients and family members who are more "successful" than you but who you deem perhaps less intelligent and less deserving of their success than you.

Two things separate you from them: Belief and action.

Belief is the more important of the two as it drives the action. Belief it can be done, belief you're the one to do it. Belief that you will succeed. I will always remember a black tie event in London when a client and I had a conversation along these lines. His view was quite simple; while others talked about it, he got out there and took action. I complained of the lack of progress, he chided me for talking, but not acting. He couldn't understand why I didn't "just get on with it" and recognised that I was potentially more capable than he was but without action it was meaningless. Self-belief was not a problem for this man and his success was self-evident.

With self-belief anything is possible.

My own self-belief at the time was a dented and fragile thing. I was always quick to talk down achievements or proclaim them as "lucky" events.

If something that happens to you is "luck" then you are not responsible for it and can't recreate it. There is no self-belief or self-confidence to be found in "luck".

My client wouldn't put any of his achievements down to luck. I would.

My client wouldn't downplay his achievements. I would.

My client was happy, fulfilled and pushing himself daily. I wasn't.

I needed to start "Acting as if" (see Chapter 4).

I needed to repair my fragile self-belief and set about changing my perception. I needed success and positive experiences to base my self-belief upon, but to achieve this I needed to take a leap of faith to create those positive experiences.

It was catch-22. As my discussion with my client continued, I realised this was how he started. In the beginning he had taken bold action and made decisions based on nothing but his faith that it would work out. He was "acting as if" and didn't even realise it. As time went on and successes accumulated, his self-belief was bursting at the seams. A self-perpetuating circle.

Modelling this "fake it till you make it" approach was my attempt to replicate his success. I modelled his approach.

And it worked.

Subconscious strategies are powerful things. For my client, he followed his belief and made things happen for no reason other than he didn't know different/better. I was proclaiming myself to not being a victim, but subconsciously playing the victim and limiting my results in the process.

I knew better but was simply unaware of my unconscious strategy. The only reason I hadn't given up and "settled with my lot" was my strong belief that I deserved more than I had.

I had some of the belief but lacked the action. My lack of confidence in myself was the gap between belief and action – and I had been in the gap for far too long.

Throughout my YOU DESERVE IT journey I was taking stock of my life, challenging my thinking and reframing my life to change my situation.

> "When you change the way you look at things,
> the things you look at change."
> **Dr. Wayne Dyer**

I began to recognise my achievements and to celebrate them as my first step toward building my confidence. In the same way you can deserve more than you think (Chapter 9) you can be thankful and proud of more achievements than you think.

Although my job didn't fulfil me, by reframing, I found my outlook changed and I could enjoy it for what it was.

Reticular Activating System

Now for the science bit. There is a part of the brain known as the RAS (Reticular Activating System) and its function is primarily to regulate the sleep-wake transition. It also controls what you focus on, which is vital with so much stimuli in our modern world; light, sound, taste, touch and so many distractions – TV, Internet, news, books etc.

The RAS helps us to filter out what we do and don't want to see. It's because of your RAS for example that if you bought a new car in blue, then you suddenly notice just how many blue cars there are on the roads. The number of blue cars hasn't necessarily changed, but your awareness of them has.

This works very well for celebrating achievements.

I had been so focussed on the negative or on the achievements of others that I didn't notice my own achievements and successes. The client I mentioned earlier? He celebrated everything and had rock solid self-belief to boot. For him, life was one long pat on the back. I celebrated nothing by comparison and suffered fragile self-confidence.

The beauty of the RAS is that once you focus on something, your brain "tunes in" to find more of the same. So you start noticing more of those blue cars.

It's perpetual.

In my case I noticed just how far I'd come.

I'd survived a parental suicide, which alone could have floored me, or anyone. I'd survived one of the largest natural disasters in living memory, which alone could have killed me, let alone floored me. I had battled with anxiety and depression and was winning. I had a good job, lovely wife, wonderful children. I was a homeowner with no personal debt and lived a relatively comfortable life. Noticing these things immediately caused a "paradigm shift" as Steven Covey would say. I was brimming with examples of successes and triumphs and my mind (RAS) was tuning in for more.

I decided to celebrate every success, however small, going forward. Until this point I'd taken the opposite approach. I focussed on the terrible things that had happened to me, the "terrible" and unfulfilling job I had, the lost deals, the failures, the missed opportunities. As I began to focus on the positive things, I saw more of them – however small.

It's no surprise that focussing on all that bad stuff had been so damaging to my self-confidence.

Much like parenting my children, I needed to "parent" myself using praise and positive action. With an increase in self-confidence I was able to take more action (to deserve more you need to serve more), I was able to move from belief I could do it (which I felt like I'd always had somewhere) to absolute 100% unshakable belief I could do it and pursue my goals of becoming a coach, speaker, author. When you feel better about yourself, you tend to feel better about the world around you too. You are kinder and more connected to others. When you are kinder and more connected to others, you are in a better position to "serve" them and to add value.

You can't pour from an empty cup.

You move from selfish, to selfless and then to Selfmore (Chapter 3). Selfmore is where you want to be, to deserve more.

Hotchkiss's 7 Deadly Sins of Narcissism

By unconsciously playing the victim, I was indulging in narcissistic behaviour. Self-pity and playing the martyr were strangely fulfilling at the time. I guess that's down to responsibility too; by not being responsible you can fail but it's not your fault.

"You can get addicted to a certain kind of sadness"
Gotye – Somebody That I Used to Know (song)

It might feel "good" if that's the right word, but feeling a victim keeps you where you are. Feeling the world owes you or that nothing is fair can lead you to feel entitled to (deserve) things which you don't. In Hotchkiss's seven deadly sins of narcissism, the subject of entitlement (deadly sin number five) is a pertinent one.

    Considering yourself "special" or expecting favourable treatment (with no real justification) can cause problems as not only do you appear difficult / demanding to others, you are taking a selfish approach when what you need is Selfmore. You are also, more importantly, not dealing with reality and are in no position to take advantage of it or be responsible for it (able to choose your response). If your view on reality is negatively biased, your actions are biased and so are your results.

Wake up calls are never pain free.

By looking closer at my own situation than I ever had before, I realised I was guilty of a number of things listed here – and possibly yet more which I didn't even realise. I was subconsciously a victim, subconsciously not expecting to succeed as I was always a victim of circumstance – despite how hard I tried to succeed. I considered myself "special" and "lucky" which may have served to help me in not giving up, but such narcissism stunted my ability to think of and to serve others. I was waiting for the search and rescue party to come and save me – but they weren't coming. No wonder I had reached the limits of what I deserved and couldn't seem to breakthrough.

"I deserve it" without action is an emotional response.

Life is tough. You think you're doing all you can, surely you deserve to have everything you want? After all you don't know how to try any harder...

YOU DESERVE IT cares nothing of sob stories, special treatment or mitigating circumstances. If you don't do what is required you don't deserve the result.

As I went through life feeling deserving of more and entitled to more without really taking any action, I was perpetuating my own situation. Perhaps this is the same for you? If you can't ever seem to achieve what you want or breakthrough to the "next level" perhaps you are sabotaging yourself through entitlement thinking?

Are you focussed more on yourself than others? Could you be subconsciously playing the victim? Are you sabotaging your best efforts to avoid the fear of failure, or perhaps even the fear of success?

Reticular activating system, delusion, narcissism; whatever the situation, it's only with relevant structured action that you can deserve the things you want.

youdeservethisbook.com

10 things to remember

1. To believe you deserve something without taking action is delusion.
2. Learned helplessness is a form of victim mentality.
3. With self belief, anything is possible.
4. Your Reticular Activating System controls your mind's focus – it seeks you more of what you focus on.
5. You are entitled to nothing except that which you work for.
6. Celebrate every success, dissect every failure – you win some, you learn some.
7. Self-esteem is built on self praise and recognising the positive.
8. YOU DESERVE IT cares nothing for sob stories.
9. Are you subconsciously sabotaging yourself? Are you afraid to succeed?
10. YOU DESERVE IT requires belief and action.

youdeservethisbook.com

Exercise – Neurobics

If you are right-handed, start to brush your teeth with your left hand, write with your left hand, carry things, do buttons and zips – anything you would do with your right hand, do it with your left (or vice versa). Travel new routes to work, rearrange your furniture, change your routine – do anything which is a change to the "norm" of your daily life.

Example

I am right handed so switched everything to my left hand. All of a sudden I noticed the trees, the different sounds of conversations and traffic (I was in central London) I noticed that the London Underground signs could be applicable as guidance for life – give up seats to those less able, be courteous and don't smoke. The world had a strange new vividness which I simply wasn't expecting.

Things you could try:

- Write with the non-dominant hand.
- Don't check email until midday each day.
- Rearrange the furniture in your house.
- Wear new (or old) clothes you've not worn before.
- Try a new fragrance, a new meal or new drink.
- Drive a new route to work or home.
- If it's new to you and not the norm – give it a go.

Guidance

We can find ourselves locked into certain thought patterns and become comfortable doing certain things in certain ways. By swapping hands, driving new routes to work and the like, you challenge your brain to create new pathways and connections.

It's literally a workout for your mind. In doing so you may notice the world in a new perspective, you may see things that would have passed you by previously and generally have more creative thoughts. Challenging your mind produces new thoughts; new thoughts help you expand your world.

youdeservethisbook.com

When complete, ask yourself:

- Why do I do XYZ this set way anyway?
- What else could I change and what other new things could I try?

What you'll need

Perseverance! It can be difficult at first to go against the norms of your life.

Duration

1 day

When completed, ask yourself:

Did you start to notice anything new in your surroundings? Did you feel more creative? More energised? More resourceful?

8 – The girl at the bar

When you change the way you look at things, the things you look at change.

- How do you view the world?
- Do you judge people?
- How would the world look if you ceased to judge?

In this chapter we'll learn how your perspective on the world defines it. How you perceive the world creates your reality, so if this is based more on emotion than fact, then your own "reality" might differ from the world in which you live which can cause issues. We'll learn that trying to stay factual rather than let emotions colour things is the way forward.

"So why does she do the job?"

Sat, Pepsi in hand (the Coke we serve is Pepsi) and with a fresh notebook in front of me, my journey began. A girl in a bar. She works behind the bar, seemed young (18-25) and appeared totally disinterested and disengaged from her job.

So why does she do it? Money? Of course. A career in hospitality? Doubtful. No idea of what else to do? Possible. Then it hit me; she doesn't realise she can do more. This poor, unhappy girl had sold herself short into bar work as she didn't realise she could do more. Or is it perhaps for her there is no career or great calling, just a job to pay the bills? I settled on that.

What a terrible life. No real prospects, unsociable hours, limited pay prospects, but plenty of discounted drinks and a raft of new friends all in the same boat. How could she just work in a bar, standing there on a quiet Tuesday afternoon, staring at music television in a trance-like state – without a thought for the future? I was trying to experiment with being non-judgemental about the world around me.

<u>Non</u>-judgemental.

Oh dear...

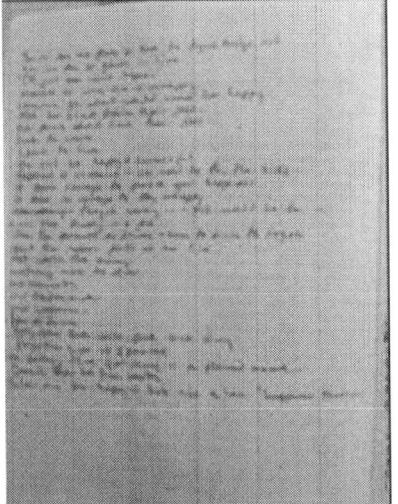 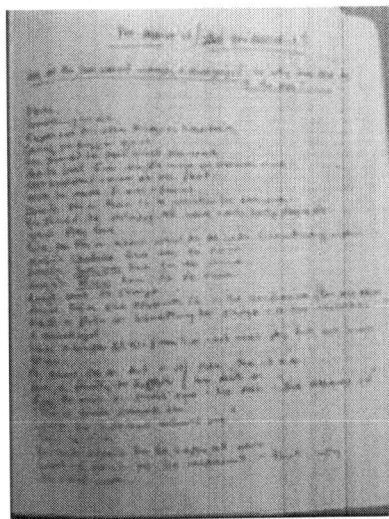

I was disappointed to have filled two pages in my notebook to realise I wasn't being non-judgemental. It was assumption, presumption. Guesswork.

"Don't make assumptions."
Rule no. 3 - *The Four Agreements* by Don Miguel Ruiz

I had to know. So I asked her. What followed was as interesting as it was unexpected. Charlotte was an 18-year-old soon-to-be veterinary student. Originally from Buckinghamshire, she was now flat sharing in North London whilst working part time in the bar to save for her gap year travels which were coming up. Coming from a long line of vets, she was continuing the family tradition, but wanted to let her hair down in South East Asia first.

As part of a hardworking family, she had not been spoilt and fully understood working for her money to pay her way. Bar work was the way to go. Having been away at the weekend she was exhausted from helping her dad at his practice and she was "zoned out" and not her bubbly self today as a result.

Wow.

I explained to her what I was doing – and even conceded my initial conclusion that she was wasting her life in a bar and perhaps she could do more. "It's funny how things aren't as they seem," she said. Funny indeed.

How many times a day, let alone in your life have you drawn "conclusions" on people, situations and problems based on no facts, just guesswork and your own biases?

Worse still, how many times have you made these assumptions about yourself? How has your perception of your own situation and your capability affected your ability to succeed?

As in the previous chapter, the issue is that we all make judgements and decisions based on our own perceptions and experiences. As such, they can feel "right" to us, but may be adrift from reality.

This is known as "methodology bias".

By having certain thoughts and opinions about the world around me, I look for things which affirm my beliefs rather than challenge them.

It's similar to the RAS (Reticular Activating System) in that you focus so much on certain things (such as when you see blue cars on the motorway) that you don't register the black, silver and red cars – but they are still there.

With so much information for us to digest on a daily basis, the RAS, methodology bias and other techniques help us to function rather than drown in choices, detail and input. The danger here is that you can make conclusions based on nothing factual at all – only to discover afterwards that your conclusions were wrong. Or you take factual evidence but draw biased conclusions from it to "find what you want to see". This explained why I found it so difficult in the beginning to be non-judgemental and why I was living proof that making assumptions can lead to an incorrect perception of reality.

Your perception is your reality.

Going back to my lack of progress and my lack of happiness, I would see that I was making assumptions and drawing conclusions about things based on no real facts. This lazy thinking was keeping me in a glass box, unable to break free. It also fuelled my frustration as I had "thought out" many options or routes I could take in my life – and set about pooh-poohing them all.

Could it be that my thinking and my perception were stunted in the same way my thoughts about the girl at the bar were?

Could it be that to deserve more you have to do more and take action, but that action must come from new thinking to be effective?

I had a great job and a comfortable life so why was I so unhappy?

Because working for this prestigious car company wasn't my "calling", I had dismissed it as a means to an end (similar to poor old Charlotte at the bar). This dismissal didn't allow me to find the goodness in my job and to be grateful for it; my perception was tainted. As I wasn't happy, I was more open to finding fault in other parts of my life and finding other things to worry about, rather than seeing the good in what I had.

My methodology bias was in full swing.

This is why I downplayed my achievements, rejected successes as "luck" and consequently suffered low confidence as a result. I perceived myself to be unhappy and was looking for "evidence" to prove myself right and support my thinking rather than challenge it.

In the 1999 film Any Given Sunday, Al Pacino gives a speech to his team and references the fact that American Football, in fact life, is a game of "inches". It's all about the small, incremental successes that build the bigger picture:

> *"We CLAW with our finger nails for that inch.*
> *Cause we know when we add up all those inches*
> *that's going to make the f**king difference*
> *between WINNING and LOSING*
> *between LIVING and DYING."*

"The inches we need are everywhere around us" is a reminder that there is opportunity everywhere in life, it just depends if you are seeking it out or not. By looking at my overall life and concluding I was unhappy, I "missed the inches all around me". The promotions, the bonuses, the company car and so much more. I knew I had a comfortable job but I dismissed it all as I was "unhappy".

*In dismissing these smaller achievements
I was ensuring I remained unhappy.*

Changing perception and recognising the good parts of my job helped me to conclude that life was actually very good; I had worked hard to deserve it, but now I wanted something else.

So rather than "everything is terrible" I began to recognise everything was actually very good, but it was now time for some new direction and that didn't downplay my achievements, it was healthy to strive for more.

Allowing myself to see those "inches" was far more constructive than focussing on the negative elements, seeking the cloud in every silver lining. My self-esteem and confidence took a boost and this helped propel me along my YOU DESERVE IT journey.

What could you be missing in your life right now? If you are focussing on what you don't have and what you want, then you can write off (or at the very least disregard and downplay) what you have actually achieved. I realise now that this was my mistake; something that kept my thinking and performance limited. Remaining non-judgemental is difficult. We are all so used to well-worn methods of thinking that any change can be difficult to make.

Above all else, we are naturally biased. It takes enormous self-courage and self-awareness to identify what you are doing non-judgementally and then conclude you may be wrong and need to correct your approach. No one likes to be wrong, but I find it's better to be wrong and correct course than to never realise (or acknowledge) you are wrong and limit your performance as a result.

"You don't know what you don't know". If this is true, then the only way to combat "you don't know what you don't know" is to undertake some more active thinking and active questioning.

Ask better questions.

In Chapter 1 we discussed "the settled" – those who don't design their lives, rather let circumstances shape them and "settle" for what is on offer. Those who achieve, those who succeed, those who deserve take a more considered and constructive approach.

The lazy thinking I had indulged in, using presumption, guesswork and opinions to make decisions, had limited my performance and brought me to my current plateau. It's only through writing this book that I was able to question my views and opinions to find out "what I didn't know". Asking direct and oftentimes obvious questions such as "will XYZ activity take me closer to my goal?" was one of the first steps to changing what I deserved.

So why had I not asked these questions before?

Fear of failure? Fear of being wrong? Not knowing what to ask? In my heart of hearts I knew the questions I needed to ask – just as you know that too much chocolate cake won't help your diet but you indulge anyway. It's one of the parts of my journey I have no conclusive answer for – except perhaps to say I wasn't ready. I wanted to deserve more, but wasn't ready to commit the energy and the time to writing this book and making everything a reality.

I knew roughly what I needed to do, but didn't do it.

The moment I started to ask questions of myself and take action such as join the speakers' club, the incremental effects began. It was down to getting started, taking small action and committing to my goals.

"When you want to succeed as bad as you want to breathe – then you will be successful."
ET The Hip Hop Preacher

Although I complained I disliked my job, the fact was that life was comfortable and there was little reason to upset the status quo. I was playing to not lose, instead of playing to win. I perceived everything I had achieved, and my income, to be the greatest it could be, so why risk going for more?

My YOU DESERVE IT blueprint limited me. My judgement (not facts) drove my inner monologue which asked me repeatedly, "Just how can you make money from motivating and inspiring people?"

There are of course a million ways, but with little faith I could replicate let alone exceed my current income, my action and progress remained limited. I was afraid of losing what I had. My belief I could not replicate or exceed my income was based on fear alone, not fact. It was based on nothing at all, but it controlled me. The income I could generate in following my dreams was just one of hundreds of considerations I had made; yet with no concrete evidence I let my methodology bias guide me.

youdeservethisbook.com

If "the settled" are those who let life decide for them and settle in their lives, the "biased" are those who don't challenge their thinking and settle on their biases.

I have learned that the only way to be "in touch with reality" is to see things as they are – not better or worse than they are. The key to this is asking questions and seeking facts. Being aware of whether or not you are being judgemental – because being judgemental, as I learned, is too easy, but can lead to bad/incorrect choices.

By seeing things worse than they are, you can affect your mood and perhaps take a pessimistic view on your outcomes and opportunities – seeking further pessimistic things to "support your view". By seeing things better than they are, you are "setting yourself up for a fall", raising your hopes and expectations only to have them dashed as you're not "in touch with reality" as you let your perception guide you.

Before a situation overwhelms you with either excitement or disappointment, remember that life is best lived with a long term approach. However devastating or amazing you may view a situation as being, your perceptions change over time.

This story illustrates how circumstances can be viewed differently by different people.

> Once upon a time, there was a farmer in the central region of China. He didn't have a lot of money and, instead of a tractor, he used an old horse to plough his field.
>
> One afternoon, while working in the field, the horse dropped dead. Everyone in the village said, "Oh, what a horrible thing to happen." The farmer said simply, "We'll see." He was so at peace and so calm, that everyone in the village got together and, admiring his attitude, gave him a new horse as a gift.
>
> Everyone's reaction now was, "What a lucky man." And the farmer said, "We'll see."
>
> A couple days later, the new horse jumped a fence and ran away. Everyone in the village shook their heads and said, "What a poor fellow!"
>
> The farmer smiled and said, "We'll see."
>
> Eventually, the horse found his way home, and everyone again said, "What a fortunate man."
>
> The farmer said, "We'll see."
>
> Later in the year, the farmer's young boy went out riding on the horse and fell and broke his leg. Everyone in the village said, "What a shame for the poor boy."
>
> The farmer said, "We'll see."

youdeservethisbook.com

Two days later, the army came into the village to draft new recruits. When they saw that the farmer's son had a broken leg, they decided not to recruit him.

Everyone said, "What a fortunate young man."

The farmer smiled again – and said, "We'll see."

This book, my entire YOU DESERVE IT journey of discovery is my effort to analyse and correct my thinking and my actions as I was not achieving everything I believed I was capable of. It's taken hundreds of hours, thousands of words of notes, research, emails, calls and discussion. Despite this level of work, you can begin to change your thinking today.

It's the beginning which counts. You can start the process today.

Are you the girl / guy at the bar?

10 things to remember

1. Your perception is your reality.
2. Don't make assumptions – always seek out the facts.
3. Methodology Bias is looking for things which affirm your beliefs rather than challenging them.
4. "The inches we need are all around us"
5. You don't know what you don't know.
6. Life is best lived with a long term, "we'll see" type approach.
7. Ask direct, constructive questions of yourself and the world around you.
8. Consider if your beliefs are presumption or reality – can you factually prove them?
9. Your misperceptions could be holding you back from everything you want.
10. Things aren't always as they seem.

youdeservethisbook.com

Exercise – Observation

This is exactly the exercise I undertook very early on in the process of creating this book. Go to a bar or pub, pick someone – it could be a member of staff or a customer – and make as many observations about them as possible. Physical observations, behavioural observations, anything and everything that would help you to describe this person to another. Speculate on who they are and what they do, how to they live their life? What is their "story"? Once complete, approach the person and ask them about their life. Explain you are challenging your assumptions and contrast what you thought about them to the reality.

Example

I observed a girl at a bar and then spoke with her to contrast my perception to her reality.

You can try this only with friendly, approachable people, I recommend:

- Taxi drivers
- Bar staff
- Waiters/waitresses
- Hairdressers

Guidance

Your perception can sometimes be adrift from reality. You can make decisions and take action based on your opinions and assumptions rather than fact. By speaking to the person and learning the facts you will understand just how adrift your thinking can be and how judgemental we all are.

Ask yourself:

- Without any evidence or fact why did I draw these conclusions?
- What else could I be "sure" of which is based on assumption and guessing?

youdeservethisbook.com

Tip
Pick a staff member rather than a customer; they will be there longer and more open to talking as they are paid to be affable.

What you'll need
A notebook, a friendly willing barperson

Duration
2 hours

When completed, ask yourself:
How did your perception of the person differ from the reality? Are you surprised by how different (or similar) your assumptions were?

youdeservethisbook.com

9 – You are right

You can deserve more than you think.

- Do you have positive things in your life you don't feel you deserve?
- Have you ever been overwhelmed by the results of your actions (good or bad)?

In this chapter, we'll look at Imposter Syndrome and how you can deserve more or less than you feel you do. We'll discover the YOU DESERVE IT Disconnect, unintended consequences and "The Cobra Effect" as well as how to be calmer in five minutes.

Just as you deserve everything in your life right now (Chapter 1), your life reflects what you deserve, the value you have added for others and the efforts you have made. You may even have things in your life (positive things) that you don't feel you deserve.

A promotion, an influx of work if you run a business, a pay rise or bonus. Positive things like this which we feel we "don't deserve" are often downplayed as luck or as "anyone could have done the same". If you have positive things in your life but feel you don't deserve them, this is a recognised phenomenon – it's called Imposter Syndrome.

> **Imposter syndrome** *is a psychological phenomenon in which people are unable to internalize their accomplishments. Despite external evidence of their competence, those with the syndrome remain convinced that they are frauds and do not deserve the success they have achieved. Proof of success is dismissed as luck, timing, or as a result of deceiving others into thinking they are more intelligent and competent than they believe themselves to be.*
> Source: *https://en.wikipedia.org/wiki/Impostor_syndrome*

If it's in your life and your actions have influenced it, then YOU DESERVE IT.

It's the same for the negative things in your life which you don't feel you deserve. "Runs of bad luck" where numerous bad things happen and you don't feel you've deserved them.

youdeservethisbook.com

Whether good or bad, you have a perception of what you feel you do and don't deserve. Anything which falls outside this perception is classified as "undeserved" as surely your perception of what you deserve can't be wrong. Can it?

In short, yes.

This is your YOU DESERVE IT blueprint; it's your estimation of what you feel you deserve, based partially on fact, but largely on assumption, perception and emotion. As we discovered in the last chapter, such perception can limit your performance as you're not "in touch with reality" and thus not able to deal with it as effectively. You're working from emotions, not facts.

I was at a stage in life where things were good, and yet I was embarrassed to be doing so well and to not feel that I deserved it.

I was exceeding my YOU DESERVE IT blueprint; the blueprint of what I thought I could deserve.

Yes I worked hard, but didn't other people work hard too? I classified my successes as "luck" and downplayed them as "nothing special", modest to the last. Such modesty can damage your self-esteem; I realise now that recognising successes and progress are important – not arrogant.

When you have more positive things than you feel you deserve; you may "discount" them or not acknowledge them, as however wonderful they may be, you don't feel you deserve them. If you feel you don't deserve something positive in your life, you may find it difficult to enjoy it and make the most of it. You may even fall victim to self-sabotage.

This can cause you to limit your achievements.

Everything beyond your limited perception of what you can deserve will not be fully acknowledged. It also means what you aim to achieve can be equally as limited.

Understanding this is so vital.

If you don't think you could deserve something then you are limiting your chances of actually achieving it. You can limit yourself based on perception alone.

Remember "Ferrariostasis" from Chapter 2? This is a form of YOU DESERVE IT stasis: you are operating within agreed tolerances of what you feel you deserve. These tolerances are self-created and self-imposed; there is nothing stopping you from exceeding these boundaries except yourself.

If you have more negative things in your life than you feel you deserve, it can cause you to adopt a victim mentality, which can, in turn, damage your self-esteem. You will amplify the negative and be incredulous as to how you found yourself in this position wondering, "What have I done to deserve this?"

We naturally have a tendency to believe we deserve few negative things in life, so this means even minor negative things can seem like a much bigger deal than they are.

Self-worth and self-esteem play a vital role here. Everything you believe you deserve is grounded in self-worth. You will draw conclusions on what you are "worth" based on biased opinion mixed with some fact and experience. Your "self-worth", in the context of YOU DESERVE IT, is decided ultimately by the value you add to others.

If you don't think much of yourself and have low self-esteem, but you add value to many people, your self-worth *should* be high. If you don't think much of yourself but reap the rewards of adding value to others – you may feel guilty or downplay your achievements as you can't see the worth that those around you can see. This was me.

Making the connection between the value you add and your self-worth is the only way to align what you think you deserve with what you actually deserve.

If you think highly of yourself, but don't add much value to others then you may be disappointed by how little you deserve.

"Self-worth" in this context relates to literally how much you are worth to others – not necessarily your monetary worth, although monetary worth is an indication of how much value you are adding in the workplace / marketplace.

So how much are you worth?

Too many of us pin our self-worth to our income. Yes, this is an important part of life, but money isn't everything. In terms of your life, you will add value to clients and customers, but also to friends, family and loved ones.

Non-monetary value can often outweigh the monetary; listening, focussing, attention, favours, lifts, surprises, there are a million non-monetary ways to add value to those around us.

If you've ever been offered a job, won a contract or been recommended by someone you know well, they are basing their actions on their estimation of your (non-monetary) worth to them.

youdeservethisbook.com

Being polite, loyal, trustworthy, caring and reliable are all pieces of the jigsaw which establish your value. Not just your bank balance.

This is also true of those in your life adding value to you. Your closest friends and dearest relatives are those who have been there for you. They have offered you advice, guidance, support, money, lifts to the airport; all sorts of things which have made a difference to you and added value. They will have done this through a desire to serve.

These people who have done so much for you are the first to benefit from you seeking to repay the favour. If you have been the recipient of kindness you are often keen to "repay" the person as soon as is possible. If someone who has offered you their support and kindness falls on hard times, you are more inclined to help them – it's almost an obligation.

In both life and business, the same rules apply. The value you add to others and the value others add to you can be distorted by perception.

The problem here is – your perception doesn't count.

This was my stumbling block and perhaps yours too. Whatever I thought I did or didn't deserve didn't matter. Only my actions and efforts determine what I deserve.

This explains why you feel you deserve some things in your life and that you don't deserve certain other things. The things you feel you deserve, that you actually have, align with your perception and your YOU DESERVE IT blueprint. You work hard at the gym and develop muscles, you feel YOU DESERVE IT as you connect the result of muscles with the hours of work you put in to achieve them.

youdeservethisbook.com

9 – You are right | **135**

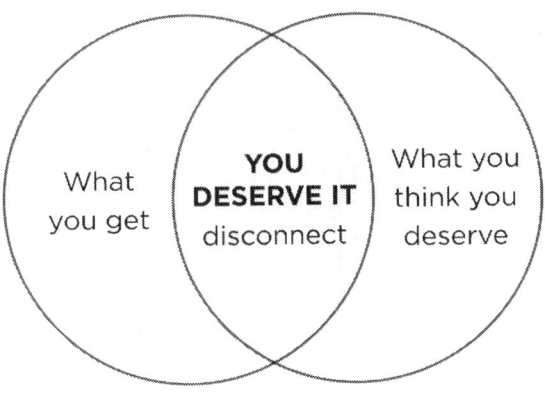

This is the YOU DESERVE IT disconnect. The things which don't align with your perception about what you deserve are downplayed, discounted and annoying.

Anything you think you deserve, but don't get and anything which you get which you don't think you deserve fall into the YOU DESERVE IT disconnect.

Establishing the reason for the disconnect is crucial to moving forward.

For example; a promotion you didn't feel you deserved is downplayed as luck. The difficulty here is that the things in your life which result from your actions are deserved, however you may feel about it. Following this line of thinking you need to align your thoughts about what you deserve with your actions.

But how?

How do you make peace with the negative things you have deserved and the positive things you may feel guilty about deserving?

I've achieved this, it **is** possible.

The first strategy is to be non-judgemental. As with my thoughts about the girl at the bar, you can think or feel how you please about anything in your life but you are never too far from the truth (reality). I took notes, made observations (tainted by my perception and methodology bias) and drew conclusions which were completely at

youdeservethisbook.com

odds with the reality. It was only speaking with Charlotte at the bar and gaining some factual evidence that I realised how dangerous being judgemental can be. You will eventually, reach a "correction point" when you challenge your thinking and change your approach if you aren't obtaining the results you want from life.

Asking questions, focussing on facts and not emotions will help you to reach this point. This book is my own "correction point" and I hope it will catalyse yours. It's my realisation that how I viewed the world was biased to such a degree that my life was staying stuck in the same place. I realised that it was not what happened in my life, but what I did about it, which would unstick me.

The second strategy is to welcome all things into your life with the same approach. From winning money to the death of a loved one, attempting to maintain a level approach can save you from the pain of things you don't feel you deserve.

This is commonly known as being "Zen-like". Zen is a form of Mahayana Buddhism which focuses on maintaining a "Buddha-like" nature. Zen focuses on the simplistic beauty of life – observing the breath and observing the mind, it also focuses on Kensho. Kensho is gaining insight into one's true nature. By observing how you act and react in any given situation you can gain a deeper understanding as to your true character and true beliefs.

It takes years to hone such skills, but trying to adopt this approach in life begins the powerful and processional process of change. Utilising breathing techniques and meditation can help you maintain a level of balance in everyday life, removing emotion and your thoughts for even a short while to help you gain perspective on the world.

Even simply attempting to remain balanced in your approach to life will put you in a better position to be more "in touch with reality" and less biased in your thinking. Simply being aware of the need to maintain a balanced approach to your life helps you to achieve it.

youdeservethisbook.com

How to be calmer in five minutes – courtesy of Wikihow.

- **Step 1.** Count to your age. If you're 28, you would count till the number 28.
- **Step 2.** Picture the word calm for ten seconds then say out loud three times.
- **Step 3.** Think about something that makes you feel happy and soothed.
- **Step 4.** Talk about how you feel to yourself or write it out.
- **Step 5** Take a deep breath... and slowly breathe out through your mouth.

So why can't you fully control what you do and don't deserve?

If you could, life would be simpler after all. You can deserve more than you think, both in the negative and the positive sense, but your actions can only influence so much. As a card-carrying control freak, this reality still irks me...

One of the reasons you are never truly in control of circumstances is the "law of unintended consequences".

This concept was popularised by the American sociologist Robert K Merton. (He also coined the phrase "self-fulfilling prophecy".) Unintended consequences are "Outcomes that are not the ones intended by purposeful action".

With the best plan, focussed action and the best intentions, you can never control 100% of the outcome – there are just too many factors at play.

Unintended consequences are grouped into three types:

1. **A positive**, often called luck or serendipity.
2. **A negative**, often called bad luck or misfortune.
3. **A perverse effect**, you achieve the exact opposite of what you aimed for – also known as "The Cobra Effect"

A cautionary tale of unintended consequences is that of "The Cobra Effect".

The Cobra Effect is an anecdote from the time of British rule in Colonial India which documents a problem with venomous cobras. The government offered a bounty for each cobra killed, believing this would help reduce the number of cobras and help to solve the issue. Some enterprising people bred cobras to subsequently kill them to get the bounty. Upon learning this, the government cancelled the bounty. The cobras which were bred to be killed were now worthless and as such released into the wild, dramatically increasing cobra numbers. The result was a perverse effect – in an effort to reduce cobra numbers, the number of cobras had actually increased.

Whilst consequences such as this are "unintended" they are deserved as they derive from purposeful action. Although the villagers may not feel they deserve to be overrun with cobras (!), the difference is what you expected the outcome to be, versus the reality.

This is your perception.

Raising your awareness of the potential consequences of your actions and being responsible for them is the most likely route to deserving everything you set out to achieve.

The consequences of your actions are important to consider. We tend to view things one-dimensionally as we are focussed on ourselves instead of others. The Indian government focussed on their problem so much that they didn't fully consider the consequences of their actions. If they did, then a different approach such as using traps or educating the population about the dangers of snakes could have resulted instead.

This is why we are all told to focus on solutions rather than problems. If you focus on the problem too much then you can limit the potential solutions.

Before you focus on potential solutions to any problem, it's a good idea to breathe slowly, rhythmically for a moment to clear your mind.

I was focussing on being unhappy and not following my passion so much that I wasn't focussing on solutions. My half-hearted attempts at trying new things, reading personal development books and strategizing about what I *could* do had yielded little to no progress. It was the Procrastination Illusion. I deserved it.

As an unintended (yet positive) consequence, the business and personal development books I had read in my quest to find happiness and branch out for myself actually improved my work at the prestigious car company and led to my success there. I wanted to leave to pursue my own path, but ended up working harder than ever, and succeeding.

Like the government in Delhi, I was trying to put out a fire whilst unknowingly fanning the flames.

I focussed my hard work and efforts on my job which yielded me a career – when what I truly wanted a calling.

The career has provided me room to pursue my calling, so it's not all bad, but it has set me back as I've focussed more on my career instead of my calling.

I was deserving more than I thought I should deserve at work and deserving less then I wanted to deserve in pursuing my happiness and purpose. I was "lucky" to be doing so well in my job and "unlucky" to not make progress towards my purpose. In this context, "lucky" means taking action and "unlucky" means not taking structured action.

My new understanding of precessional effects (see the honey bee in Chapter 3) helped greatly to change my thoughts and my actions. Like the honey bee pollinating plants as a matter of course when collecting pollen, your daily actions can have long term effects and can cause other things to happen in your life.

In "The Art of Exceptional Living" by Jim Rohn, he talks about eating an apple a day as an example and metaphor for precessional and incremental effects. The apple is representative of healthy eating habits. If you don't eat healthily today you won't be unhealthy, but if you don't eat healthily for six years, the impact is greater. If you don't save some money today it makes no difference. If you don't save money for six years it has a greater impact on your finances.

Jim Rohn defines success and failure accordingly:

- **Success** – A few simple disciplines practised every day.
- **Failure** – A few errors in judgement repeated every day.

If you are continuing to take structured action on something, you will reap a compounded return. This is a fundamental way to deserve more then you expect you deserve. The important part is that the action could be intentional or not, positive or negative. It all has consequences.

youdeservethisbook.com

If you regularly save money, you will accumulate a nest egg of savings. These savings accumulate interest. That interest then accumulates and generates more interest and so on. You may get to a stage where you receive regular interest payments yet feel you don't deserve them because you only "saved a little money" regularly over many years.

It doesn't matter.

YOU DESERVE IT.

Whilst you may perceive the habit of saving regularly to be insignificant or "anyone could do it", by maintaining the action you increase the momentum and enjoy a far greater return on your efforts.

The reverse is also true. If you're in debt, the interest accrues interest and grows over time. You have deserved this outcome through your action (inaction).

If you eat poorly and ignore your health, you may be fine for the first few years. Eventually you may become overweight and perhaps suffer liver or digestive issues. You won't feel like you deserve to suffer these ailments – yet your actions have brought you to this point.

In both cases your perception of what you feel you deserve is at play, yet the reality of what is actually deserved is unaffected by your perception; the action creates the outcome. It's a classic example of The Hidden Choice (Chapter 5).

Similarly to the saving example above, I felt I didn't deserve my success at work.

For years I had arrived early, worked lunch, stayed late, helped others, made suggestions and proved myself reliable and hardworking. Over time, this reputation and my continued efforts placed me as the likely candidate for promotion to my current role.

When the opportunity arose I was the prime candidate for the job – I felt "lucky" to get the job, but "luck", in my view now, is where preparation meets opportunity. I deserved the promotion. No question.

"All of a sudden" I was earning far more than previously, driving a company car and working on higher level tasks. The day to day stresses dissipated and I had a new set of challenges to embark upon.

My thinking about the promotion was an example of the "overnight success" fallacy where people who succeed are perceived to have done so quickly, the years of work that led them to that point being quickly forgotten.

youdeservethisbook.com

I was forgetting the years of my own hard work I had put in and was feeling guilty that I was deserving so much more "all of a sudden".

It was my perception that was off – not what I deserved.

Perception does not influence what you deserve.

Had I not progressed and had I stayed in the same job, would I have felt I deserved more eventually? Most likely. I would have felt I deserved more and wondered why I didn't have it.

Understand that your perception of what you deserve versus what you actually have in your life are often different.

When you align the two – when you accept that you are deserving of more positive things than you thought and when you celebrate your accomplishments – it is fulfilling. If you disregard this as "luck" or "serendipity" you're missing the point (and the warm feeling of accomplishment I now enjoy).

Recognising and celebrating your success is a wholesome and enjoyable undertaking. Once you acknowledge your achievements, your self-esteem begins to increase; you take a step closer to "reality" and recognise your true value in the world, not just your perception of it. When you accept that you are deserving of negative things you are putting yourself in a position to change them.

Being responsible (able to choose your response) allows you to look into why you are deserving more negative things than you believe you should. With this insight you can look to un-deserve them and remove them from your life.

Above all else, the understanding that there is sometimes disparity between what you think you deserve and what you actually deserve, that is the lesson to learn. Understanding there can be disparity and that you can change the situation will help you deserve what you want.

Sometimes you will get more than you feel you deserve, sometimes less, but you always get what you deserve from your actions.

youdeservethisbook.com

10 things to remember

1. Imposter Syndrome is believing you don't deserve what you have and are in some way a fraud.
2. You have a predefined idea of what you deserve – this is your YOU DESERVE IT blueprint.
3. It's healthy and vital to recognise the good things you deserve.
4. Self-worth and self-esteem largely dictate what you feel you deserve.
5. You can't control everything when it comes to YOU DESERVE IT, but you can control more than you think.
6. Be wary of "unintended consequences".
7. Success is a few simple disciplines, practised every day.
8. Failure is a few errors in judgement repeated every day.
9. You might feel you deserve more of less than you do, but you always get what you deserve.
10. Don't downplay your successes, don't magnify your failures.

youdeservethisbook.com

Exercise – Vision Board

You may have heard of "visualising" our future selves and future successes. This activity asks you to create a vision board based on everything you want. Take copies of magazines that display the things you want in life – nice house, nice body, nice car etc. and cut out and stick them to an A3 board to make a "vision" of your future. Get as many images and as many categories as you can, you want a board filled with numerous examples of everything you want rather than one picture of each. You want to feel immersed in everything you want when you look at the board once completed.

Example
Consider every aspect of your dream life – both actual things you want and things which represent the life you want:

- Houses / cars / boats
- Holidays / locations
- Pictures of families / ideal partners
- Clothes / fragrance
- Music / art / sculpture
- Scenery pictures

Guidance
Few of us know what we actually want from life and fewer still focus on it and define it. By defining what you want and seeking to visualise it you remind yourself why you do what you do and ultimately where your life could be if you stay dedicated to your goals. The vision board helps to define goals and to fuel motivation.

If you don't ask and consider what you want – you are unlikely to achieve it.

Tip
It's easier to focus on materialistic things in this exercise so for personality traits such as "passionate" write it directly onto the board.

youdeservethisbook.com

Every aspect of what you want and who you want to be needs to be on this board.

What you'll need
Magazines and other physical pictures of the things and life you want (the board must be physical not on the computer)

Duration
2 hours

When completed, ask yourself:
For the materialistic things – are you pursuing owning a Ferrari or merely the feelings you think you will have driving one? Focussing more on feeling and doing than having and wanting is a liberating part of understanding what you want from life.

10 – It's not fair

When something isn't deserved there is imbalance.

- If you don't deserve it, why do you have it?
- Could it be that you just don't WANT to deserve it?

In this chapter we'll look at how although you don't deserve some things, you deserve the consequences of how you react to them. We'll understand that playing the victim or having a sob story is of no value to YOU DESERVE IT. Finally we'll change problems to challenges in a bid to move forward and not be defeated.

As a child, I witnessed the attempted suicides of my father. There were five in total; the worst being when he tried to gas himself in his car in our garage. I didn't feel I deserved to be in that situation. I didn't.

As the waves rushed around me and I clung to the palm tree in Thailand, unsure if I would live even another few minutes as the debris and bodies rushed past; I didn't feel I deserved to be in that situation. I didn't.

Loved ones die, planes crash, illnesses are contracted; there are many things in life which happen to us all which are completely undeserved.

I believe we deserve everything in our lives; the caveat being everything we can *influence*.

If a mad gunman bursts into the coffee shop now as I write this and sprays the place with bullets, resulting in my untimely death, we all agree I would not deserve such a gruesome ending.

We all have things in our lives we feel we don't deserve; debt, obesity, crap relationships, death, cancer, disability – the list goes on. Sadly, dear reader, you do deserve some of these things – but only some.

If the thing you feel you don't deserve had absolutely nothing to do with your actions, then you truly don't deserve it. Cancer is an example of this, or me being caught up in the tsunami. There is nothing you could do to influence either situation and on that basis it cannot be deserved.

youdeservethisbook.com

Everything else is deserved; you just don't like to consider that you may be responsible for your credit card debt, flabby bits or underwhelming career.

It's okay, neither did I.

This book is guidance for you. Some enlightenment to help you refocus your approach to life. I'm not here to espouse and I have things in my life I don't feel I deserve, but deep down, know I do. I'm not perfect, nor will I ever be.

Remember:

It's not what happens to you, it's what you do about it.

I have had my fair (was it fair?) share of difficult circumstances that I truly have done nothing to deserve. The reason these circumstances have not defeated me, the reason this book is sat in front of you comes down to my belief that it's not what happens to you, it's what you do about it.

I did not deserve to be in the tsunami – but I am responsible for how I responded to it.

While the survivors I've met have tried to put it behind them, forget it and "move on" with their lives, I was aware I needed professional help to properly deal with the situation. If not, my night terrors, my fear of the sea and the underlying anxiety that permeated all aspects of my life could come back to haunt me in years to come. Two hundred and fifty plus hours of professional counselling ensued. Being responsible about the situations I faced was, in this instance, to ask for help.

A wonderful woman, Morag, met me at my first session. (An equally lovely woman, Tracey, helped me with Cognitive Behavioural Therapy in later years.)

With a smile on my face I told Morag I hadn't eaten or washed in days, had suicidal thoughts, was a survivor of parental suicide and the (at the time, the very recent) Asian tsunami.

I followed that up with, "Please fix me." And a laugh.

I can picture the room, the easy chairs, the lamps, and the loud ticking clock. I remember baring my soul to a relative stranger; I remember the tears – plenty of tears. I used to joke that I would eventually run out of tears I had cried so much.

youdeservethisbook.com

10 – It's not fair | 147

Did I deserve to be washed away and nearly drown? (Bearing in mind I was indoors at the time, asleep... on land)

Did I deserve to witness the breakdown of my parents' marriage and the suicide attempts?

Did I deserve my own feelings of depression, anxiety and my struggle in everyday life?

Absolutely not. I had no influence over these situations.

What I realised so early on was that if I didn't take responsibility for my situation, I would deserve to live a life of depression, alcoholism and perhaps the same sad ending as my father.

I didn't deserve it.

But I was responsible for it.

At the time I downplayed seeing a counsellor and trying medication to help me cope. I saw these as logical steps to combat the potential future issues I could face. To ask for help, although incredibly courageous, was a no brainer for me.

I believe this to have saved my life. I also recognise now what an enormous thing this was to do. It was the one thing my father didn't do; I was determined not to repeat his mistakes.

Now free from depression medication, counselling sessions and the issues such as overwhelming anxiety, which I initially battled with, I still have dark times. I realise now that I've inherited the neurological chemistry which makes me susceptible to depression. I've spent days in bed escaping the world. Days not eating at all. Days not speaking to anyone. Days not working. Days just not doing anything at all but waiting for the dark clouds to pass.

There have been countless times when I considered taking my own life. I'm not ashamed to admit that. There is no shame in depression.

Do I deserve to feel this way and to face these challenges?

No. I have done nothing to cause them.

Am I responsible for them?

100% yes.

This is the YOU DESERVE IT mindset; this is how you turn tragedy to triumph.

The YOU DESERVE IT Mindset: Taking responsibility for not only the things you can influence and thus deserve, but also the things outside of your control (such as the tsunami). Being responsible for how you deal with truly undeserved events is how you turn tragedy to triumph.

Am I a victim? No. Am I special? I'd like to think so, but no.

I realise that had I started looking to blame the world, other people and circumstances, then I was not going to get very far in my own life.

Being responsible for everything in my life has helped me to deserve the things I want. Had I not dealt with my "issues", who knows where life could have taken me?

It's impossible to say.

Having witnessed the arguments, the drink and the abuse dispensed by my father as he battled depression with no medication or no counselling, I knew that to avoid this for myself I needed to take a new approach. I needed to take responsibility.

While it feels strangely comforting to have the pity of others from hearing your sob story, eventually the Monty Python-esque arms race of who is worse off becomes tedious.

In English culture in particular, there's a perverse desire to be pitied, to continue stoically and to enhance the appearance of your obstacles to make things appear even worse than they already are.

> "'E was right. I was happier then and I had NOTHIN'. We used to live in this tiiiny old house, with greaaaaat big holes in the roof."
>
> "House? You were lucky to have a HOUSE! We used to live in one room, all hundred and twenty-six of us, no furniture. Half the floor was missing; we were all huddled together in one corner for fear of FALLING!"
>
> "You were lucky to have a ROOM! *We* used to have to live in a corridor!"
>
> **Four Yorkshiremen sketch - Monty Python**

However terrible life may be, life moves on and so should we.

After a while, no matter how bad things may be in your life, the pity stops and you are expected to "get on with it".

This is code for "take responsibility for it." In the end, only you are responsible for you.

youdeservethisbook.com

Is there anything in your life which you truly don't deserve? Is there something which is there through no fault of your own that you have to deal with? If so, are you being responsible for it?

I want that answer to always be yes. From this book onwards I want you to deliberately mis-pronounce and mis-spell the word responsible as response-able. Remind yourself that response-able is a position of power, a position of choice; you can change the situation, if you want to.

When something isn't deserved there is imbalance. I didn't deserve certain things in my life and the imbalance was that I felt drawn into a victim mentality. The imbalance was that I had to deal with the situation or be worse off if I didn't.

Had I not been response-able, I would have been an accessory. A compliant bystander, like those who watch a mugging but don't step in. Like those bystanders, I could choose to step in or choose to let it happen.

I chose to step in.

Being response-able for things you haven't deserved is frustrating. It feels unfair, but unfair doesn't exist; it's a man-made concept it's infuriating and can be very painful.

Being responsible is the only way.

I will never forget the counselling sessions when Morag (my counsellor) would try to "push me" into difficult topics and exercises. I'd feel angry, affronted, a victim, but I'd carry on knowing I needed to carry on to "fix myself". I soon realised that these difficult situations she was "pushing me" towards were catalysts to my progress.

In life, it's the perceived "difficult" things that are often the right things to do; or at least the things which bring results.

Saving money, exercising, eating vegetables, being a parent; these are all "difficult" things (especially being a parent...) but they are, in my opinion, the "right things" – the things that will push you forward.

Victim mentality will keep you from your dreams.

It's kept me from mine. If I was not response-able for the things that have happened to me, I could not change them, deal with them, conquer them.

Quite simply – victims don't deserve it.

As a victim you feel you feel you don't deserve to be in the negative situation within which you find yourself.

The other side to this is that as a victim you won't take responsibility for where you find yourself and are thus unlikely to take action to deserve anything better. In both cases, you "don't deserve it".

Going back again to Morag, the days I played the victim with her, complained about the unfairness of the suicide and tsunami and everything else and sulked, feeling sorry for myself, were the most frustrating sessions where I made the least progress. I would swear, shout, and get angry, bang the table and feel all worked up. (To her credit, she never wavered.) Despite that I would leave the session worse off than when I came.

Victims are powerless.

The sessions where I "pushed" myself and challenged my thinking, where I took responsibility to move on with situations, by contrast, left me feeling energised and optimistic. I'm not a religious person. I have no faith, no thoughts of god and I don't pray. I do however, like a certain aspect of religion and it serves me well:

I view everything as a test.

Religious and spiritual people talk about "learning lessons" and "moving to the next level" in life by passing "tests" cleverly designed as difficult circumstances.

Although not religious or spiritual, I have noticed that I find myself in the same situations time and time again – it's only when I change my approach and "pass the test" that I move on to "the next level".

Traffic was one of these "tests". I would not let people in or give way on a regular basis. I would become easily stressed, angry, and confrontational with other drivers believing everyone was "out to get me". It was always, "Me first!"

It went on for years and made parts of driving quite unpleasant and potentially dangerous. I can't choose how other people drive, but I can choose how I react to it.

Response-able. The moment I began to let people in, give way and be Selfmore about it, I felt peaceful and happy. Driving is now a pleasure.

If life is a series of tests, then I feel that I have passed this one. Never again will I be stressed out behind the wheel.

Whether you view life as a series of tests or not, it's clear that you will get the same results until you change your actions. However unfair it may feel, change your actions, and pass the test. Move forward.

Kinder driving

If you find driving stressful, feel like you are always being cut up and never let out at junctions, then this exercise will help to restore your calm when driving.

I used to never let people change lanes or let people out at junctions, I was so focussed on getting to where I wanted to go that I couldn't "waste time" and sped up to not let anyone in and get to my destination faster.

The misperception here is time. Traffic permitting, letting people out at junctions or letting people pull into your lane has a negligible effect on journey time. It only serves to make driving stressful as you feel "everyone is out to get you".

> *On a regular journey such as your work commute, drive as normal, don't let people in and don't change the way you do things – time your journey and keep a note of this.*
>
> *The next time you take the journey I want you to completely change how you drive. As you approach junctions or as others indicate to come into your lane, imagine they are a close friend or family member. If someone close to you needed to exit a junction you would let them go, so it should be no different for anyone else.*

I am confident that like me, you will notice the "kinder driving" technique makes no real difference to your journey time, but you will be happier and may even have had lots of thumbs up and gratitude from your fellow motorists.

When you recognise that letting people out at junctions and slowing down doesn't really affect your journey time, but deeply affects your happiness, you will change how you drive forever.

youdeservethisbook.com

It's not just negative things which can be undeserved. Just ask the children of the super wealthy. Through no action of their own, these children stand to inherit vast amounts of money and a unique experience of life. For those who are response-able, the situation is viewed as one with a great many possibilities; something to get really immersed in. A challenge.

For others, the drive to achieve can be obliterated by the thought that the child will be unlikely to surpass the parent in terms of achievement, so why bother? This can lead to alcoholism, depression, drug addiction.

The issue is never the situation or circumstance per se, the issue is the response.

It's decisions, not conditions, which shape our lives. Viewing the situation as a "problem" or something so overwhelming you are paralysed to act, is, again, victim mentality.

Remember – victims don't deserve it.

I believe a slight change in vocabulary and approach can help overcome this. Before we get to that, I'm aware that your personal issues and desire to achieve goals will not change overnight with the simple changing of one word. That's not the point; it's the slight change in approach.

Maintain this and over time momentum builds. I didn't conquer my issues overnight, as much as I would have liked to.

Remember; success is defined by Jim Rohn as a few small disciplines practised every day. It took years of work, but it started with a decision. A decision not to be beaten, coupled with my willingness to adapt my approach as I went (like course made good in Chapter 2) meant I was on the right track.

Let's change your vocabulary.

One of my clients used this terminology when I worked for a prestigious car company and it made them a pleasure to deal with.

It sounded a bit "cheesy" at first, but it works.

Change "problem" to "challenge".

youdeservethisbook.com

problem
/ˈprɒbləm/

noun

1. a matter or situation regarded as unwelcome or harmful and needing to be dealt with and overcome.

challenge
/ˈtʃalɪn(d)ʒ/

noun

1. a call to someone to participate in a competitive situation or fight to decide who is superior in terms of ability or strength.
"he accepted the challenge"
synonyms: dare, provocation; summons
"he accepted the challenge"

2. a call to prove or justify something.
"a challenge to the legality of the banning order"
synonyms: confrontation with, dispute with, stand against, test of, opposition, disagreement with; More

verb

1. dispute the truth or validity of.
"it is possible to challenge the report's assumptions"
synonyms: question, disagree with, object to, take exception to, confront, dispute, take issue with, protest against, call into question; More

2. invite (someone) to engage in a contest.
"he challenged one of my men to a duel"

Problem sounds unpleasant. A situation which, once resolved, will leave you in no better position than when you started is a problem. A problem is something that happens to you – it's a burden.

Problems breed negative thinking. They are onerous.

Challenges are enticing. Challenges can help you grow and leave you better off. Challenges are opportunities; they can be exciting and fulfilling.

Challenges open your thinking, problems keep it closed.

Using this approach, I haven't had a problem in years.
I've had plenty of challenges and opportunities, but not one problem.

This slightly different approach helps you to change your reaction to the situation. Being response-able is easier with challenges. Challenges are about overcoming; problems are about getting through or merely surviving.

Whatever you have in your life that you don't deserve (where your actions have truly not caused it) try looking at it through the lens of a challenge instead.

It's not fair that you have to be response-able for things and suffer at the hands of something beyond your control. It's not fair but it's a challenge – it's a chance. It's a test.

Will it make or break you?

Can you merely survive this or can you thrive?

We all face challenges in life, no one gets special treatment. It's not what happens to you, it's what you do about it which counts.

If there is something in your life you don't deserve: remember to be response-able, treat it like a challenge instead of a problem and remember that victims don't deserve it.

youdeservethisbook.com

10 things to remember

1. Everything you can influence is deserved – whether you like it or not.
2. Anything which isn't deserved creates imbalance.
3. It's not what happens to you, it's what you do about it.
4. If you don't deserve something (as you can't influence it) you deserve how you react to it.
5. You might not deserve everything but you can be responsible for everything.
6. Pity gets you nowhere.
7. Victims don't deserve it.
8. Viewing situations as a "test" can help you to dissect them to understand better what you need to do – without your feelings or perception tainting it.
9. It's decisions, not conditions, which shape our lives.
10. Turn problems into challenges.

youdeservethisbook.com

Exercise – Gratitude

Gratitude is a key component of happiness and fulfilment (as well as success). For the next week, keep a gratitude journal and write at least three things you are grateful for. This can be anything large or small, if it's in your life and you're thankful for it, jot it down. Do keep this up for the full seven days as the longer you practice gratitude the more powerful its impact becomes.

Example
I have a small red gratitude journal which I write in each day. From three things to 15 things, I make sure I write down anything which comes into my head which I am grateful for. This may be the big things such as new clients or buying something nice, or the small things such as having a warm and comfortable home in the winter. Whatever it is, be thankful for it and write it down. There are no right or wrong answers and no minimum or maximum number of things to keep track of.

Guidance
We often take far too much for granted in life. From clean drinking water, to food, loved ones, health, money, opportunity, education and countless more. When you begin, you may list the "clichéd" things you feel you should be thankful for such as your health, but as you progress you will venture into more meaningful and personal things – that's where this exercise works its magic.

Ask yourself – what am I thankful for?

Tip
Write without editing, don't worry about repeating yourself or writing what you "should" – if it's in your life and you're thankful for it, put it down.

What you'll need
Notebook and pen.

youdeservethisbook.com

Duration
7 days

When completed, ask yourself:
How great does it feel to be grateful? Are you surprised by how many great things there are in your life – many of which are "small" and overlooked every day?

11 – Gewüsst Wie

Self-worth dictates net worth.

- What are your skills?
- Could you apply them to add value to others?
- How much are you truly worth?

In this chapter, we'll be introduced to the power of Gewüsst Wie, learn about the "know where" man and the fable of the Chinese Bamboo Tree. We'll look at "the five whys", FIRO-B profiling and the power of knowing what you're really worth.
Before we start though, let me tell you a story.

> ***"Know where man"*** *Nikola Tesla visited Henry Ford at his factory, which was having some kind of difficulty. Ford asked Tesla if he could help identify the problem area. Tesla walked up to a wall of boilerplate and made a small X in chalk on one of the plates. Ford was thrilled, and told him to send an invoice.*
>
> *The bill arrived, for $10,000. Ford asked for a breakdown. Tesla sent another invoice, indicating a $1 charge for marking the wall with an X, and $9,999 for knowing where to put it.*

This story highlights the difference between the value of the work at hand and the value of the knowledge behind it; the two can be **very** different.

Gewüsst Wie is a German saying translated literally as "know-how". With know-how, your productivity can increase exponentially; so, too, what you can deserve.

Know-how is your ability to get things done, your ability to add value. Know-how gets results. Know-how, knowledge, experience, whatever you call it, it can take time to require and a lot of effort. By its nature, Gewüsst Wie is the long term approach to life and YOU DESERVE IT.

youdeservethisbook.com

Just because it's long term shouldn't put you off, in fact it should excite you. (Remember to reframe "problems" to challenges" from the previous chapter.)

Fewer people play life in the long term; the long term is planning, the short term is settling. There are always more settlers than planners as planning is perceived to be so much more "difficult". This means that those who do plan, deserve more by virtue of supply and demand. Specialist skills and Gewüsst Wie demand specialist fees. They deserve specialist fees as in the case of Tesla.

Some things in life cannot be deserved overnight no matter how hard you work.

Continued effort can move mountains, constant dripping hollows the stone.

What you deserve reflects the value you add when you serve others.

You are capable of adding more value and serving others better if you are experienced and in possession of Gewüsst Wie. With Gewüsst Wie you are in the minority, you are rarer and rarity increases value. As it can take some time, often years, to perfect skills, gain experience and qualifications, it means not everyone obtains Gewüsst Wie. While some stay the course and finish what they begin, others do not put in the effort and time, never realising the potential of this powerful tool.

It's easy to look at doctors, dentists, solicitors and other professionals and marvel at their level of pay and privilege. What isn't so obvious is the years of hard work, dedication and sacrifice that have led them to where they are today, to Gewüsst Wie. (They are another case of the "overnight success" where the thousands of preceding nights become forgotten.)

These people deserve more because they understand that to deserve more and to serve more can mean an investment of time and energy in advance. You serve before you deserve. You give before you receive, you must be Selfmore; that is, to primarily seek to add value and serve others but also with an eye on your own objectives.

I found myself in possession of Gewüsst Wie in my sales role. Through the natural course of my work, and my own personal development at the hands of the countless personal development books I read, I had accumulated 10 years of experience in a role where not too much changes over time. This meant that once the knowledge and experience were acquired, they could be used nearly endlessly. This meant I was able to achieve and maintain success with no real additional effort, just a small amount of "course made good" from time to time.

Strangely it was this boredom and lack of challenge that catalysed my decision to pursue my passion and ultimately start creating YOU DESERVE IT.

I wanted a challenge.

As comfortable as it was, I didn't want to spend my life doing the same things year in year out. At 10 years into the job, I was bored and I had potentially 30 more years to go; to me at the time, it was terrifying!

I didn't plan for Gewüsst Wie but I obtained it. I'd obtained it through my quest to serve others, add value and do a great job. I'd obtained it through persistent effort. Even though I wanted to follow my own path and ultimately considered working in cars as a stop gap, I still wanted to do a great job and be the best I could be. It's a matter of personal pride.

Doing a great job, especially one you don't enjoy, is the mark of a successful person. Anyone could slacken up but real winners keep pushing, they take pride in their work.

By adding more value, I became more valuable myself; this is the essence of Gewüsst Wie.

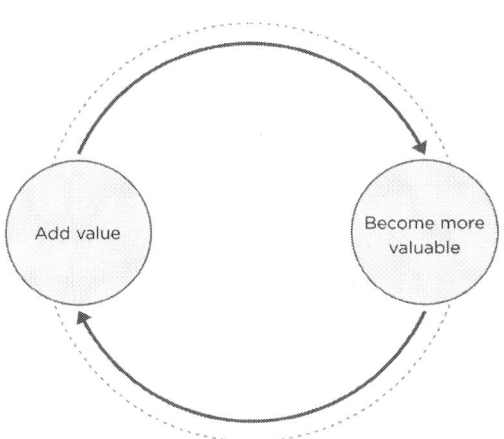

youdeservethisbook.com

Whilst I didn't have a plan to obtain it, Gewüsst Wie often requires planning, as becoming experienced enough and skilled enough takes time. If nothing else, Gewüsst Wie requires continuous effort and adaptation over time for it to be effective – it doesn't happen overnight.

Things which take time and persistence often require faith to see them through; you need to visualise the end result and use that to motivate your current actions even if you may not see any signs of progress immediately.

"Faith is taking the first step when you can't see the whole staircase."
Dr. Martin Luther King

Consider the parable of **Chinese Bamboo Tree:**

> *"When this particular seed of the Chinese Bamboo tree is planted, watered and nurtured, for years it doesn't outwardly grow as much as an inch. Nothing happens for the first year. There's no sign of growth. Not even a hint. The same thing happens – or doesn't happen – the second year. And then the third year. The tree is carefully watered and fertilized each year, but nothing shows. No growth. No anything. So it goes as the sun rises and sets for four solid years. The farmer and his wife have nothing tangible to show for this labour or effort. Then, along comes year five. After five years of fertilizing and watering have passed, with nothing to show for it – the bamboo tree suddenly sprouts and grows eighty feet in just SIX WEEKS!*
>
> *Did the little tree lie dormant for four years only to grow exponentially in the fifth? Or, was the little tree growing underground, developing a root system strong enough to support its potential for outward growth in the fifth year and beyond? The answer is, of course, obvious. Had the tree not developed a strong unseen foundation it could not have sustained its life as it grew."*

Although we all naturally have a level of experience and knowledge, gained through the natural course of our lives, Gewüsst Wie, in the context of this chapter, pertains to actively pursuing the skills and abilities necessary to add more value, making yourself more valuable and in turn capable of deserving more.

Gewüsst Wie through experience is not about just turning up, you have to seek constant improvement and take pride in what you do.

Those who deserve the most in life are often those who have actively pursued Gewüsst Wie. CEOs that have risen up through the ranks, entrepreneurs such as Sir James Dyson who have failed for years before succeeding, and sports people who dedicate their lives to their craft.

It took James Dyson years before his vacuum cleaner was a mainstream success, but it would be easy to think he developed the idea and enjoyed global success in a short period of time.

These people commit with no guarantee of success and no rigidly set path. They commit with the belief that they can do it, along with a vivid image of what they want to create or achieve and the knowledge that they'll persist and adapt until they succeed. They believe it before they see it.

Gewüsst Wie explains both why you are deserving things now "without trying" particularly in work or business, as well as why you are limited to where you are now.

Some things will come easily to you. Selling cars to my clients was simple. If I asked you to sell 100 prestige vehicles this month with no previous experience or contacts you would struggle. I'm no better than you; it's just that I have the skills, the contacts, the Gewüsst Wie to do it. When Gewüsst Wie is in place, the "impossible" often becomes routine.

It can be easy to settle for the "easy life" and to not try for Gewüsst Wie, not strive to improve or to achieve your dreams; after all, why try for more when everything is going so well?

This is certainly something I was asked as I transitioned from seller to speaker.

My life on paper was "perfect", so why would I risk losing what I had? Because I was neither happy nor passionate in my work any more. I needed a challenge.

To deserve more, you may just need some more Gewüsst Wie to make you more valuable and enable you to deserve more.

If you want to deserve more, then Gewüsst Wie allows you to serve more and to add more value to people and add value to more people.

Ultimately, your Gewüsst Wie is your calling card.

The beauty of Gewüsst Wie is that once obtained, however long it may have taken and however arduous the journey was, you will never

youdeservethisbook.com

lose it. Once achieved, Gewüsst Wie is yours to keep. The fundamentals remain largely consistent. From dentistry to medicine, law or selling, the details of the landscape may change and adapt, but the basic principles often remain quite constant.

When you put your Gewüsst Wie into action, you can continually reap the rewards of your efforts like the Chinese Bamboo Tree and the "know where" man. It's your reward for the time spent laying the foundation and putting in the work to gain the skills, experience and knowledge you need.

Think of it in terms of farming. You plant the seeds of time and effort, watering and tending to them every day. Eventually you have a crop to harvest – one that will fruit continuously. As well as reaping the rewards from your Gewüsst Wie on a near unlimited basis, another magical thing happens. As those with Gewüsst Wie tend to be in the minority, you will find that those who need your help and know-how are now magnetically drawn to you as you become a person of authority and expertise. Through recommendations, referrals and reputation, Gewüsst Wie offers a "compounding" effect.

Gewüsst Wie works like this:

> The more you know, the more you serve.
> The more you serve, the more you learn.
> The more you learn, the more you know.
> The more you know, the greater your reputation and the demand for your Gewüsst Wie.

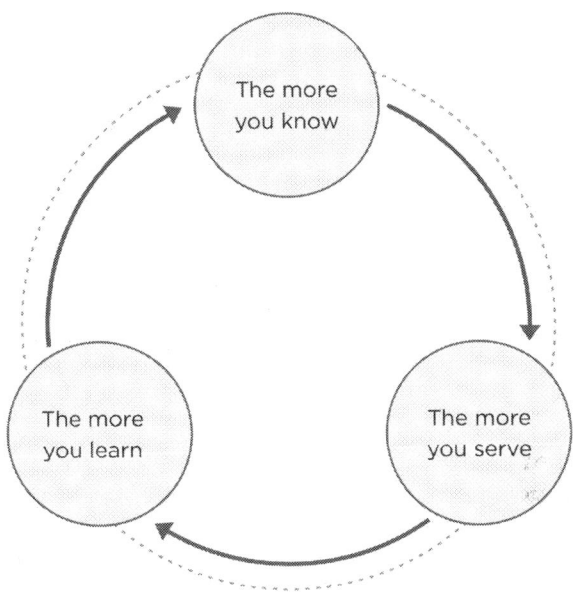

Supply and demand further catalyse this effect: rarer things are more valuable.

There will always be a demand for those people who can get the job done, but never enough of those people. It's the difficulty in obtaining Gewüsst Wie that means there will never be enough of these people, and this is where the real value lies. This is why your Gewüsst Wie is your secret weapon.

Gewüsst Wie cannot be rushed, there are no shortcuts and that's what makes it all the more important. The level of dedication and work required to obtain Gewüsst Wie is reflected in what it can help obtain for you. The more valuable the Gewüsst Wie, the harder it is or longer it takes to obtain. It's also reflected in the fact that so few people actively pursue it.

For most, it's far easier to go for the easier things to achieve that can be instantly gratifying rather than to play the longer game.

There are those who recognise the value of Gewüsst Wie but seem to not want to put in the effort to obtain it. People who "blag", who embellish, mislead and lie about their knowledge and experience. These people are eventually (often quickly) discovered. Pretending to have ability and experience and putting ability and experience into practice are two very different things.

> ***Gewüsst Wie is a great leveller:***
> ***you either have it, or you don't.***

Modelling (from Chapter 4) can play an important role here. If you have identified someone who is deserving of the results you want to achieve, you can dissect "what they have done to deserve this" in the context of Gewüsst Wie. What special skills, experience or contacts do they have? How could you obtain or model these in your own situation?

In my work, I looked to my counterparts for inspiration and noted the varying styles of doing business in play. Some would "wine and dine" clients, befriend them as loyal partners and protect their commercial interests at all costs. Others would maintain a professional distance, preferring to be a stickler for detail, reliability and punctuality. Others would dedicate themselves to adding as much value as possible through product information, regular meetings and near constant contact.

These different styles all yielded varying results and reflected the needs of the clients.

As salespeople, adapting to needs in order to add value is vital. All of my colleagues possessed years of experience; the conditions allowed you to stay in what was a very comfortable job for as long as you desired. Once you had "learned the ropes" and obtained the rudimentary amount of Gewüsst Wie, the following years would simply be a repetition of the first two or three years; very little dramatically changed in the few years I had worked there.

The fundamentals remained the same.

The years of experience for my own Gewüsst Wie could not be emulated or sped up; it would come to me one day at a time. By simply staying in my role I was naturally accumulating experience.

It was the cross section of different styles of doing the same job which interested me the most. How could I benefit from the techniques I was witnessing? What could work for me and my clients? I began to "model" my colleagues, blending together the bits I wanted and leaving out the techniques which, for one reason or another, weren't for me.

It was fascinating to observe how successful the varying techniques were. It became clear that amongst my colleagues, there was a variety of Gewüsst Wie across a wide range of disciplines.

It's natural to expect your personal experience to mix with your skills and personality to form your own unique brand of Gewüsst Wie.

Gewüsst Wie comprises the following five elements, with Desire to improve being the most important as it's the driver for growth and change.

- **Experience** Gaining experience from actually doing a task repeatedly.
- **Knowledge** The knowledge gained from previous successes and failures.
- **Skills** The skills developed as a result of repetition.
- **Personality** How you utilise your Experience, Knowledge and Skills is vitally important. Do you harness it or do you neglect it?
- **Desire to improve** Gewüsst Wie is strongest when it's created from a desire to improve and to serve others.

168 | YOU DESERVE IT

The Desire to improve is also known as "kaizen". Continually seeking to improve and seeking to become more efficient will translate into serving more and adding more value as you naturally become better at what you do.

Adding more value and becoming better at what you do fuels Gewüsst Wie and YOU DESERVE IT.

kaizen
/kʌɪˈzɛn/

noun

> a Japanese business philosophy of continuous improvement of working practices, personal efficiency, etc.

My colleagues were open and happy to share their approach with me and the techniques they used on a day to day basis.

This accelerated my learning as I replaced months with minutes, learning pitfalls, shortcuts, tips and tricks that would otherwise have

youdeservethisbook.com

taken years to find. It's amazing what people will tell you if you simply ask them.

My Gewüsst Wie grew rapidly due to this willingness and kindness to share (for which I will always be grateful), but also due to my own pursuit of expedited learning through modelling.

***Your Gewüsst Wie is your calling card;
it's personal to you.***

Through sharing best practice and advice with me, my colleagues were able to cast an eye on how they conducted themselves. It was a chance to review what they did and how they did it. Self-reflection is a vital tool to improve.

Sharing with me, in effect, became a strategy review for them, allowing them to perfect their techniques, discard old ones or make adjustments. Through helping me, they helped themselves. As always, being Selfmore was a win-win-win situation.

Being aware of your own Gewüsst Wie, of the value you add to others and the value of your knowledge and experience, can equally be a catalyst and a show stopper.

Those who know their value and who seek out those who wish to benefit from it (such as "know where man") are the ones who get the most from Gewüsst Wie.

Those who have no idea how their talents could be valuable to others miss the point entirely. Unutilised knowledge and experience are worthless; it's the belief in your Gewüsst Wie, coupled with the knowledge of how it can add value to others that make all the difference.

Although the fundamentals remain constant, not adapting and changing as your experience gradually grows and the natural landscape of work and life changes is also worthless.

From my colleagues it was clear to see those who knew their value. (Not in an arrogant way. Knowing your worth is not arrogance. Having an inflated idea of your value is.) Those who knew their value were happy to "ask a fair price" for it.

It was also clear to see those with perhaps greater experience and ability who remained subdued and limited in their approach; these people possessed Gewüsst Wie, but didn't know how to use it, nor believe in its value.

My own success was catalysed when I realised I could make certain requests or demands of my clients, in return for my own expertise.

If you don't ask, you don't get. I wanted more so I asked for more. The astonishing thing for me was that the more I asked for, the more I got.

Market data, sales figures, performance targets, anything that would help me in my role to sell more and to serve my clients better. Gewüsst Wie was my bargaining chip; the thing I "brought to the party" and over the years it obtained me a comfortable living. There was no obligation to help me, but as I'd spent years helping my clients, my requests for help were eagerly fulfilled through the magic of reciprocity.

In your work or business life right now, are there skills you are under-utilising or under-valuing? It's these skills, or the belief in the power of them, that can hold you back.

For me, the answer was a resounding YES! I had "sold myself short" in a number of areas.

One of my greatest skills was people. For too long, I'd kept those that I worked with at arm's length, never really "letting them in" to see the "real me". I saw them as my competition. We all sold to similar clients so I felt I needed to beat them, not join them. In winter 2014, we conducted a "FIRO-B" test in our team to assess the interpersonal relationships and look at how we interact with each other from our various characteristics.

If you are not familiar with FIRO-B, here it is in a nutshell:

> ***Fundamental Interpersonal Relations Orientation (FIRO)** is a theory of interpersonal relations, introduced by William Schutz in 1958. This theory mainly explains the interpersonal underworld of a small group. The theory is based on the belief that when people get together in a group, there are three main interpersonal needs they are looking to obtain –*
> *affection/openness, control and inclusion. Schutz developed a*

measuring instrument that contains six scales of nine-item questions that he called FIRO-B.

And here is my score:

	Inclusion	Control	Affection
Expressed	4	4	1
Wanted	1	1	3

I scored the lowest in the group. There are no prizes for high scores, but a low score indicates a lack of engagement. The low score meant I worked best alone, showed little emotion and did not particularly want to lead or be led. It was a wakeup call. This wasn't me.

Outside of work I was a friendly, caring and easy going person. I enjoyed connecting with my friends, sharing their lives and being there for them. It was clear that at work I was not using my Gewüsst Wie when it came to people. I was foolishly isolating myself, believing others to be a threat. This was selfish behaviour, rooted in a playing to not lose, rather than playing to win mindset.

What I needed was Selfmore behaviour and to play to win in order to thrive and to deserve.

I immediately began to take the time to speak with colleagues and seniors, to take an interest in their lives outside of work and to be a more authentic version of myself. It was time to be me again. It was time to be Selfmore.

In reconnecting and adjusting in this way, I further reduced my age old feelings that work was "terrible" and I was "trapped" doing a job I "hated". I realised there were many great people I could interact with on a daily basis and so much I could learn from so many of them. I shared some of my own know-how with as many colleagues as I could in an effort to be "Selfmore" and to "pay it forward" before I would ultimately leave. The sharing of my own Gewüsst Wie, being a more approachable and warmer person at work led to me benefitting from countless favours, help, advice and the respect and gratitude of others I had craved – where before there was nothing as I was so distant.

youdeservethisbook.com

Gewüsst Wie

Gewüsst Wie is your "know-how"; it's a culmination of your knowledge, experience and skill. Considering and cataloguing your Gewüsst Wie can help you understand if you are playing to your strengths.

Example
My own Gewüsst Wie:

Experience
I have 10 years of experience in sales and account management. From dealing with customers to creating opportunities and exceeding targets, I am most at home when looking after my clients and servicing their needs. I often make in-person visits, give presentations and write reports, monitoring performance and adjusting my actions to benefit the client and keep me working towards my target.

Outside of work I have experience of overcoming adversity, maintaining a blog and creating and exploring new ideas. I've had extensive counselling and completed courses and attended talks all based around living a life of purpose and following your dreams.

Knowledge
I have specific knowledge of the motor industry and of how our brand operates. Specific knowledge of the computer systems we use and the different customer types we deal with.

Outside of work I have extensive knowledge of the "self-help" industry and read on average a book a week relevant to the topic. I am aware of hundreds of inspirational resources, speakers, websites, books and more which can be very useful for keeping yourself motivated.

Skills
I am able to quickly learn and adapt to new situations, information and opportunities. I am able to meet clients' needs and to maximise the selling opportunities I face. Pre-empting future situations and requirements has been one of the cornerstones of my success in sales and account management.

Outside of work I have acquired the skills necessary to create and maintain websites, operate a social media presence and how to document and explore my ideas in terms of writing a book.

Personality & Kaizen

I currently am not utilising my passion for self-help and my extensive knowledge of the industry to my full advantage. My thirst for knowledge about the self-help industry displays my passion, whereas in a work setting my thirst for knowledge and new challenges has diminished.

Guidance

For each section, consider listing as many useful and relevant items as possible. Think of this as though you are writing a CV to a prospective employer – what useful skills, knowledge and experience do you have to offer?

Consider both your work life and your home life – it's often your home life activities which can reveal your passions. We're not looking for a bullet point list as such, rather a flowing description.

Experience

What experiences have you had inside and outside of work which could be considered assets. Consider your role in your employment and how you spend your leisure time.

Knowledge

Do you have detailed knowledge in specific areas acquired through your employment? Do you know about certain techniques, products or situations which could be advantageous to you?

Skills

Which skills or qualifications have you acquired and practised both inside and outside of work?

Once you have considered these areas, now consider how you utilise your skills, knowledge and experience – which do you seek to improve and which do you no longer focus on?

youdeservethisbook.com

The areas you seek to improve upon are often the areas about which you are passionate. The skills, knowledge and experience you gain outside of work is often (but not always) also where your passions lie. If your work life and passions are not aligned then you are not utilising your gifts and could consider how to align these two areas of your life.

Tip
This is a free thinking exercise. There are no right or wrong answers, consider the questions as honestly and fully as you can. By listing as many skills and experiences as you can, you will have a clearer picture of your own "know how"

What you'll need
Pen, pad, honesty.

Duration
1 hour

When completed, ask yourself:
Am I utilising my Gewüsst Wie? Do I play to my strengths and utilise my skills, knowledge and experience? If not – how could I?

It was recognising and utilising (sharing) my own Gewüsst Wie that caused so much to change.

In sharing with others, I began to assess my approach and to learn new things. I embraced my colleagues and my work and enjoyed further success as a result of the goodwill I was generating. I didn't want to stay working with cars long term, but improving performance is always my goal.

Possessing knowledge and experience is the ultimate goal in Gewüsst Wie, but pursuing it is vitally important. By questioning and analysing everything you can in your world, you will learn more about how it all works and fits together, how the people within your world work – and thus how to serve them.

Here, the "five whys" can be useful to establish the root cause of any situation.

Example:

The vehicle will not start. (The problem)

- Why? - The battery is dead. (first why)
- Why? - The alternator is not functioning. (second why)
- Why? - The alternator belt has broken. (third why)
- Why? - The alternator belt was well beyond its useful service life and not replaced. (fourth why)
- Why? - The vehicle was not maintained according to the recommended service schedule. (fifth why, a root cause)

If you do not pursue Gewüsst Wie, if you sit still in an ever changing world and wonder why others are enjoying more results than you, then you will be unlikely to deserve more than you have. You need to remain open. You need to adapt. This is why those in life who proclaim "it's not my job" or "it's not my problem" will never get as far as perhaps they could.

Being responsible for everything you can fertilises Gewüsst Wie. If you are not response-able for your continued learning and development, response-able for your life and what happens to you, you will limit what you deserve.

youdeservethisbook.com

By seeking to add value, by seeking to be as useful as you can be, you will naturally accumulate Gewüsst Wie. You will naturally evolve with the world around you as you are continuously response-able for it. I noticed those I worked with who didn't move from their role in all the many years I was there and concluded it was down to two things.

1. The first was the unwillingness to actively learn and actively pursue additional knowledge and additional responsibilities. The belief that you have nothing new to learn or no reason to try can be deadly to progress.
2. The second was that despite the years of experience and vast amounts of knowledge and skill, they didn't ask for its true value – or even understand its true value.

I was fortunate to not only pursue Gewüsst Wie naturally, but to be brave enough to ask for its true worth – this was a fundamental part of my success in sales, and latterly my success as a speaker, coach and author.

As I looked to leave and change my career, I knew a new set of skills, abilities and experience would be necessary; I would be on a new path. I would need to find new ways to serve and new ways to play to my own strengths as I had reached the end of my current career path.

Gewüsst Wie is a fluid thing.

Just as vinyl became cassettes, became CDs and then mp3s, your knowledge will constantly evolve and need to evolve to stay useful and relevant. Whilst this kind of evolution is prevalent in all areas of life, the fundamentals of seeking knowledge and experience, putting it to good use, sharing it with others and being aware of its value are fundamentals to your success.

youdeservethisbook.com

10 things to remember

1. Gewüsst Wie is the accumulation of your knowledge, experience, skills, personality and desire to improve.
2. Gewüsst Wie can take years to accumulate, but once achieved it is never lost.
3. When you add value, you become more valuable.
4. Long term success is built on strong foundations demonstrated by the parable of the Chinese Bamboo Tree.
5. The more you know, the more you can serve, the more you serve, the more you learn, the more you know…
6. Knowing the value of your Gewüsst Wie and having the courage to ask for it are game changers.
7. Being responsible for every situation you find yourself in fertilises Gewüsst Wie – nothing is ever "not my job".
8. You either have Gewüsst Wie, or you don't – it can't be faked.
9. Your Gewüsst Wie is your calling card.
10. Gewüsst Wie requires continuous improvement and effort to be fully effective.

youdeservethisbook.com

Exercise – Depth

Pick a subject, it can be anything, and seek to become a master in that subject. Dive as deep as possible, learn as much as possible and focus your energies on this one subject. It could be something whimsical (such as becoming a TinTinologist – yes they do exist), something theoretical such as learning about ancient Greece or the world wars. It could be more practical such as learning how to play the guitar, how to sew or how to make a website. Whatever it is, set out over the next 30 days to become more knowledgeable about it.

Example

I dedicate my time to finding and sharing inspiring things with those who need it via my blog Every Day Should Be Fun. In doing so I am on a daily quest to find and learn about as many inspiring and motivational things as possible. By dedicating myself to this craft daily and having consistently blogged since 2013 with no breaks, it demonstrates to me the power of learning and of persistence.

Consider what you could learn in your own life:

- An instrument
- A language
- Computer coding
- Painting/drawing/sculpting
- Juggling
- The origins of everyday objects or sayings
- History of your local community
- Research your family tree
- The list is endless.

Guidance

Once you focus upon something, and it really doesn't matter what it is, you can increase your skill, your knowledge and your proficiency just through the power of focus and intention. If you want to achieve something in life and are unsure where to begin, set out to become an expert first, have a fact finding mission and you should notice your enthusiasm and skill grow as you learn more.

You could pick something useful, such as learning a skill, or recreational such as learning about local history – what you learn isn't as relevant as the pursuit of knowledge and seeking out the information.

Tip
Pick something you have an interest in or a passion for. If you enjoyed trains as a child why not become a master at train spotting? It's not what you pick that matters, it's the dedication to mastery that matters.

What you'll need
A subject you are passionate about and want to explore further.

Duration
7 days

When completed, ask yourself:
How enjoyable is it to focus on one thing? How surprised were you about just how much information is available on the topic you have chosen? Do you feel more motivated to learn more now you have begun?

youdeservethisbook.com

12 – Ennui

Disappointment – feeling you deserve things but not taking action.

- Why don't you have what you want?
- Are you doing all you can?
- Have you let life just happen to you?

In this chapter we'll learn how ennui is a warning sign to change your approach. We'll understand how deadly ennui can be to your ambitions, how to keep it at bay with mindfulness and meditation as well and that to beat boredom you can choose to do nothing.

ennui
/ɒnˈwiː/

noun

a feeling of listlessness and dissatisfaction arising from a lack of occupation or excitement.
"he succumbed to ennui and despair"
synonyms: boredom, tedium, listlessness, lethargy, lassitude, languor, restlessness, weariness, sluggishness, enervation; More

In life, we have warning signs, prompts that urge us to take action or to change course.

Smoke alarms, speed limits, crash prevention systems*; there are countless mechanisms in place to protect us from continuing our current course of action if the outcome is expected to be detrimental.

* The crash prevention system continuously monitors the distance from the vehicle ahead, warning the driver when there is a danger of a crash and optimising the braking power according to the remaining distance.

Ennui is the warning sign for YOU DESERVE IT.

Ennui is the fancy word for boredom. Boredom is one of the most frustrating and difficult situations I used to find myself in on a near daily basis.

We all suffer boredom / ennui from time to time; it's a natural part of life. You might think boredom is a period of "nothing", a void where nothing is going on. The reality is that boredom is not nothing and there is no void. Boredom is not restful or empty; it's frustratingly full of... frustration!

Boredom comes about as a result of incongruence between what you're doing and what you want to do or think you should be doing.

You want to be on that flight, but you're stuck, delayed in departures. You want to be on holiday but can't afford it. You want to be an author and a speaker but don't think you have the skills and courage to pursue it...

Whilst researching this chapter, it was telling to see that mentions of the word (in the literature Google tracks) have increased dramatically since 1900. The more technology we have, the more "connected" we've become, the more we mention the word boredom in our literature. Coincidence?

youdeservethisbook.com

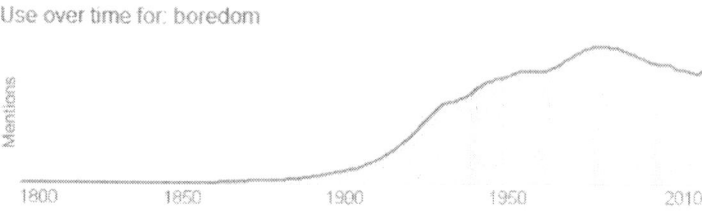

Boredom is more common in the young. There is a need in children and teenagers for instant gratification, everything now and not later. My children have certainly schooled me in the art of impatience!

> *Adolescence is driven by dissatisfaction, the young person no longer content to be defined and treated as a child anymore, wanting to become older but not sure how, more boredom part of the price they pay for the uncertain developmental journey they now undertake – having more times of not knowing what to do with themselves.*
>
> *The adolescent dilemma is this. More than ever before the young person wants freedom to be independent, but what he or she discovers is that freedom is one birthplace of boredom. Now that you have more choice, what are you going to do with it? In many cases, the adolescent simply doesn't know. The past is much clearer ("How I don't want to be any more") than the future ("How I want to be instead"). So rather than feel excited, the teenager feels at a loss to know how to fill the void of opportunity that has been created.*
>
> Source:https://www.psychologytoday.com/blog/surviving-your-childs-adolescence/201208/aspects-adolescent-boredom

Boredom drives impatience.

The urge just to get to the point now, get it done now and destroy any obstacles in your way. Impatience can be destructive, but if you harness it, impatience is rocket fuel.

We know we can never be fully in control of everything in the world around us; there will always be some impatience and boredom in your life. There will always be points where what you're doing and what you want to do or think you should do just won't tally.

This is normal. This is life.

The problem for me wasn't just "some" boredom. EVERYTHING was boring.

I'd struggle to explain to my wife that I found my life dull and boring; but that she wasn't dull or boring...

She wasn't part of it. I love my wife and children dearly, they are my world. The issue I had was that I felt unchallenged and bored in my career; the place where I spent most of my waking life, and this boredom was seeping into everything. Slowly but surely it was sapping the joy from everything else in my life.

This was ennui.

This was my warning. My crash prevention system.

Like all great warnings, such as car alarms and smoke detectors, I ignored it, suspecting malfunction. I disregarded the warning and reset the smoke alarm / car alarm / ennui and continued on for years.

For *years*!

Imagine leaving a house alarm going off for years. Surely they can't ALL be false alarms? Looking back now, I have no idea how I didn't see the signs. Perhaps I didn't want to see them? Through YOU DESERVE IT I learnt that any warning is worthless without action.

Yet again it was clear that to deserve it I needed to be responseable. The feeling of ennui was a trigger to act. A trigger to take action.

Feeling bored, especially proclaiming this boredom to others, can be a sign of a lack of responsibility for your circumstances. (Another alarm bell.) You are proclaiming you are bored in the hope of outside help to alleviate it, or at least some pity to make you feel better.

This is certainly where I found myself. Proclaiming boredom to my wife, my brother, close friends and family at regular intervals, expecting / hoping someone to intervene and help.

Sadly, the life rafts weren't on their way – it was all up to me.

Like the boy who cried wolf, they eventually lost interest in my tales of boredom and I was no less bored as a result, just more frustrated.

I needed to take responsibility – just why was I bored? My head was full of thoughts such as "nothing exciting ever happens" and "it's all just the same old routine".

These statements swirled around my head for years; all of them indicated that I simply wasn't challenging myself, I was abdicating responsibility, expecting others to help resolve my quandary.

youdeservethisbook.com

I had reached the limits of my current lifestyle and was literally "spinning my wheels" as I had run out of things that challenged and inspired me. This made sense.

Although I didn't want to make a "career" out of cars, it had provided challenges and opportunities to grow which had kept me occupied (distracted) for years. Now, in my tenth year at the company, there was little more I could achieve in my limited working arena and the ennui was flooding in, the alarm bells were ringing. I was there through lack of planning (the settled, Chapter 1) I had let life take me where it took me, with little thought or planning for the longer term. I didn't decide to stay in my job for so long; I let the favourable circumstances decide for me. The fact that my hard work had provided a comfortable living happened without any forethought, though I am deserving of it and grateful for it nonetheless.

When circumstances stopped "deciding for me", when there was nothing else to "fall into" or "stumble upon" I was left where I started. No true idea of my destination but plenty of time and fuel to get there still. It's as though working in the motor trade was a pleasant detour on my journey, but now the detour was over the focus came back to my lack of destination.

Through the distraction of life and work I'd found material happiness, but no fulfilment. Once the material happiness subsided I was left with ennui and it was an unpleasant and uncomfortable place to be. I didn't know where I wanted to be in life, but I knew where I didn't want to be. Every moment spent not knowing where I wanted to be felt wasted. It was utterly frustrating.

So many of us know what we don't want, but don't know what we do want. But why? I discovered there is a power in vulnerability. Brené Brown covers this in her famous TED talk. For me it was the "vulnerability" of being authentic.

Admitting to myself that I wanted to inspire others in the way I had been inspired through the books I had read and speakers I had heard.

There is no shame in what I wanted to do, but I placed too high an importance on the opinions of others and over-focussed on the "what-ifs?" of failure.

Once again I found myself playing to not lose instead of playing to win. Who cares what other people think? I needed to be happy for me.

In focussing so much on the opinions of others (or at least my perception of their opinions) I was limiting my beliefs and thus limiting my ability to achieve. These beliefs held me back from realising my full potential and everything I felt I deserved. These beliefs were also based on nothing more than opinion, assumption and guesswork; fear by any other name.

If you find yourself at a point of ennui, if there's so much you want to do but feel you "can't", then it's time to question that "can't".

Unless what you want to do will harm others (highly unlikely) then the reasons to do it should always outweigh the reasons to not do it simply based on the pursuit of your own happiness.

Happiness should always be the destination (It's also the journey). We fall short from focussing too much on the "why not" rather than the why. Remember, when you change the way you look at things, the things you look at change.

When I re-immersed myself in the books and talks I had previously been motivated by, when I spoke with friends I had helped to inspire, when I began to experience the warm feelings of positivity that all of this brought me – I focussed on it.

These warm feelings of positivity were what I wanted for others, not just myself. I wanted to inspire others and to help them achieve all they can.

In limiting myself I wasn't serving myself and I certainly wasn't serving others by holding back my passion. I was in a similar position to my colleagues, in possession of Gewüsst Wie but not utilising it fully.

With no serve there is no deserve.

I deserved to have everything in my life right now, but no more. To deserve more, I had to serve more (which included serving myself).

Reconnecting with these feelings, reminding myself why I wanted to become a coach, speaker and author helped motivate me to action. By simply shifting focus from why I "couldn't" and "shouldn't" follow my heart to why I should made all the difference.

Taking action was the answer (and so frequently is).

Taking action to actually set out to deserve what I thought I could deserve started the momentum that caused me to find fulfilment in my life. I just needed a reminder of why I wanted to be a speaker.

Ennui is the result of not taking action, of not reaching your full potential. Ennui is for all those who wonder "what if", for all those who feel they deserve more but do nothing about it through fear.

"Our deepest fear is not that we are inadequate. Our deepest fear is that we are powerful beyond measure. It is our light, not our darkness that most frightens us."
Marianne Williamson

There are a number of reasons you may not respond to your feelings of ennui.

You simply may not know what to do, where to start or even what you want. You feel you are capable and deserve more, but are unsure what that could be.

I suffered with these frustrations, not knowing what to do, not taking action and feeling trapped in ennui for the foreseeable future.

I felt anxious about this for years. I focussed so much on "not knowing what I want to do when I grow up" that my ennui perpetuated because I was focussing on why I couldn't change or that I simply didn't know what to do.

Fear was my prison, ennui was my sentence.

My Reticular Activating System was focussing on more of the same and as such focussed on the problem, rather than seeking solutions.

I know now that one of the most effective ways to deal with ennui is to do nothing. It was those times through mental exhaustion from constantly worrying and feeling trapped, that I "gave up" and allowed my mind to clear and my body to relax. It was then that I began to think most clearly.

No phone, no email, no people, no books, no music.

When the constant chatter of my worrying mind lessened, I was able to actually think (instead of run through the same tired old thought patterns I had on repeat). Instead of running the same thought patterns of "what should I do with my life?" and stressing out about time ebbing away, I let go of everything I could and tried just to "be".

I now understand the power of mindfulness and meditation. "Emptying your mind" or at least focussing on the here and now and being present can free you from the shackles of over-thinking.

> *"Your mind will answer most questions*
> *if you learn to relax and wait for the answer."*
> **William S. Burroughs**

Ennui is the warning sign that you can do more and be more, for me it was also the sign I needed to take some time out and to relax a little. To let go of thoughts and worries as best I could and just be present. I was always afraid of such "letting go" and "letting life happen" for fear of it running away with me. I crave control; it's part of my character, so to give up controlling thinking and to just let myself exist, even for a few minutes, was difficult at first. But remembering I'm not truly in control of everything (it just feels as though I am) has helped me to loosen the grip.

We'll cover later in the book what happened when I gave up email and working evenings and weekends. At first I thought this may adversely affect my performance at work and potentially be an issue. The reality was that I spent more quality time with my family, felt more relaxed and in control as well as enjoying continuing results.

By taking even small steps (although giving up email in the evenings was a huge step for me) I could experiment and see what happened. I could see what worked and what didn't, picking and choosing what I wanted. I thought the world would end if I stopped working far too much – and it didn't.

What could you be doing (or not doing) out of this same fear of letting go?

How could you experiment with it? Could you have a positive outcome as I did, when you feared a negative one?

What could you let go of in order to relax and refocus?

In tackling ennui I also made more time to do things for myself such as reading and soaking in the bath. By spending time on myself and "looking after" myself better, I noticed improved performance at work and more clarity for YOU DESERVE IT. Looking after yourself is serving yourself and respecting yourself. We all deserve our own respect.

It seemed that I got better results the less I forced myself to work or to think about something. By simply letting go, even for a short while, I felt in control again as I had *chosen* to let go. As this happened, the ennui subsided.

My alternative strategy for ennui was focussing on motivation.

We all need some motivation and inspiration to get moving and to build some momentum. In 2013 I had finally started to collate all of the motivational and inspiring things that I had found when dealing with difficult times in my own life. Having sources of inspiration (and plenty of them) collated in one place is an effective way to tackle boredom and lack of "oomph".

Like an emergency kit, the sources of motivation and inspiration I had compiled have helped me on countless occasions – and still do. I keep everything online at my website **everydayshouldbefun.com**. It's a 100% free resource for inspiring things which I update regularly.

My hope is that others will be inspired and motivated in the same way I am, because when you're pursuing your dreams, you need to be fired up and ready. You need to stay focussed on the positives and the possibilities.

Focussing on motivation can also be about focussing on previous victories and accomplishments. Allowing yourself to enjoy the good things you have achieved and to acknowledge that you deserve them. To feel you deserve something positive is a fulfilling experience; it can help lift you from ennui, frustration and boredom. Focussing on previous successes can also remind you that ennui is impermanent. I focussed on never, NEVER missing a sales target in all my time in sales – an amazing feat and one that I am deeply proud of.

I focussed on the achievements of Every Day Should Be Fun, this book, my journey to following my passion and more. Allowing yourself to enjoy your successes feels just great!

However frustrated and listless you may feel (I think my personal record is about two full days and nights in one sitting), you will always come out the other side.

"It's always darkest before dawn."
Proverb

Just as you've had successes and they are now in the past, so too the feelings of not knowing what to do next will pass. Nothing is permanent.

Ennui can be frustrating, overwhelming and deeply unproductive. It is a warning sign that you are capable of more and can deserve more but aren't pushing yourself. Shifting focus from what you're not doing to what you could do or would like to do can help you make the next step to escape ennui.

If you feel you don't know what you want to do or what you could do, then ennui is a reminder to take a "time out". Take some time to just be you, to enjoy a walk in the park or a coffee with a loved one.

Free your mind and the answers will come.

A wise man once told me that you don't need to have all the answers – you are the answer.

youdeservethisbook.com

10 things to remember

1. Ennui (boredom) is a warning sign for change.
2. Boredom drives impatience.
3. Boredom is not taking responsibility.
4. You don't need to have all the answers – you are the answer.
5. Free your mind and the answers will come.
6. Ennui is impermanent.
7. Action cures ennui.
8. Inaction causes ennui.
9. Ennui can result from "settling" rather than "planning".
10. Boredom is a natural part of life, but it serves to warn us that we're not at the limits of what we can achieve.

Exercise – 3 questions

This activity utilises the following questions: "what have you learned from me", "what joy have I given you" and "what trouble have I caused you". These three powerful questions will help you to better understand your relationship with those around you and the impact you have on others. (Often you will be unaware of the impact – both good and bad.)

Example
I asked my mum and my wife these three questions. I was curious as to the trouble I may have caused them (strange how we focus on the negative first) my mum's answers were:

What have you learned from me?
That there is no point wasting time worrying about things, better to address your issues and solve problems calmly.

What joy have I given you?
A loving relationship, that every mother would envy. Watching you grow into a wonderful young man, personable and polite. The joy of my beautiful grandson and the lovely calm home environment you have created for him. Whenever I think of you, or describe you, I always say "my James is fun with a capital F"

What trouble have I caused you?
In your formative years, when you were often angry (understandably). I remember the driving tests in particular! I would add that you have worked extremely hard to turn your life around and overcome these issues.

I then asked my wife:

What have you learned from me?
I have learned from you… planning for the future (I never used to think about it much before. Mainly financially).

youdeservethisbook.com

What joy have I given you?
Joy you've given me... our family and making plans for our future.

What trouble have I caused you?
Learning to live with someone who struggles with depression. Not necessarily a trouble. Maybe that should go under what I've learned...

Guidance
We have an impact on those around us and your perception of that impact may be incorrect. By understanding the facts of how you are seen by those close to you, you can highlight areas of improvement and celebrate what is working.

Ask only those closest to you, from whom you can expect an honest and frank answer.

Tip
Ask only those closest to you who can be trusted to give honest and unbiased answers. Sugar coating won't help anyone in this exercise.

What you'll need
Three people to ask these three questions.

Duration
1 day

When completed, ask yourself:
How do the answers sit with what you thought they would be? Are you overwhelmed by the positive or the negative?

youdeservethisbook.com

13 – Lucky tattoo

Luck is the opposite of deserve.

- Do you feel lucky?
- Are you "cursed"?
- Is luck dependent on effort?

In this chapter, we'll look at how luck is a matter of perception and consider that it may not actually exist. We'll consider a world without luck, discover the confirmation bias and learn how I use luck to my advantage even though I don't believe in it.

I have lucky tattooed on my back. Not literally the word "lucky" but the Thai word for lucky.

I had the tattoo inked in 2008 on Phi Phi Island, Thailand, using the traditional bamboo method as my way of drawing a line under the events of the tsunami on Boxing Day 2004 and to remember how lucky I was to survive.

Remember, however, that luck is a man-made concept.

I feel lucky to have survived the tsunami, I lost no limbs, suffered no long term physical damage, lost no loved ones and was of course alive myself.

Having seen the destruction, the bodies and the number of people who were killed or seriously injured, I considered myself extremely lucky indeed.

youdeservethisbook.com

But am I lucky to have survived or unlucky to have been there in the first place?

A very good question. The reality is both. I am lucky to have survived, but unlucky to have been involved at all. Luck is subjective. Luck is open to interpretation. More importantly, luck has nothing to do with me at all.

I did nothing to cause the tsunami, it could have happened at any time and was due to an underwater earthquake; nothing to do with me!

My survival was nothing to do with me either. The bungalow collapsed and I popped up seconds before drowning. Pure luck.

This is "circumstantial luck", when events "haphazardly occur". I was held underwater for circa two minutes in my bungalow but didn't drown. I now know that this was due to me remaining in a relaxed, sleep-like state (I was asleep as events initially unfolded) again, nothing to do with my actions. As the bungalow collapsed and I gasped for air, clinging to a tree, I was responsible for holding onto the tree, but not for the fact that I wasn't struck by any of the passing debris or that the tree didn't give way and uproot. When I then ran to higher ground, narrowly escaping the next waves, I was in more control and no longer at the complete mercy of outside circumstances. That said, what if I had tripped on some debris or not made it to safety in time? Would that have been luck?

For me, luck is positive thinking, it's focussing on the good things in life, especially the good things we can't explain and call luck. I actively seek out fortunate circumstances that I can influence and attribute them as good luck. I no longer believe in luck, only chance, but the *idea* of luck helps me more than it hinders me.

By believing myself to be "lucky" I am more bold and confident in my actions – actively seeking the good in the world and focussing on it. By focussing on good luck, I am naturally aware of more of the "fortunate" things which happen and am happier as a result. This is textbook playing to win, instead of playing to not lose (Chapter 5).

I use my Reticular Activating System to focus on lucky things – *not unlucky things.*

It's a form of "act as if"; I act as if I am lucky, seek out "lucky" things and feel "lucky" as a result.

It would take no more or less effort to focus on bad luck. If I focussed on the negative in life and deemed myself "unlucky" then surely I would be miserable as a result. If I tuned in to all the bad things that happen, I not only miss the good things, but also damage my self-esteem and self-confidence as "nothing lucky ever happens to me".

Given the choice, I choose lucky every time. Life is always about choices, it's decisions, not conditions that shape our lives.

Although being a "lucky" person by choice allows me to notice more positive things and to be more positive, "lucky" is inherently unfulfilling. It's not a strategy for life, it's a mindset.

Luck is nothing to do with your actions.

Luck is not repeatable.

Luck is not really anything at all; it's just an idea, a way to make sense of random events.

> *"Hope is not a strategy; luck is not a factor,*
> *fear is not an option"*
> **James Cameron**

As "luck" has little to do with your input, it can never be as enjoyable or fulfilling as something that is. Those who win the lottery or those who survive natural disasters can sometimes be left wondering "why me?"

And they'd be right.

Survivors' guilt is the most pertinent example of this. In an event where people die randomly and others do not (such as the tsunami) some feel guilty that they lived and that it was pure chance – nothing to do with their actions.

Why should I have survived when others died?

I personally (and thankfully) didn't suffer with survivor's guilt following the tsunami simply because I am more open to the fact that the world is a collection of events which can seem to happen randomly and indiscriminately.

I'm comfortable with the notion that I survived purely by chance and that I was "fortunate". I don't feel as though I deserved to survive or that I deserved to die that day – it all just kind of happened. I'm thankful to have survived and consider myself lucky to still be here to be able to share my experiences and my story.

My liberal acceptance of luck and chance is, I am aware, quite uncommon. So often we try to find or to affix a meaning to circumstances. Surely all those red traffic lights are just for you or that winning lottery ticket is because you've had such a tough time of late and "deserve" a break, not just because you randomly matched the numbers.

This is known as confirmation bias:

> *Confirmation bias, also called my side bias, is the tendency to search for, interpret, or recall information in a way that confirms one's beliefs or hypotheses.*

Life is not the Truman Show. Sadly it's not all about you or me, life just happens. Things collide together and we find them lucky or unlucky based on our perception.

Luck doesn't exist; it's a man-made concept, a perception. Even so, I choose lucky every time.

> *"Perception is nine tenths."*
> **Michael Newell**

We feel we deserve the "good luck", the "lucky escapes", and the "bank error in your favour" without question. We enjoy these lucky events either believing we deserve them or believing we're entitled to them. This is my strategy. I focus on and enjoy as many of the "lucky" things I can find in my life, deliberately maximising and enhancing how lucky they are as it makes me feel great.

Don't get me wrong, I don't use luck to rely on as a strategy. I use it to make sense of the world when something positive happens for seemingly no reason. Unlucky events are unwanted and unpleasant. No one wants to accept responsibility for unlucky events as it's "just luck" and "it could have happened to anyone".

For "unlucky" events I ask myself if I could have influenced the situation (you can only deserve what you can influence) and then what I've done to deserve it as a means of avoiding repeating the situation.

You win some, you learn some.

Strange how our logic around luck is so off balance. We are quick to disown bad luck and quick to claim the good luck. The reality is there is no luck, there's what we feel we deserve and what we feel we don't deserve.

But what if there was no luck?

What if things happened and we assigned no concept of luck to them?

Personally, I would be worse off as luck is a great motivation for me. Constantly seeking the good "luck" helps me filter the negativity and focus on being positive and upbeat. Seeing "good luck" is my Reticular Activating System looking for the good in the world – however small.

What about "unlucky" people? Those who believe they are doomed, avoiding ladders and black cats? If they had no bad luck, nothing to link situations together, would they be so aware of their "unluckiness"? And perhaps would it dissipate?

Without any luck, would we all take more responsibility (responseable-ity) for creating our circumstances and futures? Would we accept random positive and negative events as just that: random? Just as every person is unique, so too are the situations when people "collide".

Without "luck" as a factor, would we seek to influence and control more in our lives? Would we put more in, and in due course receive more back?

Luck is an excuse not to act. An excuse not to be responsible for everything you can be.

Luck is an alibi; it's an impediment to success as well as a catalyst.

Lucky or unlucky, luck is what you make of it.

If you want to succeed in deserving what you want then you need to disregard luck altogether. Luck is the opposite of deserve.

To deserve, you need to plan, take action and add value – it's an incremental learning curve. Luck shortcuts the system and although having what you want is appealing, if you feel or know you don't deserve it, then it's a hollow victory.

This is why some lottery winners claim to have been happier before their wins.

Far better to achieve what you can and to be proud of it, than to defer taking action, relying on luck, achieving very little in the meantime while you're waiting for that "lucky break".

I used to take a half-hearted approach to business and life as I "knew" I would win the National Lottery (in the UK) at some point. I was, after all, a "lucky" person; I even had "lucky" tattooed on my back. Through writing this book and examining my life in detail, I now see that the lottery was an excuse for me. Escapism. A vehicle for hope.

I didn't have to try as hard or worry about failing because "one day" I'd win enough money that everything would be just fine. Money solves all problems after all… doesn't it?

It was just a matter of time. One day my numbers would come up, one day…

> 6 numbers are drawn at random from the set of integers between 1 and 49, which means there are 49! / (6!*(49-6)!) combinations of numbers (the draw order doesn't matter). The means that the jackpot chance is 1 in 13,983,816 or approximately 1 in 14 million.
> Source: http://lottery.merseyworld.com/Info/Chances.html

As soon as I realised the harsh reality I stopped playing immediately. I was "relying" on luck as a strategy. I was being lazy and irresponsible, not focussing my efforts on achieving what I could.

I was sabotaging myself through limiting my efforts.

The result? I played the National Lottery every week (give or take) since circa 1994 (I began playing before I was even old enough to play, which was 16). As it's now 2015 my expenditure on lottery tickets must be way into the thousands (I liked playing instant scratch cards too) but I had nothing much to show for it except a ton of wasted time looking at flashy cars and houses I would buy "when" I won.

The hopeful feeling of checking my numbers was always outweighed by the disappointment of not winning. "Maybe next time," I'd tell myself.

"Maybe next time…"

Of all the realisations, this was the most difficult (it took three failed attempts to quit playing until I finally managed it) and it was the most embarrassing thing to admit. I'm embarrassed to think I "relied" on the lottery to provide hope and considered it my best chance of financial success. I have so much to offer, so much ability, why could I not see it? Why did I think I had more chance of winning the lottery than of achieving my goals?

This led me to realise that those who believe in luck as a strategy often don't believe in themselves. If you don't believe in yourself then you're not serving yourself. If you believe in luck and rely on it to "fix" or advance your life (as I did) then you are pinning your hopes on random, unconnected events and pure chance. You are side-stepping responsibility.

You have more faith that you will guess six lottery numbers correctly, with odds in the tens of millions to one – than in your own ability to realise your dreams.

How terribly sad.

And yet, that was me.

I was using luck, and in particular the lottery, as a crutch. I was low on self-esteem and self-confidence, so the prospect of overnight millions naturally appealed as the easiest solution. It was escapism territory. It alleviated my ennui and my lack of progress. And it was only £1 per ticket.

Overnight millions? It had been a long "overnight" though. Approximately 6205 days and nothing yet...

This explained yet more about how I'd made so little progress on my dreams. I was attempting to rely on luck as a strategy to move forward rather than taking control myself.

Although luck is all around us, fortunate events are random. If they're not random, then by definition, they are deserved.

Luck can't be planned for or relied upon and no one is responsible for it.

If you're not responsible for it, you can't influence it and thus you are deluding yourself to think otherwise.

I was so unsure of what to do in life, had so little faith in myself, that the easy lure of luck was too tempting and I spent 17 years hoping and procrastinating on something that was less likely than me simply making a success of myself.

I had more chance of getting hit by lightning – 960,000 to 1.[1]

---

[1] Source: https://en.wikipedia.org/wiki/Lightning_strike

Had I spent the time, energy and money on my dreams instead of the lottery, I have no doubt that without it, I would be more successful than I am at this point.

But I deserved to be where I was, based on my action and inaction. By choosing to rely on luck as a strategy, I was choosing to not rely on myself. It hindered my progress and I deserved the hindrance.

As well as being more successful, I would also feel more deserving of my success and entitled to it.

One of the "final straws" in my lottery playing obsession was the realisation that if I did actually win, if I did actually become a multi-millionaire overnight as I wanted so much, it could potentially warp and destroy everything I had ever known. All the things I had worked so hard for could be rubbished as "meagre" and replaced with newer, shinier stuff.

My efforts would be overshadowed by the enormity of newfound wealth. I may even feel as though I had "failed" previously in life as I couldn't acquire the money myself and was only rich due to this "hand out".

Just what did I want with all that money anyway? Security was the best answer I could conjure.

If financial security was my goal, how could I focus so much on the most unreliable way to obtain it?

The answer? A combination of laziness, fear, low self-esteem and hope.

Financial security is a steady, incremental, solid base which is built over time, perhaps by saving a few pounds each week instead of playing the lottery... It's a plan of saving more, spending less, earning more, investing. It's about changing your mindset first, then your finances.

Once I let go of "relying" on luck, I knew I had to focus 100% on my own goals and success. The only way I'd achieve financial security or the flashy cars would be through my own endeavours. I removed luck as a strategy. I removed the false hope. I removed the blockers. With no plan B I'd have to focus on plan A.

It was a daunting prospect at first, but now I'm further down the line I'm happy to be 100% in control of my destiny and making my own luck. I'm also happy to save my lottery expenditure to use for something more constructive.

You don't deserve to be lucky, it just happens. All you can deserve are the things you work towards and focus on. Luck is not to be relied upon or even acknowledged; its pursuit can rob you of time, money and energy which you could be spending better elsewhere.

The moral of the story?

Don't believe in luck. Believe in yourself.

youdeservethisbook.com

10 things to remember

1. Luck doesn't actually exist, it's a man-made concept.
2. Luck is the opposite of deserve.
3. "Hope is not a strategy, luck is not a factor, fear is not an option" – James Cameron.
4. Luck is an excuse to not act.
5. Believe in yourself, not luck.
6. Remove luck, focus on action.
7. No one deserves luck.
8. Luck is rare.
9. Using luck as a strategy wastes time and energy.
10. Luck is subjective; it's what you make of it.

youdeservethisbook.com

Exercise – Push your luck

Try as many things as possible, enter competitions, play the lottery, gamble on the horses, predict coin tosses – do anything which will result in you being either "lucky" or "unlucky". Secondly, consider how many lucky things you've entered into previously (such as playing the lottery since 1994 in my case) and any instances of being lucky or indeed unlucky – jot it all down and tally your lucky versus unlucky scores. We're looking for instances of luck rather than magnitude so if you have won £37M on the lottery that only counts as one instance of good luck.

Example

I am a recovering 16-year lottery veteran so I tossed a coin 100 times, predicting that heads would come up more times than tails. The result was in fact that I had 70 heads and 30 tails. Luck prevailed! Repeating the activity twice more have me 40 heads/60 tails and then 42 heads and 58 tails. I was "lucky" once and then "unlucky" twice in a row.

Try non-monetary luck experiments such as coin tossing – you may not have the joy of winning money but you avoid the pain of losing it.

Guidance

Luck cannot be relied upon and that you are more "unlucky" than you are "lucky". This is because your "lucky" circumstance is more definitive but the number of potential "unlucky" circumstances is often greater. The lottery for example requires you to pick six balls out of 59 – there are 53 balls which are "unlucky" for me and only six which are "lucky". It's the instances of "luck" rather than their magnitude that best demonstrate using luck as a strategy. A strategy implies it is regular, can be repeated or influenced.

Ask yourself:

- Why am I betting on luck and not on myself?
- Am I using luck as an excuse or a way to avoid blame or failure?

youdeservethisbook.com

Tip
Try not to spend too much money, you can predict coin tosses or "pretend play" the lottery to test the theory.

What you'll need
Competitions, prize draws, lotteries, coin toss, anything that tests "luck"

Duration
1 day

When completed, ask yourself:
Are you closer to realising that luck is not something to be relied upon?

It's a random thing which can't be influenced – and certainly not a strategy for life.

youdeservethisbook.com

14 – Let it be

The YOU DESERVE IT blueprint.

- How does your view on the world affect your results?
- Could you deserve more by expecting more and changing your standards?

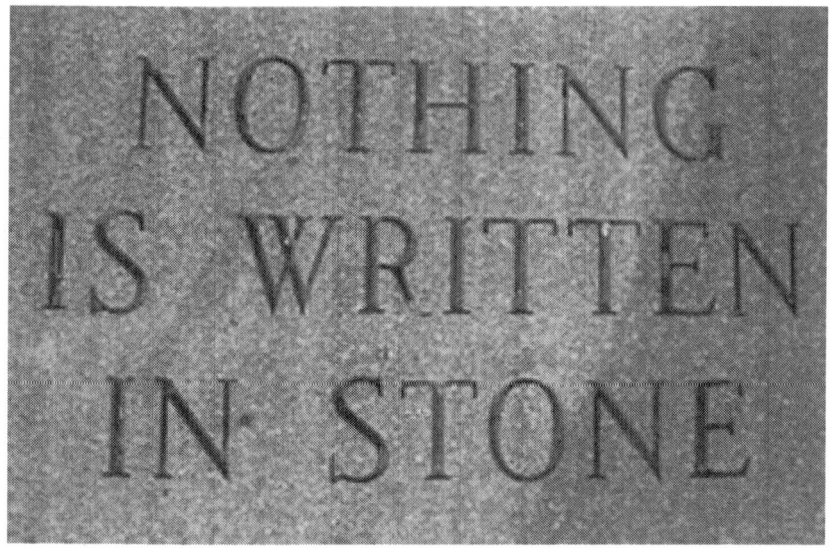

In this chapter we'll look at the various factors which can affect what you think you can and do deserve. I call this collection of factors the YOU DESERVE IT blueprint. We consider how the factors combine to form your view on the world and remind you that you can change and adapt; your blueprint is a dynamic thing, it's not set in stone.

So what are the defining factors which combine to give your perspective on what you feel you deserve?

- Past experiences
- Peers, peer pressure and expectations
- Traditions and norms
- Fear
- Luck
- Self-esteem / self-belief
- Gewüsst Wie

- Ambition
- Desire

What you deserve and what you think you deserve are both determined by your actions and your environment. What you act upon and what you think you deserve are both based entirely upon what you believe you deserve.

What you believe you deserve is your YOU DESERVE IT blueprint.

Just as homeostasis (or Ferrariostasis) kept me within boundaries, so too, your YOU DESERVE IT blueprint determines everything about what you deserve (Deserveostasis).

Change the blueprint and you change the self-imposed limits as to what you can deserve.

If you feel you deserve a lot more than you have, the evidence will be in your drive to succeed and comes from your blueprint. Likewise, your lack of action despite feeling you deserve more than you have, also comes from your blueprint.

It's possible to feel you deserve much more than you have, but to take no action which results in resentment. For many, "feeling" you deserve more should encourage the "more" to manifest, why do you need to work for it?

On the other hand, if you feel you don't deserve much more than you have, then your actions will be limited as you have reached the boundaries of your YOU DESERVE IT blueprint and won't believe that you are capable of any more.

If you feel you deserve a lot more than you have, this is evident in your drive to succeed and determines the actions you take to obtain all you feel you deserve. Your drive to succeed and the compulsion you feel to obtain what you feel you deserve comes from your blueprint. It's the self-imposed expectation of what you are capable of.

Just as when you're full, you stop eating, so too when you have what you feel you deserve you stop acting. You have reached your "limit".

All limits are self-imposed.

Your blueprint is linked entirely to your self-worth. A small and limited blueprint evidences low self-worth and a larger blueprint evidences higher self-worth.

While neither is a small blueprint bad nor a large blueprint good, what matters is that they reflect your level of self-worth.

- **Small blueprint** = Low self-worth.
- **Large blueprint** = Higher self-worth.

As you're reading this book we can presume you feel you deserve more than you're getting but aren't setting out to "claim what is yours" as you don't feel you are deserving of it on some level. There is something missing – which is why you're reading a book on how to deserve.

This is my own YOU DESERVE IT blueprint, or at least it was.

I realised I had great desires and a strong drive to deserve so much more, but there was a disconnect. My actions didn't match my drive and as such it limited my performance.

This limitation was self-imposed; a hesitance to pursue more because I didn't feel I was capable of achieving it. Maybe I was confusing desiring with deserving (Chapter 20)?

To finally break through and to align my actions with my goals, I needed to understand why I was hesitating and limiting myself. If this was everything I wanted why would I stop myself achieving it? Why wouldn't I pursue it with everything I had?

We all have a pre-determined value, an amount (not necessarily monetary) that we think we are worth. A set of standards. The disconnect lies in what we think we're worth and what we believe we're worth. You can *think* you're worth £100,000 a year for example, but *believe* you're worth £50,000 and settle for this more "realistic" number.

What we think we deserve is unlimited. It's more about desire than deserve, more about feelings than facts. What we believe we deserve is more grounded, it's based more on facts and reality.

What we believe we're worth (the YOU DESERVE IT blueprint) is dictated by multiple different factors.

youdeservethisbook.com

YOU DESERVE IT Blueprint

What you deserve and what you think you deserve are created and limited by your blueprint. A number of factors make up your blueprint and some of them can be holding you back. Here we consider the factors in a free thinking exercise.

Example

Before I set out to become a speaker, coach and author I felt embarrassed about my dreams. Being a "motivational speaker" sounded gimmicky and flimsy. I didn't even admit to myself I wanted to pursue this dream for 10 years. Those 10 years were lost because I was afraid of what others might think. Looking back it seems silly, but at the time the fear was very real.

I asked myself some questions in an attempt to move forwards:

How have past experiences influenced my thinking?

With no background in speaking, no training and no content to deliver I didn't feel qualified to be a speaker.

Do I feel obliged to act in a certain way – even though I disagree?

I didn't pursue my goal because I had a job and bills and family life – I felt obliged to be a "normal" person and not to pursue my "far-fetched" goal.

Am I afraid to be myself?

I was 100% afraid to be myself and that was purely because I cared what others might think.

I had fragile self-esteem so any negative feedback or mockery would have cut deep.

What am I afraid of? Why am I afraid of it?

I was afraid of the opinions of others but also afraid that I didn't have a clue about where to begin or what to do. It all seemed so far away that I didn't know where to begin and was afraid of the unknown.

youdeservethisbook.com

What can't I pursue more?
I felt like I couldn't pursue more than I had, but why? No-one in my family or circle of friends had done anything like this so I felt like I couldn't.

What facts do I have to prove I can't pursue more?
I can't find any good reason that I couldn't have pursued more, aside from lack of knowledge and experience which I could acquire.

Am I afraid of the opinions of others?
100% yes but writing that down seems like a silly reason to hold back on my dreams...

Am I utilising my passions and skills? If not, which unutilised passions and skills could I bring to the front?
I wasn't living my purpose or fully utilising my gifts in my job – I had so much more to offer as a speaker from my unique ideas to my passion for helping others.

Why have I settled on this goal? Why not more? Why not less?
Becoming a coach, speaker and author feels like the right fit for me – I didn't settle on more as I need to make a start somewhere but will grow my goals as my experience grows. I didn't settle on less because there's no reason to settle for less other than fear of failure and what others may say.

Guidance
For each section of the blueprint, consider:

- How have past experiences influenced my thinking?
- Do I feel obliged to act in a certain way – even though I disagree?
- Am I afraid to be myself?

- What am I afraid of? Why am I afraid of it?
- What can't I pursue more?
- What facts do I have to prove I can't pursue more?
- Am I afraid of the opinions of others?
- Am I utilising my passions and skills? If not, which unutilised passions and skills could I bring to the front?
- Why have I settled on this goal? Why not more? Why not less?

Tip
This is a free thinking exercise. There are no right or wrong answers, consider the questions as honestly and fully as you can.

What you'll need
Pen, pad, honesty.

Duration
1 hour

When completed, ask yourself:
What is holding me back? Can I eradicate any of these items? Is there any evidence or is it assumption?

youdeservethisbook.com

Past experiences

Past successes and failures are one of the most important elements that lay the foundations. If success has always "come easy" to you – achievements, recognition and rewards – then your blueprint will reflect this.

When starting new endeavours or considering what you could achieve and deserve, you will use past successes as a basis for the future and have a high expectation of what can be achieved.

This makes sense. Why would you expect less?

If you've achieved much before, then you are unlikely to expect less going forward. If you do expect less in the future, then it's a sign you don't feel you deserve what you already have; perhaps you consider you have been lucky (luck is the opposite of deserve) perhaps not, but if you expect less of the future than you've had in the past you are limiting yourself. You're not doing yourself justice.

Through expecting less and thus limiting yourself to achieve less, your actions fall in line with this lower expectation and you actually do achieve less. A self-fulfilling prophecy.

Yes, it's a cruel world.

If success has evaded you or been extremely tough work then you may limit what you believe you deserve as surely you can't just suddenly deserve more than you've had before… can you?

By limiting your thinking and actions you limit what you're capable of and find yourself to be "right" in your thinking about deserving more.

This crystallises the YOU DESERVE IT blueprint. We all seek to be "right" or "correct" or for everything to align and to work together in harmony. This is the confirmation bias at work.

Call it a self-fulfilling prophecy, a blueprint or fate; your achievements reflect your actions which will always reflect your thoughts and emotions.

To deserve what you want, you have to change (or at least align) your thoughts so that your blueprint reflects a destination you are happy with.

If you want to earn six figures a year, you have to believe you are capable of deserving of it in the first place to then set about achieving it. If you don't believe you deserve your goals you will never achieve them, and if you don't believe it, self-sabotage will never be too far away.

Peers, Peer Pressure and Expectations

It's not just your successes and failures that affect your blueprint. If every member of your family has a PhD then you are more inclined to pursue this for yourself and believe you should. As a member of the <insert family name> family, you may feel it's your duty to obtain a PhD and are capable of deserving it to carry on the family tradition. On the other hand, if no member of your family ever graduated from school let alone university, you may feel that nothing much is expected of you academically, after all "the apple never falls too far from the tree".

That may be true – but you're not an apple.

What you can think, believe and achieve are limitless. Only you can limit yourself and this must be rooted in your thinking for you to succeed. Only you can limit yourself.

The opinions of others can be equally uplifting or limiting. Friends and family members may push you to achieve and support you every step of the way, they may also however, warn you of potential hazards and having "ideas above your station".

While it's wise and sociable to discuss your goals and thoughts with others, and it's worth contemplating advice, it should always be your call. Only you can limit yourself.

Advice is often dispensed by those who haven't been able to achieve what they wanted. These people either believe it's not possible to succeed and want to warn you of the "inevitable" failure and save you the heartache, or they don't want you to succeed in something they were unable to succeed in themselves.

Traditions and norms

Society and norms are a form of "stasis" within which we all operate. It was once madness to think you could fly people over an ocean in a metal tube – until it was a reality.

> "You see things; and you say, 'Why?' But I dream things that never were; and I say, 'Why not?'"
> **George Bernard Shaw**

Television, the internet, sliced bread; sometimes you have to challenge the norms and go against society's accepted ways of thinking in order to achieve and deserve more.

It's not wise to go against society and norms just for the sake of it though. Things such as sliced bread, the internet, and the wheel are tried, tested and proven to work. They don't need changing per se, but at the very least they are your starting point for innovation. Times change, things become outdated (Betamax to VHS to DVD) and knowledge / technology advance. Question the status quo if you can improve upon it, just don't accept it as a limit without question. (Remember the five whys.)

Fear

Fear is a defining factor in your own YOU DESERVE IT blueprint. Fear exists to protect us; as a species we need to survive to procreate and ensure lineage, but in today's modern society we can feel the same compelling urge to run from being eaten by a tiger that we get when our credit card bill is larger than expected. This is known as "fight or flight".

Our fears exist to keep us alive, but with so little to threaten our lives (versus early human history) these powerful fear messages from the prehistoric part of our brains warn us of dangers with the same life-threatening importance, often completely out of perspective.

Fear, in small doses, can work for you.

Fear, kept in context, can work for you.

That's the key – don't let fear dictate to you, keep perspective, make it work for you.

I found I was limiting my own YOU DESERVE IT blueprint by "playing not to lose" instead of "playing to win". My fear of losing what I had limited my actions and my potential. Had I feared less and "played to win" I would have taken more and diversified action and perhaps deserved more in the process. I would have certainly put myself in more situations which could have allowed me to succeed, rather than simply protect what I had.

Reward comes from risk, with no risk, there is no reward.

It's about having an abundance mindset.

> *Steven Covey coined the idea of abundance mentality or abundance mindset, a concept in which a person believes there are enough resources and successes to share with*

> others. He contrasts it with the scarcity mindset (i.e. destructive and unnecessary competition), which is founded on the idea that, if someone else wins or is successful in a situation, that means you lose. Individuals with an abundance mentality reject the notion of zero-sum games and are able to celebrate the success of others rather than feel threatened by it.
> https://en.wikipedia.org/wiki/The_7_Habits_of_Highly_Effective_People#Abundance_mentality

The fact was that I could deserve more than I had (you're reading my book after all...) but I let fear limit me and limit my blueprint, "cutting my cloth accordingly" with my actions. Only I could limit myself.

This fear limiting mindset has largely driven my work with YOU DESERVE IT. I was previously consciously unaware that I was limiting myself. I wonder if you are too?

Could you be limiting yourself right now without really even being aware of it? Perhaps you do realise you are limiting yourself but aren't sure what to do about it.

I could deserve more and you can deserve more too, remember that limits are there to be challenged.

Just as fear limited me, the next factor, that of luck, actually *empowered* me.

Luck

We've established that luck is a manmade concept and is never really a factor; it is simply our interpretation of events. Even so, believing I was lucky (and having it tattooed on my back) pushed me to believe I deserved more.

If luck doesn't exist, then belief in luck is a very real thing. Just as I believed I was lucky and deserving of more good fortune, the belief you are unlucky can limit what you expect to deserve as "things like this always happen to me".

Your blueprint can be limited or enhanced through luck, it's your choice.

Good luck is not a strategy; believing you are lucky, in my opinion, is also not a strategy, but it does cultivate a positive mindset.

I am an advocate of focussing on "good luck" and minimising the focus on "bad luck". You always get more of what you focus upon, so it makes sense to focus on the positive. It feels better too.

The factor underlying it all is your self-esteem. How you value yourself (evident in how you treat and take care of yourself, how you serve yourself) dictates much of what you believe you can do and what you are deserving of.

Healthy self-esteem empowers you to explore your limits, enjoy life and express yourself effectively. Poor self-esteem limits you to not expect too much from life and in turn not get too much or have as rich an experience as you could.

Knowing that you matter, that you have a right to be here as much as any person, and ensuring you treat yourself well and respect yourself – these are the building blocks of self-esteem.

To serve others, you must first serve yourself.

My own self-esteem has been terrible for years; depression destroys self-esteem. Despite triumphing over major life setbacks and then going on to enjoy successes and a happy life, I would often dismiss good events believing I didn't deserve them when I did. At my lowest ebb, my low self-esteem led me to not take basic care of myself, to not eat and to have suicidal thoughts; at points I didn't even feel worthy of living.

Self-esteem / self-belief

When I began to examine my own beliefs about what I deserved, I realised self-esteem was a major issue.

Whilst I felt I deserved so much more than I had and was trying to pursue it, I felt like I wasn't quite making progress, there was always something holding me back. These "somethings" were my belief that I didn't deserve more. I've spent years trying and working hard, always feeling held back in some way, and now I see it.

If you don't believe in something, it has no real worth to you.

If you don't believe in something, you don't act upon it, you doubt it and hesitate.

If you don't believe in something you can think what you want, but the thoughts will remain thoughts.

Belief drives action, belief exudes passion.

Belief is a secret ingredient to YOU DESERVE IT. But what is a belief? Why do we believe some things and not others?

belief
/bɪˈliːf/

noun

1. an acceptance that something exists or is true, especially one without proof.
   "his belief in extraterrestrial life"
2. trust, faith, or confidence in (someone or something).
   "a belief in democratic politics"

A belief is not actually based upon fact – and I think this is where we go wrong (or at least where I went wrong).

You need to believe it before you see it.

I look for proof to believe something, where instead I should actually believe something and then the proof will appear (also known as faith).

faith
/feɪθ/

noun

1. complete trust or confidence in someone or something.

If a belief is not based upon fact, then past successes and events should have no bearing upon what you believe. A belief is an assumed truth, it's a conclusion we draw and is unique to our perception and our circumstances.

We use beliefs to anchor our understanding of the world around us and once they are formed we tend to stick with them through familiarity and the need to be in control. The way to challenge your beliefs is to simply reframe them. To look at them from all angles and to ask questions and seek information.

youdeservethisbook.com

If beliefs are not based upon fact, they are malleable and can be reformed. In the same way I focus on and pursue "good luck" I also focus on and pursue good beliefs, disregarding the negative beliefs as they do not serve me.

Gewüsst Wie

If you have developed a certain level of Gewüsst Wie – perhaps you are a qualified driving instructor, plumber or optician – then you have a definite set of skills and value which you can bring to the table.

With the accumulation of Gewüsst Wie comes an expectation of return. If you have spent years studying medicine to become a doctor, you expect to work as a doctor and be rewarded accordingly, you don't expect this Gewüsst Wie to be discarded and to end up in a non-skilled role.

My own Gewüsst Wie; that of selling thousands of vehicles each year, raised my personal standards about what I could and couldn't achieve.

Where some colleagues struggled to sell one car I could do deals for 20–50 or more and didn't feel like it was too much effort. I felt this way as I had accumulated the Gewüsst Wie to make it possible. My belief about what I could achieve was greater as my skillset and experience could deliver greater value.

The confidence provided by Gewüsst Wie enlarged my blueprint when it came to what performance I deserved to achieve at work.

Ambition

My ambition to become financially successful, to be independent, to provide for my family, to right the wrongs of my early life have been a huge driver when it comes to my own YOU DESERVE IT blueprint.

My ambition to succeed was based on nothing more than a deep desire and the first hand experiences of the life I didn't want. Ambition is a form of desire, but it's a desire that drives you to act, rather than a desire that keeps you trapped in perpetual hope.

ambition
/amˈbɪʃ(ə)n/

noun

a strong desire to do or achieve something.
desire and determination to achieve success.

Desire

If ambition is desire + determination, desire alone is the starting point.

What you desire is not restricted by what you believe you can or can't deserve, it's based purely on what you want.

Desire alone is ineffective and will leave you static and frustrated, but desire combined with planning and appropriate action is where YOU DESERVE IT begins to take shape. "I want" doesn't get, but it's a great place to begin.

Your own YOU DESERVE IT blueprint may be affected by all of the factors mentioned here, or just one or two. Some factors may be more dominant and others less so.

Being aware of your preconceived ideas about what you believe you deserve is an important part of the YOU DESERVE IT process.

Awareness is the first step towards change.

If you feel you deserve more than you have but never seem to quite get there and feel held back (as I did), spend some time considering your blueprint and the factors which combine to form your beliefs about what you deserve.

Whether you feel you deserve a lot more than you have, or that you don't deserve what you already have, the YOU DESERVE IT blueprint will give you some insight to be response-able and to change what you need to.

Aligning what you believe you deserve (through examining and questioning your current blueprint) with what you think you deserve, is a pivotal activity that until this book you have probably never considered doing.

I urge you to consider and explore your blueprint today so you can begin the process of getting what you want.

youdeservethisbook.com

10 things to remember

1. You have a pre-determined idea of what you deserve.
2. Many factors combine to create this idea.
3. You are in control of all factors.
4. All limitations are self-imposed.
5. Your blueprint reflects your self-worth.
6. Thinking you deserve it and actually deserving it are very different.
7. Your blueprint is a form of self-fulfilling prophecy.
8. In a work context, Gewüsst Wie determines what you deserve.
9. Reframing your beliefs is the first step to challenging them.
10. Your blueprint controls what you think you deserve and what you think you deserve controls your actions.

Exercise – 1001 Tolerations

For one day, and no longer so you don't become overwhelmed, focus on the things in life which you are tolerating. From leaky taps to squeaky doors to friends who never return calls, manipulative people, untidy rooms, not earning enough and everything else – list the things in your life which you don't like or want, but which are allowed to continue.

Example
I was astounded by how many things I tolerate in my life. From the small – rooms which need decorating, to poor food in restaurants, people being late, letting me down, clothes I should have binned years ago, to the larger issues of toxic people, heavy workload and poor eating habits – there is much about my life which I don't feel I like, yet which I tolerate.

It's the accumulation of the millions of smaller details that really adds up and clarifies just how much you may be tolerating.

Guidance
There is much in life which we don't want or actively pursue. Much which we simply put up with and tolerate, even though we don't want it. Once you identify the things you are "tolerating" – and you may be surprised by just how much and what you are tolerating – that you can take control and seek to eradicate it from your life.

Ask yourself:

- What am I tolerating in my life which I am not 100% happy with?

Tip
Spend a VERY short amount of time on this to begin with – too much time spent focussing on the negative makes you negative.

What you'll need
Notebook and pen.

youdeservethisbook.com

Duration
1 day

When completed, ask yourself:
Firstly are you surprised by just how much you tolerate? Now that you have a list of everything that you are tolerating, what can you do to put things straight and to "undeserve" what you don't want?

15 – Circles of Truth

Action Changes Things.

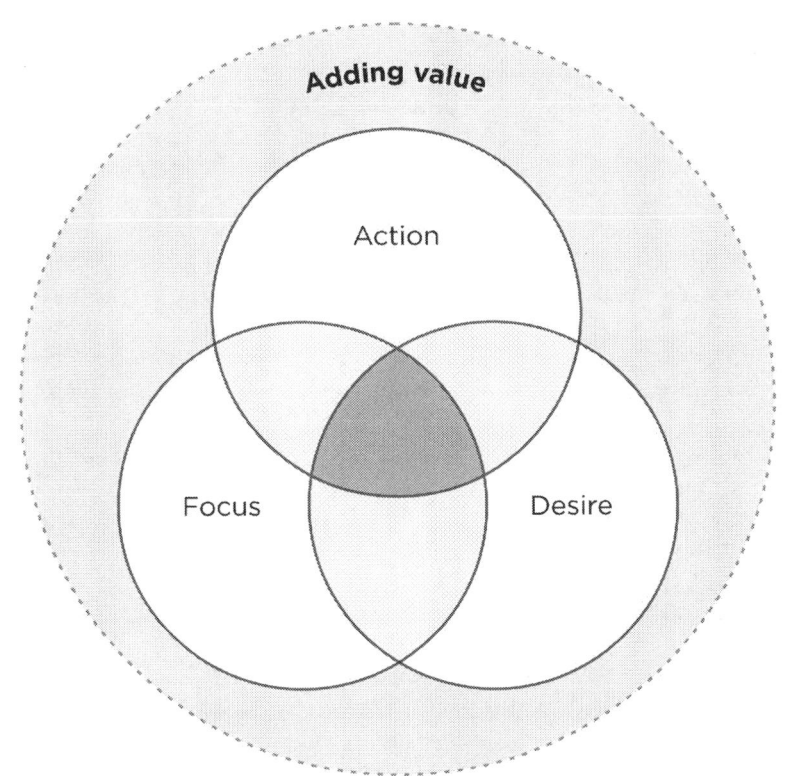

- Do you think YOU DESERVE IT?
- Do you just want it?
- Or do your actions deserve it?

In this chapter, we'll learn how what you want, what you focus on and what you act upon interact with each other to form what you deserve. We'll learn about being realistic, taking appropriate action and how adding value is the secret ingredient when it comes to deserving more.

I call this concept the circles of truth, because the truth is, you will always get what you deserve, not what you think you deserve.

(With the caveat here being anything you can influence, so terminal illness, accidents etc. are off the menu – see disclaimer.)

Anything which your actions have influenced is deserved, not forgetting that inaction is a form of action, so you can deserve things by doing "nothing" as well – these are hidden choices (Think obesity, debt, poor relationships).

Whatever you think, feel, wish, hope, plan or pray for, it all falls away.

Your actions are the defining factor. There is no negotiation. There is no escaping the truth. You can't change the truth, but the truth can change you.

As much as we can explore how you can deserve things, why you may or may not have all you think you deserve and so on, if these ideas are left as words on the page in this book then you don't deserve any of it to work for you.

The reality is if you don't act you don't get.

The circles of truth are my way to visually codify the concept of YOU DESERVE IT and give you a tool to act with (instead of just words on a page). You can use the circles to explore your own life of deservedness and act upon the results. You can use the circles to understand more about the interaction between wanting something, focussing on it, and acting upon it.

If you have anything in your life which you have and don't feel you deserve, or anything you feel you deserve and don't have, it provides the framework to question the situation.

Crucially it removes emotion and bias to reveal the truth. Hence "Circles of Truth".

So how do the elements of Desire, Focus and Action interact?

To begin with, you have to understand that your feelings are a result of your thoughts. Your feelings are not a result of the world around you and your circumstances, but rather your response to that world.

An example: You are late for a meeting.

Person 1. If being late was commonplace for you and not something you were ever troubled over, then another late arrival makes you feel no different. You think you will be late, which is no problem as it's the "norm" for you, so you feel nothing and do nothing as a result.

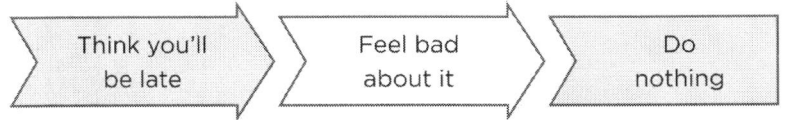

Person 2. If, however, like me, being late is a cardinal sin, then you may think that being late is terrible, you will feel guilt or embarrassment and may run to your destination and apologise profusely to those who were waiting for you.

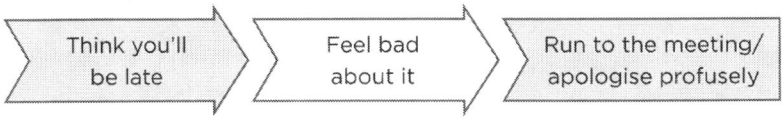

The same situation can cause you to feel differently purely by how you think about it and have habitually thought about it. What you think is dictated largely by experience.

Person 1 has been late before and suffered no consequences as a result. They deem lateness to not be an issue and thus think it is fine and certainly not something to worry about.

Person 2 has been reprimanded previously for being late so thinks it's a bad thing, feels bad and acts to put it right.

We use the past as our starting point for our future expectation. Although this logically makes sense, it's entirely possible for something different to occur and makes me think of the financial industry disclaimer line: *Past performance is not necessarily indicative of future results.*

Neither scenario is right or wrong, but it highlights how your reaction to situations can make the difference.

Your perception is your reality.

Over time, we all develop habitual patterns of thought through our experiences which allow us to "short cut" our reactions in any given situation such as lateness.

With so much data to process, the brain uses these shortcuts to aid everyday life – it's a form of adaptation. Although habitual, your thoughts can be changed but it is an involved process of considering and challenging your perspective on the world.

To change your thoughts, you first have to question their accuracy. You need to be aware that your perception may be limited or adrift from reality, however "sure" you may feel about them. This is an uncommon practice given the levels of self-awareness and courage required to challenge your own thinking. Being able to challenge yourself with the possibility of finding your thinking is "wrong" is one of the most powerful abilities in the world.

In the lateness example, I have personally experimented with being late deliberately to see what happens. I can report that my fears of "insulting" those waiting for me and losing their respect are largely inaccurate. By arriving late and apologising, most understand that lateness is a part of life and nothing to worry too much about.

By experiencing lateness and having no real negative repercussions, I'm able to change how I think about it and thus how I feel about it. I still dislike being late, but I feel it's far less important that it once was and as a result don't run or over-apologise.

My actions changed, because my feelings changed, because my thoughts changed. My thoughts changed because I actively experimented with the situation and have a new reference point for the future.

If you want to challenge your own thinking then you first need to experiment with how you react. Face your fears and see what happens

When it comes to YOU DESERVE IT, there are three factors which affect it:

- What you want.
- What you focus on.
- What you act upon.

The circles of truth help to illustrate how these three factors interact, but the bottom line is:

No action = No deserve

Let's start with what you want. This is where it all begins. We've all heard "I want doesn't get"; that may be true, but it's a great place to start.

We all have a YOU DESERVE IT blueprint; a collection of boundaries and preconceived notions about what we believe we deserve. The YOU DESERVE IT blueprint is an amalgamation of your experiences, your peers, expectations, good or bad "luck" (even though there is no such thing), traditions, norms and other external factors.

Your response to these external factors creates thoughts, then these thoughts create feelings, which drive actions and they become habitual over time.

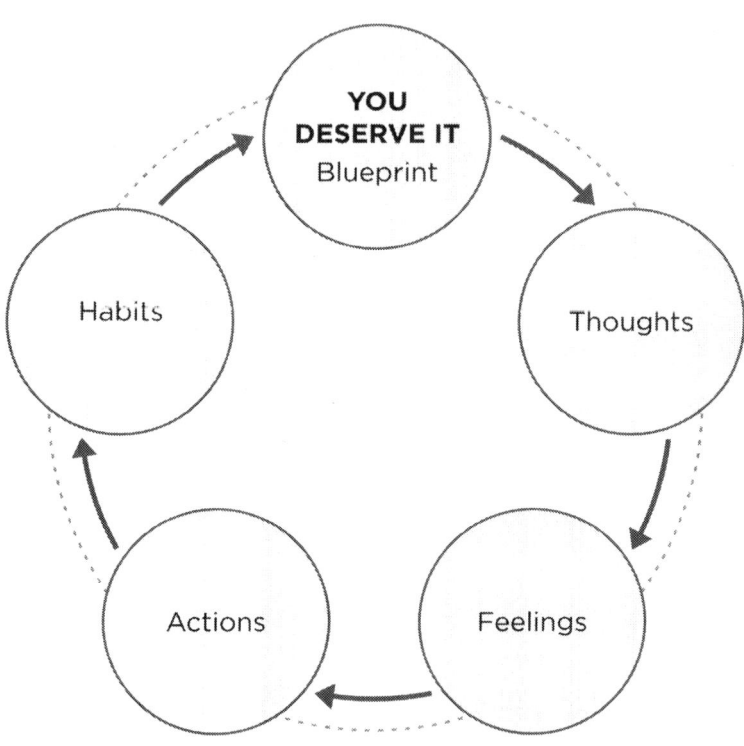

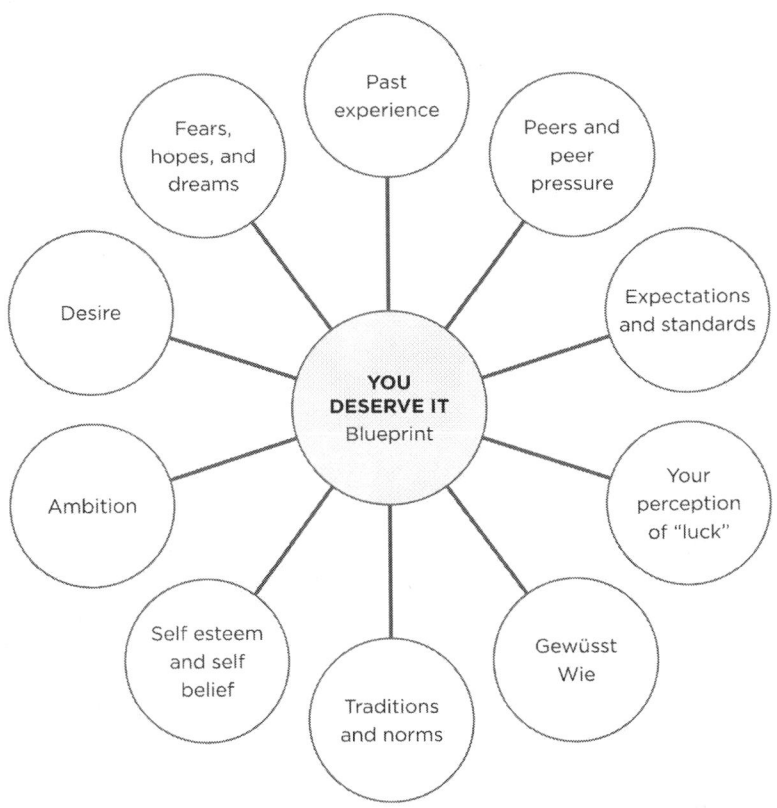

As such, you are left with a set of boundaries and responses to any given situation (such as being late – which I hate). These boundaries and responses may not be healthy for you but they explain why you behave the way you do in any given situation.

Next up after what you want is what you think you deserve. It all starts with what you think you deserve.

Desire alone = No deserve

What you think you want is influenced by the same factors as the YOU DESERVE IT blueprint: your responses to society, norms, experiences and so forth.

The difference with wanting is there are no limits. You can want anything at all and not feel the need to justify it or anchor it; you are emotionally free to want whatever you want, however conservative or ridiculous it may seem to others.

I want my own private island, for example. I want it because I think it would be amazing to live in a tropical place in seclusion to write and enjoy my life away from the pressures of the rest of the world. I don't think I deserve a private island because I don't think I've done anything to deserve it and nothing I am doing currently (unless this book does really well...) will result in me buying said private island. Whilst I don't think I deserve it, I am free to want it and to fantasise about what it would be like to live there and what I might call it and so forth.

What you act upon reflects both what you want and what you think you deserve. For some people, millionaire status isn't enough; they need billionaire status whereas others are happy earning £25k a year. What you want is unlimited, what you think you deserve is limited by your YOU DESERVE IT blueprint.

What you act upon is the crossroads (or compromise) of what you want and what you think you deserve.

youdeservethisbook.com

What you want + think you deserve = what you act upon.

Going back to my example of the island, I think I could deserve a 5-star holiday (instead of an island – I am limiting myself by being "realistic"). I would want the holiday as it allows me to play out my island fantasy and is more reachable and realistic than the island. As I think I can deserve this and as I want it, I act to save money, make the booking and jet off.

realistic
/rɪəˈlɪstɪk/

adjective

1. having or showing a sensible and practical idea of what can be achieved or expected.
   "I thought we had a realistic chance of winning"
   synonyms: practical, pragmatic, matter-of-fact, down-to-earth, sensible, commonsensical; More

2. representing things in a way that is accurate and true to life.
   "a realistic human drama"
   synonyms: true to life, lifelike, true, truthful, faithful, real-life, close, naturalistic, authentic, genuine, representational, graphic, convincing; More

The interesting part here is that of being "realistic". This is my YOU DESERVE IT blueprint in action. I don't think I could ever deserve a private island – after all, no-one I know has one and I suspect they cost millions to buy and maintain; how could I make millions to finance my dream? The answer is I could make those millions if I believed I could and dedicated myself to that path, but as I can't even imagine it being possible I will take no further steps towards it.

Lack of self-belief limits action.

This is different for someone such as Richard Branson who actually has a private island; he thought he could deserve it and took action to make it so, for him this was "realistic" as it reflected his reality and what he believed he was capable of.

youdeservethisbook.com

Thinking you can deserve something is the first step

I don't believe I could deserve the private island so I don't focus upon it; I also don't act upon it. The net result is that I don't deserve the private island. It's a self-fulfilling prophecy limited primarily by my thoughts.

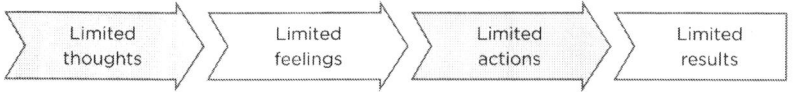

The power of limiting yourself through your blueprint and of being "realistic" is not to be underestimated. The word "realistic" is like the word "normal" – there is no real definition, it's totally subjective.

I limit myself to believe I can't get an island and settle on the island holiday instead, taking action to achieve it. My thoughts have limited my actions.

Action is the key to deserving anything. The important part about action is that it must be *appropriate*.

> ***Appropriate action:*** *Actions that will help advance you towards your goal rather than indiscriminate or vague action which keeps you busy but gets you nowhere.*

By appropriate I mean it must cause or help to cause the outcome you seek. Action for the sake of it, with an unknown or undefined result, may not lead you to what you want. Appropriate action will. I'd spent years taking "action" but none of it was appropriate to my goals (as my goals were undefined) so I was kept "busy" and feeling as though I was working hard when in reality I was wasting my time. This is how you can feel exhausted and though you've worked really hard, but get nowhere.

This is The Procrastination Illusion at work; taking action that won't necessarily advance you toward your goals, but that will keep you busy and feeling productive.

It was pretty tough to finally admit that to myself.

Let's use the circles of truth to determine firstly how you don't deserve something.

This is an important place to begin as it will help clarify in your mind exactly what you should avoid.

Had this book been written and available to me 10 years ago, the circles of truth would have saved me years of trial, error and heartache. I could have identified everything I was doing and where it would lead me – and then correct course.

This is my hope for you and a reason this book exists. We have such a poor understanding of the concept of deserving, and of the importance of appropriate action that I wanted to codify and to explain how it works.

This is the first ever book dedicated to deserving which I am aware of; this says a lot about our understanding on the subject.

I thought for a long time about being an author and a speaker. I thought I could deserve it and realise my dreams, someday. I definitely wanted to be an author and speaker – thoughts of the talks, travels, signings, fans – it all seemed very appealing. I read books, watched seminars, fantasised about my own sell-out talks and appearing on TED, writing books, appearing on television and so much more. I realise now that I took no *appropriate* action and as a result I didn't deserve to make progress. I was taking action – so where was I going wrong?

> **The Procrastination Illusion (Chapter 2):** *The Procrastination Illusion occurs when you think, plan, want, dream and research the things you want but take no appropriate action towards them. You remain theoretical in your approach, or take small inappropriate action which is unlikely to advance you.*

I read countless books and blogs, fantasised about the talks I could give and even what my book cover would look like – I did all the thinking you could possibly do. Despite taking this "action" reading the books, watching talks, fantasising about it all, nothing I did was actually going to get me closer to my goal; nothing was appropriate. I was consuming the content but was at the point in my life where I didn't fully understand that the power of books was putting the ideas into action – that's where the real magic lies. I was trapped in the Procrastination Illusion.

youdeservethisbook.com

Desire alone = You Don't Deserve It

YOU DESERVE IT requires you to want something as this drives your thoughts and actions. If you stop at simply wanting something, either through lack of self-belief, laziness or any other limiting thoughts – then you don't deserve it as you won't pursue it further and you won't take appropriate action to achieve it.

Worse than not taking appropriate action is just thinking you deserve something and taking no action to pursue it. This is very much a childlike way of thinking, a lazy way of thinking which is absent of any responsibility. I thought I deserved a pay rise at work for some time but didn't actually pursue it – I felt I should have it just based on my current performance and that someone should recognise this for me without me having to request it.

We all feel we deserve something good from time to time, but get side-tracked by "real life" and forget about it, discarding the ideas as "unrealistic".

"Realistic", like "normal" is subjective and doesn't really exist.

Thinking is the foundation to success in life, just as digging holes are the foundations when building a house. If, however, you do nothing more than think you will be left with the foundations but no house. Thinking is where it starts, but action brings thinking to life.

Wanting money, time, freedom, fast cars, a nice body, health and more besides are common place, most of us want these things (curious why money is nearly always first on the list), it's what you do with that desire and with those thoughts which determines if YOU DESERVE IT.

Now you know how to not deserve things using the circles of truth, think about all of the things you want, think you deserve or think you could deserve. The circles of truth will help you to visualise where you are right now, and more importantly why you are there.

I wanted to be an author and thought I deserved it but took no appropriate action, so I didn't deserve it. Now that I'm taking appropriate action and working towards it, I can use the circles to see that without action there will be no progress.

If that is how to not deserve it – then how do YOU DESERVE IT?

Action is the key. Appropriate action. By taking action you are demonstrating that you think YOU DESERVE IT. This could be conscious or subconscious but appropriate action makes it possible.

youdeservethisbook.com

Taking Appropriate Action = YOU DESERVE IT

Taking appropriate action (action that will cause or catalyse your result) is the lynchpin to YOU DESERVE IT.

How do you know if your actions are appropriate? Ask yourself honestly if they will result in the thing you want to achieve. Can you prove or demonstrate that the action will help achieve the result?

If you can't factually demonstrate the action will achieve the result, then it's not appropriate action.

If you are honest with yourself, eating Nutella straight from the jar won't help you to be slim, but having a banana instead is a more appropriate choice that will help result in your goal.

Appropriate action is a compass you can use at any point and in any endeavour to ensure you are on the right path. It's also the pitfall for many of us, myself included.

We see action as the necessary component to achievement. But indiscriminate action gets indiscriminate results. Focussed, appropriate action is what you need to deserve.
Ask yourself:

- "Will this honestly help me towards my ultimate goal?"
- "Can I prove this will move me towards my goal?"

Or

- "If I haven't achieved what I want, is this action honestly helping me?"

It's as simple as that. Your perception and lack of self-honesty may steer you off course if you truly believe that eating Nutella straight from the jar forms part of a balanced and healthy diet. It's stopping to ask the question which provides a sense check and some consideration, rather than blindly pursuing the same course of action.

Challenging your thinking is vital as your thinking drives your feelings, which drives your actions, which drives your results.

Let me explain how the circles work:

youdeservethisbook.com

236 | YOU DESERVE IT

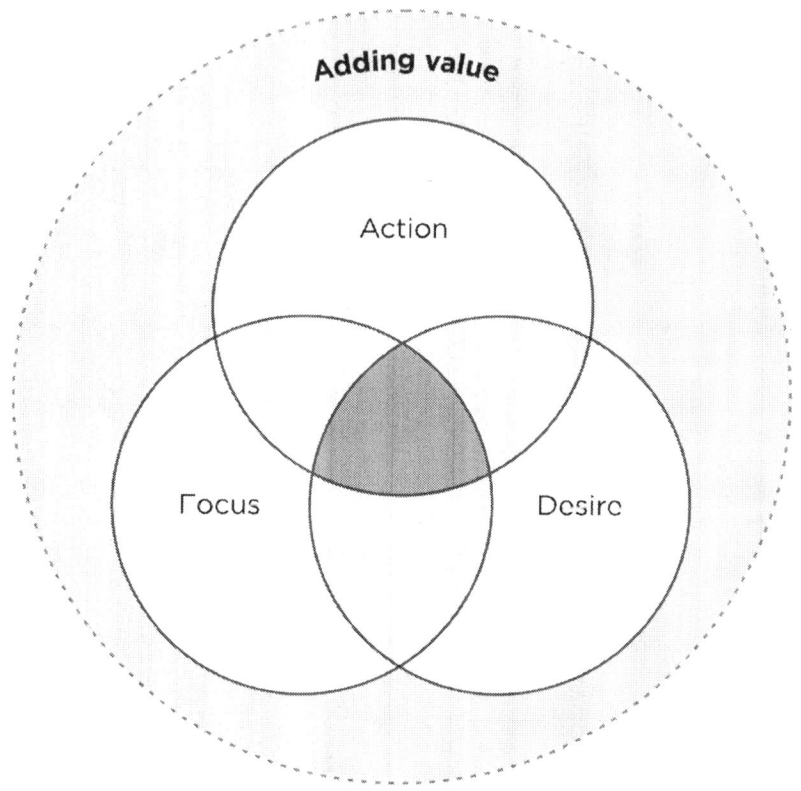

- **Desire** – This is what you want; this can be anything, from a private island to fame and fortune, your thoughts about what you want are not limited in any way as they never need to be justified or made "realistic".
- **Focus** – This is what you think you deserve. If you think you deserve something you begin to focus on it – as I did with becoming a speaker. I focussed on other speakers, authors and talks seeking to learn more about it. What you focus on and what you think you deserve are limited by your YOU DESERVE IT blueprint.

- **Action** – Appropriate Action is the key. Appropriate Action comes from knowing what you want and understanding how to get it. Action alone is no good – it must be appropriate.
- **Adding value** – The secret ingredient to YOU DESERVE IT is to look at life through the lens of adding value to others whilst getting what you want (also known as Selfmore). If you can add value to others whilst achieving your goals then YOU DESERVE IT.

Desire alone = you don't deserve it

If you simply want something but take no action towards achieving it then you don't deserve it. I want a private island but have done nothing about it – so I don't deserve it.

Focus alone = you don't deserve it

I focussed on becoming a speaker and author, researching and reading all I could. I did nothing more with this information, which left me not deserving my goal and frustrated as it felt like I'd been "working" on it.

Desire + Focus = you don't deserve it

I wanted to be a coach / speaker / author and I focussed upon it by learning more, but didn't take appropriate action to go any further. As such, I didn't deserve it.

Action = YOU DESERVE IT (but you might not want it)

If you take action on something you can deserve it, but you may not want it. I worked very hard at my job to achieve the results necessary for my job but I didn't want them as such. You may spend a lot of money on your credit card and accumulate debt – you have deserved the outcome but you don't necessarily want it.

Desire + Action = YOU DESERVE IT

If you want something and act upon it, then YOU DESERVE IT.

This is true of the smaller, easier things in everyday life. I want to go out for dinner so I make a booking; I want to buy a film on DVD so

I go online and buy it. Simple, everyday transactions fall into this category.

Focus + Action = YOU DESERVE IT
(But do you want it?)
Focussing on something and then acting upon it helps you to achieve greater goals. I focussed on achieving sales targets and as such I never missed one and was always full of ideas and plans to improve and drive sales.

Desire + Focus + Appropriate Action = YOU DESERVE IT
This is the sweet spot. This is where you've identified something you want, have focussed upon what you need to do in order to deserve it and have then taken appropriate action to make it so.

For me, this book exists because I wanted to create it, I spent a great deal of time planning and researching it and then I took appropriate action to write it, edit it and have it published. As such, I deserve it.

The secret ingredient: adding value
When you look at what you want to deserve through the lens of adding value to others, you take YOU DESERVE IT to the next level.

This is the concept of Selfmore, where you act in the interests of others but with an eye on your own interests.

Selfmore opens the doors to deserving even more as it creates reciprocity and goodwill amongst those to whom you add value. You are likely to deserve more as those you have helped are motivated to help you.

youdeservethisbook.com

The Circles of Truth

This activity looks at what you want to deserve and then looks at what you are doing about it. By contrasting the two you are able to appreciate if you are on the right path or need to make any adjustments. You can then create an action plan to correct your efforts and move you towards deserving.

Example

I wanted to be an author when I set out on my journey; I considered the following based on if I were already an author:

Action – As an author, I would have written at least one book, perhaps written a blog, but certainly would have kept regular writing part of my daily life.

Focus – I would have focussed on my subject matter, brainstormed it, and tested new ideas, researched ideas, read other books for inspiration on style, layout and content.

Value – As a published author, my ideas would help others improve their lives by giving them a new perspective from which they could pursue their goals.

Considering my goal versus my current position:

Action – I have written parts of the book, but haven't yet edited it. Haven't established a blog yet but plan to. Not writing regularly.

Focus – I'm still working full time so I spend what time I can researching the ideas for the book.

Value – Without my book published I'm not yet adding any real value to others. I am adding value to myself through pushing my boundaries, trying something new and pursuing my goal.

youdeservethisbook.com

Conclusion

Although I am writing parts of the book and jotting down ideas, I need to explore the ideas further and conduct some research. I need to start looking at different styles of writing, layouts of books and similar books to gain ideas which could help me. Although not yet published I could circulate my ideas amongst friends and family for testing but also to add value to them, I could also achieve this through writing a blog about my journey and connecting with others.

Action plan

- Conduct research into ideas for the book.
- Explore similar books for layout and writing style inspiration.
- Share ideas with friends and family for feedback
- Create a simple blog to share ideas and connect with others.

Guidance

Consider firstly something you want to deserve. Imagine for a moment you have achieved this – you already fully deserve it.

Action – Now consider what actions would you have taken and would you be taking to be deserving of this.

Focus – What would you have focussed on to have achieved this goal? What would your focus be on now you have achieved it?

Value – How would you be adding value either to yourself or to those around you now that you have achieved your goal?

Considering once more the goal you want to deserve, consider your current position.

Action – What action have you taken in pursuit of your goal?

Focus – What are you focussing on and how much of your time and focus do you spend on your goal?

Value – What value are you adding to yourself or those around you in pursuit of your goal?

Once you have completed both sections, consider the difference between the two. What action would you need to take to achieve your goals versus the action you are taking now? What are you focussing on currently versus what you would focus on to have achieved your goal? What value would you be adding versus the value you currently add?

The variance between these two sections is what stands between you and what you deserve. If you aren't taking appropriate action, focussing where you should or seeking to add value then you are limiting what you stand to deserve.

Tip
Don't overestimate what you're doing now and don't underestimate what you may need to do to achieve your goal. Honesty will bring clarity – sugar-coating will keep you from deserving.

What you'll need
Pen, pad, honesty.

Duration
30 minutes

When completed, ask yourself:
How does my current action and focus differ from what I would need to achieve my goals – can I make any adjustments?

youdeservethisbook.com

10 things to remember

1. Action is vital to YOU DESERVE IT.
2. You get what you deserve, not what you think you deserve.
3. Inaction is a form of action.
4. Thoughts dictate feelings, feelings dictate actions.
5. YOU DESERVE IT begins with what you want.
6. Lack of self-belief limits action.
7. Appropriate action is action that will help advance you towards your goal.
8. You can deserve things you don't want.
9. Adding value is the secret ingredient to YOU DESERVE IT.
10. Your blueprint determines what you feel you deserve.

Exercise – Ask better questions

The quality of your questions dictate the quality of the answer – this simple principle is often overlooked. Asking better questions is a key component for personal and professional development. For the next week, seek to ask better questions. Better questions challenge assumptions, encouraging stretching and growth, are open and positive, lead to more questions and encourage learning and investigation. This week, log each question you were going to ask and its "better question" equivalent.

Example
When you are told something, instead of "why" ask "what makes you say that". Seek to understand more than the answer, but the reason for the answer. When you are asking for something, be as specific as you can; add a timescale to your request. Look for ways to add specificity and detail to your requests and questions.

Guidance
The quality of the question will dictate the quality of the answer. Taking a moment to consider if your question is good enough to help get a better answer. Ask yourself – how can I be more specific with my question?

Tip
Keep the list of better question characteristics to hand to remind you.

What you'll need
Notebook and pen.

Duration
7 days

When completed, ask yourself:
Do better questions get better answers? How could you structure your questions in the future to get more relevant and specific answers?

youdeservethisbook.com

16 – Be afraid: a case study

> No news is good news.

- Why do we consume the news?
- Why is it always bad news?
- Could we eradicate it from our lives and be better off?

On Thursday the 3rd July 2014 I bought my last ever newspaper and resolved to never read the news again. The boldness of the headline that day, coupled with my increasing dislike for the news, was the tipping point. BE AFRAID, it proclaimed.

Until this point, I was a frequent visitor to the Daily Mail website; a UK website renowned for its reporting on immigration, benefits, minorities, and of course, celebrity.

I would find myself wasting hours every day and that's no exaggeration; I could spend 2–4 hours per **day** trawling the site at various times learning of Kim Kardashian's latest exploits or why the

UK was becoming a more likely target for future terrorist attacks and why perhaps we should all "be afraid".

Not only did I read the same stories and look at the same pictures (there is an extensive showbiz section) over and over again, but I began to find myself on the site throughout the day through sheer boredom, looking for something to occupy my mind and entertain me.

What a terrible waste of time.

Far from being entertained by constantly checking news websites (I didn't limit myself to the Daily Mail) I became increasingly annoyed at myself for wasting my time in this way and, more importantly, I was becoming increasingly anxious and aware of all the terrible goings-on in the world.

Something had to change.

The news was not serving me. It didn't deserve me.

I deserved more than this, but felt trapped in the cycle of becoming bored, reading the news, becoming anxious, becoming annoyed for wasting my time in this way, and then repeating the cycle daily. Sometimes hourly.

As I was writing this book at the time, on my own journey of discovering the many facets of YOU DESERVE IT, I decided to eradicate news addiction from my life once and for all. I didn't deserve to waste my time in this way.

With not much thought at all I stopped checking the news websites, ceased to buy newspapers and even changed the TV channel or radio station when the news was about to come on.

I became anti-news. The results were astonishing.

As a result of stopping my endless 24/7 news consumption I felt immediately calmer and less anxious. This in turn made me feel more present in my daily life and less distracted by things that had little or no bearing whatsoever on my life. I recovered hours of time each day which I could use for other, more productive things which made me feel less hurried and certainly less concerned about wasting time as I had been.

Above all else, I felt a sense of achievement. I was being responsible. I was choosing to give up the news. I was in control, and it felt great.

Through writing this book (and with my new-found extra time) I discovered I am a type-A personality. As I would learn, anything which helped me to feel less hurried and anxious was a very good thing indeed.

> **Type A:** *The theory describes "Type A" individuals as ambitious, rigidly organized, highly status-conscious, sensitive, impatient, take on more than they can handle, want other people to get to the point, anxious, proactive, and concerned with time management. People with Type A personalities are often high-achieving "workaholics" who multi-task, push themselves with deadlines, and hate both delays and ambivalence.*
> http://en.wikipedia.org/wiki/Type_A_and_Type_B_personality_theory

By eradicating the news and discovering my Type A personality, I felt I had achieved something. I'd taken control of my situation, changed it to enjoy a new outcome and enjoyed the results accordingly.

Determined to make my experience of giving up the news part of this book, as it was part of my YOU DESERVE IT journey, I began to look more closely at what I had actually achieved. I was able to distil my actions and the situation into five steps. From identifying why I didn't like the news to eradicating it, I'd followed five distinct steps to make it a reality.

This chapter distils those steps so that they are actionable and more defined. You can use them to deserve better in your own life or learn how to "un-deserve" things also. Un-deserve is covered fully in Chapter 19, but you get a taste of it here.

Step 1 – Notice

A fairly obvious place to begin, but the first and most crucial step is noticing that something is wrong or that you want to change something in your life. I was acutely aware of the negative impact my constant news consumption had had on my health, well-being and productivity.

Driven by the desire to change and to deserve better, I began to question just why I was checking the news so frequently. I used the five whys to break this down further.

16 – Be afraid: a case study

So why was I doing it? It was firstly through sheer boredom and my need to constantly feel productive or as though I am in motion. As a type A personality, sitting still and being peaceful are nearly impossible (nearly – nothing is truly impossible) for me to do. With the news I'd found a 365 24/7 way to keep in motion and to keep absorbing information to feel like I was learning. The news works in such a way that it rolls on forever, there is no end point, it will never be finished or complete and as such I was hooked on the never-ending treadmill.

I could feel busy and in motion forever by checking the news, whilst getting nowhere other than more "afraid".

I noticed (realised) that I enjoyed seeking out the stories of war, terrorism, death and so on as it gave me an adrenaline boost. With the personal history of my childhood, the suicide and the tsunami I was no stranger to danger and adrenaline. The news helped me to top up this excited / scared feeling on a daily basis.

FOMO – the Fear Of Missing Out (covered later in this book) was the final motivation. I noticed that friends and colleagues loved to share the details of stories in the news, the more detail the better. Particularly if it's a bad news story, which most of them are. The competitiveness surrounding the details of how many survivors in that plane crash, or how many Ebola victims there are in the UK right now, appeared to be a reward to those still hooked on the news treadmill – the more detail you could recall and share, the more validated checking the news appears to be.

The next time you are at work, or even in a public place, listen out for what people mention about the news. It will be all of the terrible stories, with lots of detail.

A high percentage of the news is bad news. War, murder, rape, shootings, epidemics, financial crises and so on. Although some good news stories do get reported on, the majority are bad news stories – sex sells, fear sells.

If you want some good news, check out:
http://www.huffingtonpost.com/good-news/

The next time you overhear or are involved in discussing the news I would almost certainly guess it will be a bad news story – with competing recollections of the level of detail too.

As terrible as the world's events may be, it's all so irrelevant and meaningless to your everyday life. Of course I don't wish war, plane crashes and the like on anyone. These are terrible circumstances and I feel for those affected.

That said, if a plane crashes in Indonesia and I am in London what can I do about it?

Nothing. It only serves to make me more nervous of air travel and the fragility of life.

If there is a terrorist attack in Paris, what can I do about it?

Nothing. It only serves to make me nervous of visiting Paris and reminds me of the fragility of life.

By ignoring the news will these bad things cease to happen? No.

By ignoring the news do I care less? No.

By continuing to read the news will these bad things cease to happen? No, but I will continue to feel anxious and fearful of plane crashes and the like.

I reasoned that to stop reading the news I would alleviate my anxiety and time wasted, whilst having no negative impact on the world at large.

When the headline was published that day it was the tipping point for me to abandon the news.

BE AFRAID? I'm alright, thanks.

Step 2 – Target

Noticing what is happening or what you don't want is the beginning and the easy part. Deciding what you want instead is much more difficult.

Many of us know what we don't want but don't know what we do want. Step 2 is crucial as with no defined end point or timescale you are unlikely to succeed. My target was multi-tiered. I wanted to be more peaceful and less anxious in daily life, I also wanted to waste less time and in doing so be more present and productive.

The news was holding me back from all of this; I couldn't see why I was continuing to check the news other than force of habit. I needed to kick the habit once and for all. When I set a target that was desirable to me – being more present (especially with my children) – I began to question not only why I was checking the news but also what else was standing in my way.

Your own target is likely to be the opposite of what you have noticed and what you currently dislike. If you notice you are unfit your target is to improve your fitness, if you notice you don't read often then your target is to read more etc.

The more enticing, attractive and relevant you can make the target, the more motivating it will be.

For me, being present was important, but being more present so I could enjoy time playing with my children was what moved me to act.

Find what moves and motivates you most – then find how you can incorporate that into your target.

When setting your target, remember that slow progress is better than no progress. Start small and build up. If you have an ambitious target and fail it will hurt, potentially deterring you from trying again. Creating a more manageable target or using smaller milestones will keep you interested and motivated.

My goal was to cease checking the news, but in the beginning to go without it for an evening, or a day, or even an hour was an achievement.

By starting small I was able to quickly notch up "successes" and this helped me build momentum. If I'd tried to quit from day one for good, then on day one in the afternoon when I drifted onto the Daily Mail website I would have considered myself a "failure" and perhaps abandoned my plans as "too difficult".

Step 3 – Control

You have noticed the current situation and thought about how you'd like to change it. The next step is to determine what you can actually control. For me this was straightforward. I wanted to be more peaceful, less anxious and more present and had already identified my news consumption as the largest obstacle in my path. What else could I control? Checking my phone? Checking email? Doing anything which makes me feel "busy" and "in control" but which is ultimately adding no value to me.

To determine what you can control, you utilise the very core of YOU DESERVE IT – the cause and effect of action (or inaction). What is producing the current situation and how can this be modified or eliminated to produce your alternative desired result?

Depending on your circumstances there may be one thing, there may be many things, it doesn't matter so long as you can control them.

youdeservethisbook.com

It's easy to fall prey to identifying things you *can't* control, abdicating responsibility and perpetuating your current situation as there's "nothing you can do about it".

I could have complained that the news is everywhere and that I can't escape it. I do still see newspapers and magazines in shops and sometimes I see the news on TV or in public places. It's no longer enough to hold me back and to keep me procrastinating.

If you find yourself blaming others, or feeling helpless, you simply need to reframe and look at things from a new perspective.

> *"It's not what happens to you, but how you react to it that matters."*
> **Epictetus**

I couldn't change the news, but I could change my consumption of it. If you're really stuck with identifying what you can control, then keeping a thought journal is an effective way to help you reframe and change your perspective. Jot down your observations about the thing you want to change – how it makes you feel, what you think, the facts, opinions of others, dates, times, as much information as you can muster.

What makes it onto the paper will provide clues as to what matters to you. Seeking out patterns and "connecting the dots" from your seemingly random thoughts will help reveal what action you need to take and how to proceed.

Step 4 – Response-able

Once you have identified what you could change, you need to determine how to change it and how to change your behaviour so you are more response-able (able to choose your response). I had identified the news to be the main culprit, so it was a case of minimising, or better yet eliminating, the news from my life.

To do that, I needed something to fill the void that would be left once the news was gone. I was planning to avoid the news as it was negative, so it would be better to fill the void with something positive instead. When I felt the urge to check the news I would look at positive quotes online, read inspiring stories or watch motivational videos on YouTube.

This is where my blog, Every Day Should Be Fun, helped me. There are countless positive resources to call upon, all in one place. It's a place for positive procrastination; if you don't want to do anything constructive and just want to browse the internet then it might as well be uplifting and inspiring.

Whilst it didn't immediately help me with being more present and less "busy" – it was my first step to weaning myself from being a newsaholic.

As per step 2, small progress is better than no progress, so although I would stop reading the news as abruptly as possible, I needed something in the short term to fill the gap. Eventually I would reduce that consumption back and thus close in on my target. As per step 3, the thought journal works well here; you may notice you always experience the thing you want to change at a certain time, day, or after something else happens.

These are all triggers. Find the triggers and you can control them.

I noticed I read the news just before I went to bed at night, so I made sure I had a book by the bedside for when the urge came ensuring I could pick up and read something other than the news. Completing a thought journal for a few days or a week or two (the longer the better) will help you to identify and collate any triggers for your own situation. This is a sizeable step forward, but the true power lies in harnessing these triggers for taking alternative action to pursue your goal.

Step 5 – Results

You've noticed what you don't want, established a target and a timescale to eliminate what you do want, you've identified what you can control and what your triggers are. You've taken action and now you have results. So what now?

Changing parts of your life, your behaviour and your thinking can be difficult, but never impossible. It's important to be ambitious in your aims, but pragmatic in your approach. Progress can be small and incremental to begin with – don't let this deter you.

If you didn't achieve what you set out to achieve then you need to consider why this is the case. This process will allow you to do so – you just go back to step one and begin again.

youdeservethisbook.com

Perhaps your target was too unrealistic or difficult? Could you reconsider and begin again on a smaller scale to ensure some success next time?

Perhaps there were things you could have taken control of which you weren't aware of when you set off?

Perhaps some things are beyond your control when you thought they weren't?

Perhaps you need to identify better triggers or better alternative behaviours to realise your goals? Maybe the changes seen were too small to be of use or the triggers too rare to be relevant and actionable.

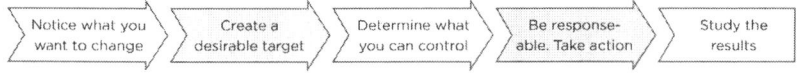

If you want to change something about yourself, it starts with considering where you are now as realistically and unbiased as possible. You then consider where you would like to be in an ideal world.

> *"You can't connect the dots looking forward; you can only connect them looking backwards."*
> **Steve Jobs**

Finally, you "connect the dots" and look to see how and what you can change to deserve your preferred outcome. This is why information is key. The information about what you want to change are the dots; more information, more dots.

I am one of the most impatient people you could hope to meet. For years I would attempt processes such as the one I am suggesting here, set an unrealistically high goal, see no sizeable improvement, lose heart, abandon the idea and be no further forward.

That is of course if I bothered to implement at all – for most of the time these types of chapters stayed as words on the page and never became action. Without action, you can't undeserve anything.

After years of going around in circles I got fed up with not making progress and committed to following through.

That's when it all changed.

I began to celebrate the smaller wins and dissected my "failures" as opportunities to learn something and improve. In the same way I only focus on good "luck" (Chapter 13) I began to only focus on successes I'd had; amplifying them and enjoying as much about them as I could. I focussed on success and dissected failure.

When I stopped being so impatient, so hard on myself, so quick to give in, so type A – I began to taste success.

Giving up the news may seem like a small thing to you, but for me it was significant. It was a large part of my daily life and I am pleased to report I haven't returned to my old ways since. I do of course hear of national and international news stories through friends and colleagues as a matter of course but they are irrelevant to me – I have literally unsubscribed from the news.

And it feels liberating.

What the "step by step" processes such as this and all the "self-improvement" and "self-help" literature fail to explain properly is this:

If you start small and make sure no matter what that you finish, then you build momentum.
That momentum fuels your larger goals.

I may have started with the news, but I moved on to giving up phone addiction, checking emails, alcohol, toxic people and a host of other things that I have decided no longer deserve a place in my life.

To achieve all this, I had to start somewhere. Starting small and staying committed are key to progress. Don't let lack of progress dishearten you, let it push you to try new things to try and help you remember.

I urge you to use this five-step process to change something in your life for the positive. It doesn't matter how small it is so long as you follow through.

The difference with this book is that I have been just like you – I have read chapters like these and taken no action. I have considered what could be done, maybe even taken some notes, but it ended there, along with my dreams. It all seemed too difficult, so I gave up.

I know that without action these words are meaningless – both to me and to you. I also know that small incremental action builds momentum and you start to achieve truly great things.

youdeservethisbook.com

254 | YOU DESERVE IT

This book was written one chapter per week until it became what you are holding in your hands now. It was also reviewed, edited and rewritten over months, after the first draft was complete.

Had I tried to write the book in a weekend or even in three months I would have likely failed. Writing a chapter a week was manageable and allowed me to complete all chapters on time without exception.

I wrote this book, yes, but I did so incrementally. I achieved the goal through persistence, commitment and celebrating smaller goals along the way.

What seemingly impossibly large goal (like writing a book) could you work towards with small incremental effort and smaller wins along the way?

I have bought one newspaper since I gave up the news, but with this headline I just couldn't leave it on the shelf.

youdeservethisbook.com

10 things to remember

1. Not everything deserves your time.
2. It's not what happens to you, it's what you do about it.
3. You can always change what you don't like.
4. Focus on your successes, learn from your failures. "You win some, you learn some".
5. Not all progress is visible.
6. Real change comes from small incremental action which builds momentum.
7. You have to start somewhere, start where you are.
8. Responsible – you are able to choose your response.
9. Lost time is never found again.
10. Ask yourself, "Will this help me advance towards my goal?"

youdeservethisbook.com

Exercise – Achievement Inventory

Take a sheet of A4 paper or notebook and list absolutely everything you have achieved in your life to date. Everything. Passing your driving test, learning to dive, passing exams, landing a job, buying a house, travelling the world, learning a language, collecting stamps – whatever you have achieved thus far in your life – however small – needs to be logged here. Decide on five of your "largest" or "most significant" achievements. Now ask those close to you, your family, partner, or friends to list 5–10 of your "largest" or "most significant" achievements.

Example

I asked my mum and my wife to complete this exercise – it's funny how my list of achievements were tangible things such as writing this book, running my blog and so forth, but they concentrated more on parts of my personality and life which were non material.

My mum:

- Overcoming childhood shyness
- Overcoming early childhood setbacks
- Commitment to all you set out to achieve
- Your drive and enthusiasm to try something new
- Proving that you have learned lessons from life's challenges and worked hard to show that you can rise above them
- Your wonderful sense of humour
- Your outlook on life that we don't have problems, just challenges
- Your strong relationship with your brother
- Being a wonderful husband
- Being just the best dad
- The love and pride I feel when I think of you as your mum

My wife:

- Overcoming life events (difficult childhood, tsunami)
- Dealing with problems in a responsible and proactive way with

counselling
- Going after your dreams
- Success with being a good salesman
- Being a supportive husband and father and great role model for our children

Guidance
We seldom, if ever, take the time to list our achievements and the good things we have accomplished in life. By focussing on the positive things we have achieved, rather than everything we have yet to achieve, we get a boost of motivation and the feel good factor of all the great things we deserve.

Tip
List everything, however large or small, that you have achieved. The longer the list the better you will feel. No achievement is too small.

What you'll need
Notebook and pen.

Duration
2 hours

When completed, ask yourself:
Are you surprised by just how much you have achieved? Are you surprised by how many "small" things you remember – and are these really less important than the big things, or is an achievement an achievement?

youdeservethisbook.com

17 – FOMO: a case study

Open 9–5 Monday–Friday only.

- What are you missing?
- Could it be nothing?
- Is the grass greener or the same(ish)?
- What are you avoiding?

I have been known to check my work email on weekends, bank holidays, Christmas Day... even my honeymoon. I'm not proud of it, but at the time it felt natural, it felt good, it felt reassuring. I couldn't imagine what terrible things might happen if I didn't check it.

This was clearly a problem.

At work, I was known by colleagues and clients as an organised person. I would pre-empt the needs of others, over-deliver and as such I found myself deserving of the success I enjoyed. (I was "serving vigorously" – the very origin of the word deserve.)

Although my eagerness to please had ensured I was deserving of more professionally, personally it was killing me and I knew, like checking the news, that I had to give it up if I wanted to find peace and a balanced home life.

It was as the result of a conversation with a close friend that we decided I should experiment with not checking email outside of my 9am to 6pm working hours.

The thought of not checking email and of subsequently "missing out" and not being in control chilled my blood. It felt like sure-fire professional suicide as I based much of my success on being available and working 24/7. Surely without my 24/7 attentiveness my productivity would suffer?

Despite these reservations and others, I recognised that to deserve something different you have to take different action. Yes, I was nervous I may affect my performance at work, but with a wife and young family I needed to be there for them – especially at evenings and weekends when I was supposed to be off work.

Keen to make progress and to prove to myself that I was committed to doing whatever it takes to reach my goals – I dove straight in. That evening at 5:59:59 my trembling finger hit the power button on my BlackBerry.

I braced myself for impact. The world did not end.

For the first time since I had a BlackBerry, I had successfully unplugged to carve out the "me" time and family time that was so lacking.

"Action cures fear."
David J Schwartz, *Magic of Thinking Big*

Seemingly insignificant to an outsider, but incredibly enormous to me, I was offline and unavailable for the first time in a long time. It felt so strange.

I felt rebellious, as though I was deliberately causing myself an issue. I anticipated switching my phone on the following morning to angry messages, missed opportunities and who knows what else? The lack of connectedness had caused me to catastrophise about what may happen. I worried about what may happen, I worried about what may not happen too.

It was a long night.

Like a drug addict craving their next hit, I felt myself reaching for the phone and had to stop myself from turning it on a few times. Eventually the urges subsided and I managed to switch off more than I ever had before. That night I slept like a log, a log in the middle of the woods with no Wi-Fi.

The next morning I turned on the phone, five minutes early; the suspense was too much to make it to 9am but I'd proven to myself I could be without my phone so allowed myself this treat.

Not a single voicemail, SMS or email. Not one.

I was surprised at the time, but on reflection this was to be expected. My out of hours work was nearly always *outbound*. There was the odd genuine emergency or out of hours request, but in the main my customers kept office hours and as such didn't email me throughout the night. I was never actually "available 24/7" to them, I just thought I was, this was my perception.

I felt relieved. Relieved to have "survived" the night, relieved to have been no worse off for it and relieved that I'd proven to myself I could do it.

There is a good reason they are known as "CrackBerries".

That was the first night I got my "CrackBerry" addiction under control and I'm pleased to report that from that day to this I have never gone back, I have stayed with digital sobriety.

Like giving up the news, it feels great. I am in control and at peace all at once.

Throughout my digital sobriety, only one "urgent" request has come in from a client, and even they conceded that as it was 8pm when they sent the email and that they'd have to wait until the morning for a reply. It's ridiculous to expect someone to work 24/7 and always be available... isn't it?

My fear of missing out (in a work context) was under control. I was able to be more present with my wife and children and for the first time I started to feel relaxed rather than wandering into my own thoughts, wondering "what if...?"

I had changed my actions and as such deserved a different result. The Notice, Target, Control, Response-able, Results structure from Chapter 16 had proven successful.

So what is FOMO?

FOMO
/ˈfəʊməʊ/

noun informal

> anxiety that an exciting or interesting event may currently be happening elsewhere, often aroused by posts seen on a social media website.
> "I realized I was a lifelong sufferer of FOMO"

The fear of missing out, the fear of not knowing certain information or missing certain opportunities, was driving my behaviour. Until it was highlighted to me, I wasn't even aware this was the case. I simply hadn't noticed the amount of time and energy I'd spend nervously anticipating situations and the needs of others over my own.

The thought journal from Chapter 16 helped bring clarity to the situation. There was a selfish element – I worked in sales and any missed opportunity in sales is to be avoided, especially if I could have seized it – albeit at 2am on a Sunday morning, whilst on holiday...

youdeservethisbook.com

I was selfishly trying to capture sales and unselfishly looking to serve my clients better than the competition. It's noble to want to serve vigorously and especially to deserve more and realise your goals, but I was over-serving and the result was detrimental to my personal time and ability to relax.

I wasn't serving myself, or my wife, or our children – work was my top priority. Remember that I didn't even enjoy my work at this point and wanted to escape; I was dedicating my best efforts to something I didn't want anyway. And I wondered why I felt so unhappy and so lacking…

FOMO is a classic case of playing to not lose instead of playing to win. When you play to win, you have a clear idea of what needs to happen to realise your goal. When you play to not lose, you have no clear idea of what to do and as such focus on what not to do.

By focussing on what not to do, you miss what you should do or could do and thus limit your chances of success.

> *"Whether you think you can,
> or you think you can't – you're right."*
> **Henry Ford**

I was focussing on not missing opportunities at work, which, like the news, is a potentially 24/7/365 never ending task to keep me "busy" and in motion, but won't help me achieve much in the longer term. It's the Procrastination Illusion at work.

The time I spent on work out of my official hours, in a job that I no longer truly enjoyed, was simply wasted. Had I spent that same time constructively pursuing my dream, perhaps I would be further along the road than I find myself as I write this.

Until I realised that the constant FOMO email and phone checking was a hindrance to me, I was doomed to repeat it.

The first step is always to notice what is wrong, before you can change it.

YOU DESERVE IT requires appropriate action, desire and thought. Acting from fear, as in "fear" of missing out, is not appropriate action. FOMO is predicated on the belief that you don't want to miss out on something. Until you challenge that thought and try missing out (as I did) how can you know it is to be feared?

You need to stick to facts, not emotions.

As I discovered, if you can take action to challenge FOMO, you can master it. FOMO is a nagging feeling of things you "should" or "could" be doing. If you actually wanted to do them, you would make the effort to do them.

- **"Should"** is based on obligation rather than choice.
- **"Could"** is based on possibility.

What you should or could be doing are irrelevant. It's what you NEED to be doing which counts.

I discovered something more powerful than FOMO. Something that helped me and will help you to ensure your actions are appropriate and advancing you towards your goals.

I discovered FOMO's arch-enemy.

JOMO.

The Joy of Missing Out is a far more enjoyable situation to find yourself in, not least because you are making a decision and being response-able – not acting out of some undefined fear or obligation.

Turning FOMO into JOMO can be accomplished with this simple question:

> ***"Will missing out on X keep me
> from achieving what I want?"***

This question directs you to appropriate action. I may fear missing out on Facebook updates or the news, but if I do actually miss out, will I be worse off? Is it even "missing out"?

If you answer the above question with yes – as it would have been for me and my constant work email checking, then I have a qualifying question to help:

> ***"Have I actually missed out on X and has this kept me from
> achieving what I want?"***

This is where experimentation comes in. I truly, 100% believed that stopping working out of hours would be career suicide. This was based on perception, not reality. The only way to know is to have factual evidence and for that, you need to experiment.

youdeservethisbook.com

You may have something in your life that you fear missing out on and truly believe it would be devastating. If you can summon the courage and the curiosity, I encourage you to try deliberately missing out.

I deliberately missed out and realised my fears were based on assumption. I can factually prove that my sales continued, if not increased, since I have not been checking things 24–7. If I had actually missed out on something or if there was a negative outcome then my constant checking could be factually justified and more palatable.

By never having missed out, I was guessing what the result would be, which is a common approach to the unknown. The problem was, this guessing was costing me my peace of mind and quality of family life. Was all that checking worth that cost? I can report that it wasn't.

Fear Of Missing Out also has a lot to do with avoiding failure and allowing myself to "tread water". For me at least, FOMO could just as well be "Fear Of Moving On" – by constantly checking things, thinking about things and being constantly "ready" – you have no energy left to consider alternative action. It's also a form of excuse – you're "too busy" to do what you need to. It's the Procrastination Illusion.

I wanted to become a coach / speaker / author, but FOMO allowed me to remain so "busy" that there was never any real time to pursue my goal.

I realise now this was a convenient excuse for inaction, a way to justify to myself why I wasn't getting anywhere. By working as much as I could, I was avoiding any potential failure of trying new things; I was playing to not lose.

The moment I became response-able and turned FOMO into JOMO, I started to see progress and feel a whole lot better too.

One final factor to consider here is Parkinson's Law:

> **"Work expands so as to fill the time available for its completion."**

With FOMO, there is no limit on time. I feared missing out at work and this feeling expanded into a 24/7/365 activity as there was no defined time limit. It felt far more important and pressing as my checking became more and more habitual – it was an ever reinforcing cycle of checking, fearing, and checking.

When you repeat behaviour, you reinforce it. I didn't challenge my FOMO and as such the "fear" grew to the point I was constantly online and available, fearful of what would happen if I wasn't.

I was an addict, always needing a hit.

If you have goals you are aiming for and things you want to deserve then Parkinson's Law can be a potential hazard. With the limited time and energy we all possess, we must ensure it is spent appropriately and in the pursuit of what we want. Whether or not you suffer with FOMO, when you become engrossed in activities which keep you from appropriate action (such as excessive computer game playing, television watching etc.) Parkinson's Law is one to focus on.

You can lose nights, days, weeks, and years of your time if you set no limits or boundaries on how you spend your time.

YOU DESERVE IT requires appropriate action and appropriate action requires appropriate use of your time. FOMO was a distraction for me; it kept me from appropriate action and progressing towards my goals.

Questioning how you spend your time and limiting / defining it where possible is the solution. I now ask myself at regular intervals:

"Will what I'm doing get me closer to my goals or am I just being busy?"

This idea (which I first discovered in The Four Hour Work Week by Tim Ferriss) helps you to realise that "busyness" is a form of laziness. It's a lack of priorities and a lack of direction.

Just as weeds grow in a garden with no boundaries or discipline, the time you spend on things which won't advance you towards your goals will expand without boundaries or discipline to the point that they threaten your success.

Just as it's difficult to tell some weeds from some plants, it can be equally as difficult to separate the productive appropriate action from the "busyness".

A garden requires regular weeding to keep things under control and your success depends upon the same principles.

The grass is green where you are now and elsewhere – it's what you do about it that counts. Don't let inappropriate action, such as constantly checking and worrying about other things, keep you from what matters.

Don't waste your time checking emails or checking on others – spend that time on yourself. By focussing elsewhere you may hinder your own achievements and progress.

Which actions or behaviours (such as FOMO) can you weed out of your own life to ensure you reach your goals?

10 things to remember

1. The grass is always greener in your head.
2. FOMO is the fear of missing out.
3. Stick to facts, not emotions.
4. Ask yourself "Will this help me towards my goals?"
5. Work expands to fill the time allotted for its completion.
6. "Busyness" is a form of laziness – it's a lack of priorities.
7. Focus on you and your own efforts, not what you're "missing out" on.
8. Some things need to be undeserved.
9. Taking control is motivating.
10. When you repeat behaviour, you reinforce it.

youdeservethisbook.com

Exercise – Reframe

Looking at the world differently changes your perspective; this is known as "reframing". For the next day pretend that you are the person you want to be. You are the success and have everything you've ever wanted. Consider how you would feel, how you would act, how you would treat yourself and others, what language you would use. Introduce yourself to new people as the person you want to be and sample what it feels like.

Example

From the outset of writing this book and pursuing my career as a coach, speaker and author I pretended I was already all of those things. I began to talk more confidently, be more compassionate, make notes about ideas and situations which inspired me. I adopted a more peaceful and confident persona where I knew what my goals were and I was pursuing them. This boost in confidence helped me to write the book and to acquire my first clients and to make the dream a reality.

Ask yourself:

- How would I think, feel and act if I was already the person I want to become?
- What do I do now which the future me definitely wouldn't do?
- What don't I do now which the future me would do?

Guidance

Even when you have achieved what you want, you will still be you. Try to understand that you can adopt the characteristics you believe you will possess when you have achieved your goals right now, and this will actually help you advance towards your goals and enjoy the journey.

Ask yourself:

- • How do I want to feel?

youdeservethisbook.com

Tip
Act as if is easier with people you don't know; introduce yourself as the person you want to be and notice how you are taken at face value.

What you'll need
An idea of who you want to become and how they would behave

Duration
1 day

When completed, ask yourself:
How did it feel to pretend to be who you aim to be and to have all you aim to have? Why are you waiting until you "get there" to feel like this? How could you try feeling like this more often to keep you charged and inspired?

youdeservethisbook.com

18 – Funnelling

YOU DESERVE IT is about serving,
serving is selling.

- Are you in sales?
- Isn't selling, life itself?
- Is selling serving, or is serving selling?

In this chapter we'll look at the connection between selling and serving. We'll consider the approach I took to sell tens of millions of pounds' worth of vehicles at my peak, and how the same principles apply for us all.

I don't consider myself a salesman. The truth is I am. We all are.

We sell ideas, thoughts, opportunities and much more besides on a daily basis, inside and outside the workplace.

In my role I was a "sales man" of sorts, but sales is still such an emotive word for me; images of boiler room style cold callers, pie charts, motorway travel, targets, bonuses....

YOU DESERVE IT is all about selling. Serving is selling.

The word deserve ultimately derives from the French word Deservir – to serve zealously.

Serving. Now there is a word which is less emotive and more accessible than "selling". To serve is to add value to someone else, regardless of money.

I prefer serving to selling, as deserving things and serving others isn't always about money.

Money can distort YOU DESERVE IT.

Friendships, marriages, favours; these are all based on value given and received and not a pound sign in sight.

Given my view on sales and my preference to view it as serving, it's no surprise that I *found* myself in my role, rather than seeking it out specifically.

I never considered myself a salesman and I still don't really. I used to say I was "a man who sells cars, but I'm not a car salesman". I simply enjoy adding value to others and to serving them. It's this simple and selfless (Selfmore) attitude which is a game changer.

True sales is truly Selfmore. It's about the value you can add. Success in sales comes when you add value to others. You add value to others by focussing on what they need and want. Once you know this, you can serve them.

If you serve enough people or add enough value then you are rewarded financially and find yourself deserving of more than when you began.

Add value, become more valuable.

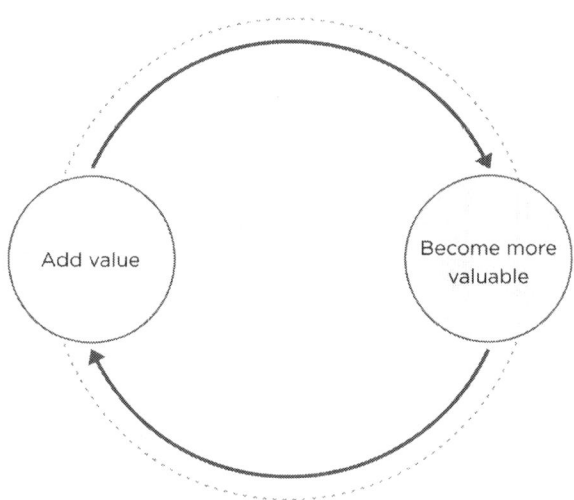

In the context of sales, deserving more means more money, but in the context of serving, deserving more means love, trust, respect, support, reciprocity.

When you don't focus on the money, you deserve what money cannot buy anyway.

youdeservethisbook.com

Focussing on money will, at best, only obtain money. Focussing on serving brings loyalty, trust, gratitude and so much more. Focussing on money is selfish, focussing on serving is Selfmore.

This principle has changed so much about my understanding of YOU DESERVE IT, sales, serving and life.

YOU DESERVE IT is about changing your perception. It's about looking outward, not inward, about what you can give, not what you can get. You get back so much more when you focus on serving and adding value to others first, rather than focussing on what you can get.

> *"You can have everything in life that you want, if you will just help enough other people get what they want."*
> **Zig Ziglar**

Although this chapter is about "sales" and although sales is the axis on which much of the world's progress is made, it's important to separate money and sales. Money is not sales. Sales is not money.

When you focus on money, either how much you do or don't have, how much you will earn or the price of fish that day – you are taking a step back from YOU DESERVE IT and from adding true value. Money is the by-product.

If I set out to make as much money as possible and focussed solely on money (in a business context), I would keep margins tight, maybe even skimp on product quality or rewarding staff correctly (amongst other cost saving techniques) to obtain my ultimate goal of as much profit as possible.

By focussing solely on money I may lose customers through cheaper product quality, lose staff through lower wages and poorer conditions and ultimately not find myself making the profit I focussed on as I was too focussed on the result rather than how it was deserved. Focussing on money shifts your focus to money related items. As such, your judgement is coloured with the context of monetary value and numbers on the page, rather than how you can serve and add value.

People are more important than money.

youdeservethisbook.com

By focussing solely on money you hinder your success as you focus on the end result (the money) rather than how it is obtained. It's the same as focussing on what you want more than focussing on how you could get it. You may make some progress, but until you focus on how to earn the money or how to add the value, the end result will elude you.

Outside of work, I focussed on wanting money and success and all the material things more than how I could possibly get there. As a result, I was stuck in the focus / desire phase not deserving what I wanted.

YOU DESERVE IT is based on serving others and adding value. It reminds us to shift focus from inwards to outward and from what you can get to what you can give.

I was subconsciously running an early concept of YOU DESERVE IT when I began my career in sales. Yes, I was motivated by money and of earning more, but I realised that to be liked by customers, to add value to them and to prove myself reliable were the keys to selling more.

I realised that earning more meant selling more and selling more meant serving more. Serving more meant focussing on others and adding value. The more I served, the more I sold and the more I earned. As such, serving was my focus. Not money. By shifting my focus away from money and what I could get, to what value I could add for others, I still ended up benefitting and being rewarded.

I call this the YOU DESERVE IT paradox.

I'll explain with an example:

Let's consider now that I wish to start a business and make a lot of money. The shift in thinking I need to make is that I need to consider how to serve more first of all, rather than just focussing on making money. What can I do for others that will add value to them?

It could be anything large or small, the important part is that I have to add value and serve them in a way they either can't or won't do for themselves.

When you add value you receive value back, either in the form of reciprocity or in the form of growing as an individual. Serving more, then means selling more. I would need to think about how I could sell a product or service based on the value I am able to add to my customer, focussing on their needs first, not my desire to sell.

Seek first to serve, then to sell.

A fine example here is Google. Google operate a "freemium" business model. Much of the value they add is available for free, from Gmail to YouTube to Google itself and so much more.

freemium
/ˈfriːmɪəm/

noun

a business model, especially on the Internet, whereby basic services are provided free of charge while more advanced features must be paid for.

They have added value to millions if not billions of people since they began reorganising the way the world stores and searches for its data.

They have done this to serve, to add value.

Even on Google's corporate website they state the following:

> **Focus on the user and all else will follow.**
> Since the beginning, we've focused on providing the best user experience possible. Whether we're designing a new Internet browser or a new tweak to the look of the homepage, <u>we take great care to ensure that they will ultimately serve you, rather than our own internal goal or bottom line.</u> Our homepage interface is clear and simple, and pages load instantly. Placement in search results is never sold to anyone, and advertising is not only clearly marked as such, it offers relevant content and is not distracting. And when we build new tools and applications, we believe they should work so well you don't have to consider how they might have been designed differently.
> http://www.google.com/about/company/philosophy/

By serving in this way, for free, Google has proven itself to be a reliable, trustworthy company and a source of massive value for internet users across the globe.

Over time, the "Freemium" model has created a loyal user base that will possibly never move away from using Google for search in their lifetime. These potential lifetime users are loyal because Google sought to serve first, to add value, and then to consider selling later on.

youdeservethisbook.com

The value Google adds is repaid in loyalty which over time becomes revenue. Google are one of the most valuable companies and brands in the world at the time of writing. Had Google sought to sell first, to charge us to use their extremely powerful services, I'm sure they would not enjoy such universal appeal; they may not even still be in business.

By adding value and asking nothing in return, they laid the foundation for one of the fastest growing and largest companies the world has ever seen, as well as a new way of doing business through the "Freemium" model.

Google took their potentially lifetime loyal user base and then set out to monetise them selling targeted advertising to businesses. Google leveraged the number of users they had, along with the data they were searching for, to sell billions of dollars of advertising annually and to become the number one dominant player in their marketplace. This was only possible by focussing on serving first, rather than profit.

This is textbook YOU DESERVE IT.

You cannot argue that Google does not deserve the success it enjoys. Years of adding value and years of innovation provided for free has left them in a position to be rewarded for the value they have added. They deserve it.

The difference was their approach.
They sought to serve first and to reap the rewards later.

Back to my example, once I have decided how to add value to my customers, I can, nay I must, find a way of delivering some of that value for free. I must find a way to serve (not sell) my customers in the first instance.

If I produce a widget which is the fastest, most efficient widget in the world, it means nothing until customers can experience the value it can add to them. Free trials, taste tests, free samples are examples of this – but they tend to be limited by time. Finding a way to add value to customers, for the foreseeable future, for free (like Google) is a more robust way to harness the power of YOU DESERVE IT.

Ensuring you can add value to your customers for free in a non-time-limited way demonstrates a commitment to them. It

youdeservethisbook.com

demonstrates that you are looking to serve them first and not sell them. You want to help them more than you want their money.

Remember, people are more important than money.

This is not to say you establish a pro bono or charitable business; far from it. Adding value for free and charging for other components or services is the effective way to monetise YOU DESERVE IT. Adding value breeds loyalty, goodwill and encourages customers to spread the word about your business. If someone adds genuine value to you and asked nothing in return, you feel inclined to "repay" this kindness and are more likely to recommend them to your circle of influence.

I took this approach in my own selling. My target was to sell as many vehicles as possible, but I knew my real target was to help as many customers as possible. My real target was to help grow my clients' businesses in any way I could, to serve them first, not sell them. If I served first, added value, proved myself reliable and professional, then they would look upon me favourably when they did need to buy (the Freemium model.) I'd provide market insight, feedback, ideas, and tips, anything I could that would potentially be of value to my customers. From how to target customers using Search Engine Optimisation to finding contacts at other (rival) suppliers, I did anything I could to help and to serve.

My ethos was and still is that I am here to serve first, and sell second.

This was not a quick fix approach to sales, it took time to establish, but like the Chinese Bamboo tree in Chapter 11, I knew that if I planted enough seeds and kept nurturing them, that eventually I would be rewarded. The rewards were worth working for and could continually be harvested.

It also differentiated me. I was seeking to serve, there was no "hard sell" – there was no pressure, no aggression. Just a deep desire to be of value and to ask nothing in return.

There was no specific day when things changed, but gradually my sales and my performance began to grow exponentially. Referrals to other new clients poured in, repeat business increased exponentially, deals were struck, sales were made, targets were smashed, and people were served. The value I had added had begun to come back to me.

Remember, add value, become more valuable.

youdeservethisbook.com

Not once had I "sold" anything to anyone. I made sure there was never any pressure. I'd present "potential opportunities" to clients with a "take it or leave it" approach. There was great internal pressure on me to sell and perform, but I knew that if that pressure reached my customers it would destroy the freemium approach and shift focus away from adding value and back to "sales" and money. It's like trying to pick fruit before its ripened.

I had customers ordering 10 units a year and others 500+; they were handled with equal respect and given equal opportunities. Focussing away from money and towards adding value meant it didn't matter the size of my customers, it only mattered what value I could add for them.

This meant I would benefit when smaller customers expanded over time and ordered more. I was with them from the beginning adding value and helping them to grow, when most other salespeople perhaps wouldn't have bothered due to poor sales figures; my loyalty to them was reciprocated when the customer was able to do so.

I was being Selfmore years before I knew what it meant. The good news here was that seemingly small customers overnight became enormous customers. If I had focussed on how "little" they bought rather than adding value to them, then they may have remained small customers to me. This differentiated me from my colleagues.

The YOU DESERVE IT approach to sales left me selling tens of millions of pounds of product each year at my peak. I never missed a target in all of my time in sales. NEVER.

Focussing on adding value levelled the playing field; it allowed things to flourish in a healthy, long term, sustainable manner, which is exactly what I needed to meet my targets.

Had I focussed on the short term, the quick sales and on the money and the targets, then my success would have been limited – and perhaps a lot more stressful too.

Sales is about serving and serving is about people.

Help enough people get what they want and you will find yourself getting what you want – and more importantly what you deserve.

youdeservethisbook.com

10 things to remember

1. YOU DESERVE IT is selling, selling is serving.
2. When you add value, you become more valuable.
3. Freemium is providing products or services for free at the front end and having another element which is paid for.
4. The YOU DESERVE IT paradox is focussing solely on what you want to deserve with no regard for other factors – it can be counter-productive.
5. Focus on adding value, not selling.
6. Serving is about people.
7. Selfmore is the act of helping others to achieve their goals but with an eye kept firmly upon achieving your own goals.
8. People are more important than money.
9. The value you add comes back to you.
10. To succeed in sales, focus on people, focus on serving, not selling.

youdeservethisbook.com

Exercise – Persuasion

Find someone in your close circle. A colleague, family member or friend. Attempt to persuade them to do something differently using the power of positivity. Be positive, accentuate the benefits of the new activity and be enthusiastic about it. It could be something small such as going out to a movie or event they wouldn't usually go to, or for them to help you with something or lend you something. Whatever it is, the outcome must be positive rather than negative for the other person.

Example
Before becoming a coach, speaker and author I was a successful sales account manager. I realised that selling the positive outcomes was the best way to get my clients to buy.

Ask yourself:

- What's the positive outcome for the other party?
- How can I make this appealing to them?

Guidance
We are not only more persuasive than we believe, but also more open to persuasion that we believe. Persuading somebody to do something using the positives is far more motivating than using the negatives. When you seek to add value and benefit to the other party, you are beginning to experiment with being Selfmore.

Tip
Pick something small to begin with and build your confidence – choosing new food on a menu, seeing a different film, something small and recreational is a great place to start.

What you'll need
A friend or colleague who is open to change.

Duration
1 day

When completed, ask yourself:
How easy was it to persuade the person? The power of positivity versus negativity is a powerful one. Positivity invites openness and suggestibility, negativity puts up barriers.

19 – Unsubscribe

How to un-deserve it.

Thank You

You have been successfully removed from this subscriber list. You will no longer hear from us.

 Did you unsubscribe by accident? Click here to re-subscribe.

- What could you "un-deserve" if you could?
- Why do YOU DESERVE IT in the first place?

Whilst it's important to know how to deserve things, it can sometimes be more important to know how to un-deserve things. In this chapter we'll look at how I gave up working on evenings and weekends using a step by step process anyone can follow.

YOU DESERVE IT is based on cause and effect. It takes no prisoners and there are no special favours or extenuating circumstances. As such, you can deserve things that you don't actually want. The things you deserve and don't want are almost always negative – debt, ill health, poor career.

There is almost certainly one or even a number of things in your life right now which you feel you don't deserve (but actually do). From debt to bad relationships and obesity, being passed over for promotion and so much more. All of these are undesirable circumstances – but they aren't un-deservable.

Many undesirable things are deserved through lack of action or lack of taking responsibility.

Remember, inaction is action and indecision is decision. Failing to act to take control of your health, your finances or whatever is going wrong is actually committing to allowing them to deteriorate. This is what I call a Hidden Choice.

It's hard to accept this is the case, or to even understand that choosing not to act is opting for a potentially negative outcome. But this is reality. Your action (or inaction) deserves the outcome. By not acting, you are deserving the negative outcome – you just don't want it.

"If you are willing to do only what's easy, life will be hard. But if you are willing to do what's hard, life will be easy."
T Harv Eker

Whilst this book focuses on how to deserve things, this chapter focuses on those things you already have in your life which perhaps you don't want.

Trying to deserve things involves getting out there, taking action and looking forward; quite the opposite is being mired in a circumstance or life you don't feel you deserve and not knowing why this is the case or what to do about it.

When I started my YOU DESERVE IT journey and ultimately this book, there were many things in my life I felt I truly didn't deserve. I was "stuck" in my job; unsure of what else I could do, but desperate to make changes. I'd felt like I'd worked hard and was doing all I could and didn't deserve to be "stuck" and so unhappy.

The victim mentality of feeling I didn't deserve to be stuck actually helped me to stay stuck as it cemented the incorrect notion that I was not responsible and thus unable to change my situation.

You are always response-able. You can always change either the situation, or your reaction to the situation.

When I broke down why I found myself stuck I realised that I hadn't taken much appropriate action towards my goals at all. I was a victim of "the settling" from Chapter 1. I'd let circumstances decide my fate.

Appropriate action is something that will help advance you towards your goals in some way. This seemingly small difference over time makes the difference between success and failure. Success is incremental.

Action alone leads to the settling, appropriate action leads you towards YOU DESERVE IT.

I'd read a lot of books and consumed a lot of videos about speaking and being a coach, but not acted upon them and taken appropriate action to move forward. I wasn't at my desired destination because I hadn't even pulled off the driveway yet. In hindsight it was obvious and made perfect sense. At the time, however, it was a mystery.

I wanted to become a coach / speaker / author, but felt trapped in my job as though someone else was responsible for holding me back. It wasn't until I accepted that I deserved to be in my current position that I was able to begin to un-deserve it.

You can't un-deserve something until you accept that YOU DESERVE IT.

I accepted that I deserved to be where I was, but needed to find out exactly how I got there so I could begin to un-deserve the things I didn't want.

To get some ideas, I flipped the situation on its head. If I was already a coach / speaker / author what would I have had to have done to deserve to be in this position?

I'd have talks, presentations, a book, a website and clients for starters. I would have established exactly what my subject matter would be, refined it, delivered it and gained experience giving talks, perhaps even for free to begin with. I would have taken public speaking lessons, brushed up on my presentation skills, and maybe even joined a networking club. And more besides. When I started to consider everything I could have done to deserve to reach my goal, I looked again at what I'd actually done...

The problem was obvious. I'd thought about it a lot, talked about it a lot, even read some relevant books and watched some online talks and videos.

But that was it.

"A little less conversation, a little more action please."
Elvis Presley

I deserved to make no progress as I'd taken no appropriate action.

It was disheartening to realise I'd been fooling myself into thinking I was "working" on my dream when I was just treading water. I was avoiding risk and playing not to lose rather than playing to win.

To contrast this, my job received my full attention nearly 24/7. I'd submitted new ideas, created countless opportunities, brought on new clients and gave it my all. As a result I was successful at my job (surprise!).

Writing these words it's obvious my actions and my goals were incongruous. I was working so hard at my job that I had little or no time and focus to work on myself. By working hard on one thing I had the perfect excuse to avoid the potential failure of pursuing my dream. The perfect excuse to not act. I was avoiding being responsible.

> *"Learn to work harder on yourself than you do on your job"*
> **Jim Rohn**

I wasn't avoiding failure, it was worse. I was avoiding trying – which is the biggest failure of all.

I was oblivious to this at the time and it cost me so much wasted time and energy that I was determined to include in this book a structure to help you to identify and eliminate the unwanted things from your own life and to ensure your actions and your goals are congruous.

So here we go.

Step 1 Choose something you don't feel you deserve

Choose something in your life you feel you don't deserve (just one thing at a time please). It must be something you have *some* influence over – so war, illness and other situations caused by outside factors are excluded.

You have an influence over so much more than you think so don't be too quick to decide what you aren't responsible for. Even if you can't influence something, you can be responsible for how you react to it.

Step 2 Admit YOU DESERVE IT
Even if you don't believe you do deserve it, and even if it's difficult to even think about – admit YOU DESERVE IT. Take responsibility for your actions and where you find yourself today. If it's a situation you haven't caused then you deserve the results of how you respond to the situation.

Admitting and realising YOU DESERVE IT is the only way forward as it allows you to be responsible for it. If you don't take responsibility, if you blame others or circumstance, you can't un-deserve it.

Step 3 Determine what is causing it
Determine what is causing you to deserve this thing you don't want. What could you have possibly done to have deserved this outcome? This bit takes real courage. To make it less painful you could imagine a friend has deserved something in their life which they don't want and you are helping them to un-deserve it.

Reframing your problem to that of "a friend" creates emotional distance and provides clarity.

To find out what is causing you to deserve this outcome you can also consider that if you did want to deserve this outcome, from a fresh beginning, what would you have to do to reach the goal? List as many possible causes as possible – try not to self-edit.

Step 4 Choose the most likely cause from your list
Choose **one** item from the list of possible causes in step 3 that you feel is most responsible for the outcome. The one thing that if you changed it, would have the biggest impact.

Step 5 Identify specific action
Identify the specific actions linked to the main possible cause from Step 4 and eliminate, modify or replace them.

YOU DESERVE IT is cause and effect. Change or remove the cause and you change or remove the effect.

youdeservethisbook.com

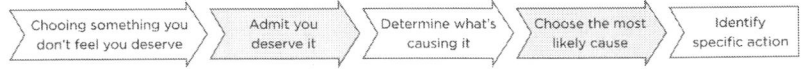

In my examples of giving up the news and giving up checking work email after hours (Chapter 16 and Chapter 17), let's look at these again through the framework of un-deserve it.

Step 1 Choose something you don't feel you deserve
I felt constantly on edge, anxious and hyper-vigilant at all times. I hated the constant near paranoia of being so alert 24/7 and had no idea why I felt like this.

Step 2 Admit YOU DESERVE IT
I accepted that whatever the reason, I deserved to feel constantly alert and exhausted, double checking things and carrying out "just in case" activities. I was reinforcing my situation (albeit habitually) but nonetheless I was perpetuating things. I deserved it.

Step 3 Determine what is causing it
I drew up a list of reasons why I could feel so hyper-vigilant and on edge all the time. From my historical anxiety and bouts of low mood to diet, sleeping, news consumption, email checking, vitamins, green space and more.

When I started to consider what could be causing my feelings, I was astonished by the possibilities (rather than feeling trapped and not able to change). The list was broad.

Step 4 Choose the most likely cause from your list
Of all the items on my list, I decided that the one with the biggest impact and that I could change immediately was my news consumption.

Step 5 Identify specific action
I decided the best resolution was to eliminate the news from my daily life entirely. I would replace it with music in the car instead of radio

youdeservethisbook.com

and books instead of newspapers. The principle was to replace negativity with positivity.

Action reinforces behaviour.

I found the process clunky at first. I'd mindlessly drift onto a news website or TV news channel and fall into old habits. It took perseverance and vigilance to catch myself each time I was "lured in" by the news and to take alternative action.

To help keep myself on track I would ask myself these questions if I found myself drifting:

- What is my goal? (to be more relaxed)
- Will what I'm doing help me achieve my goal? (no)
- Do I deserve to reach my goal? (yes)
- Then why am I doing it? (I don't know!)

The answer to the last question was almost certainly "I don't know" or "out of boredom" which helped to keep perspective and stop me drifting into endless news-checking loops. I had no reason to do it. So I stopped.

Eliminating the news helped me feel more relaxed. It was replaced with music, inspiring videos and collating content for my Every Day Should Be Fun blog.

Had I not first taken responsibility for my actions, then I would have been unable to change them and the situation would have perpetuated. I would have deserved it.

"Taking responsibility" sounds like such a heavy guilt-ridden concept but the reality is, it's about choice.

If you eat a steak in a restaurant, you are responsible for having steak for dinner as you chose it. Responsibility focuses on obligation, but where there are few real obligations, there are nearly always choices; you either choose something, or choose how you react to it.

Choice and choosing are liberating words which put you in the driving seat. You are responsible, but changing your vocabulary can make all the difference.

The belief that we can't choose or can't change "the way things are" is a perceptual myth. Such thinking derives from fear; fear of failure, fear of the unknown, fear of reality, fear of taking action.

youdeservethisbook.com

Whatever the situation there will always be some part of it you can choose and control, even if that's only your response to how you deal with the situation itself.

You are always response-able.

The power of NO is another factor when looking to not deserve the things you don't want.

Most of us fear "NO". We make up stories about why we can't come to X, Y or Z party or dinner when the reality is we simply don't want to go. Saying "NO" seems to be a near socially violent act. We avoid it because we don't want to cause offence or hurt feelings but have to lie instead which is potentially worse.

It's understandable. I've done it. We've all done it. But saying no is a powerful tool when used correctly.

It's the same for habitual parts of your life, it's easier to "go with the flow" than to question if this is what you want to do or what you should be doing. No one wants to be a "trouble maker" or seen as disruptive.

When was the last time you said no to something?

Or did you say "I'm not sure" and then backed that up with a story to help further postpone the "NO" hoping to avoid the issue or for the other party to get the point without you having to say the word? Exactly.

"NO" is sometimes more important than "YES".

There are likely far more things in your life you need to say "NO" to rather than "YES" to.

"NO" is your first line of defence against deserving the things you don't want.

Do you want to come out and eat Chinese takeaway when you know you're on a diet?

"NO!"

If you're not brave enough for "NO" (it can seem a little harsh through its lack of use) then try: "NO, I'm alright thanks." You certainly don't need to provide reasons or justification. No on its own is powerful enough.

youdeservethisbook.com

If the steps to un-deserve are your means to eradicate undesirable things from your life, "NO" is the defence that will stop them getting there in the first place.

Out of a social context and back into your own framework for deserving your goals, "NO" helps you to stay on track.

Ask yourself:

- "Does what I'm about to do get me closer to my goal?"
- "If I stop doing this will I still reach my goal?"
- "Have I done everything I can to deserve this?"

"NO" to any of these questions steers you back on course and back towards focussing on taking appropriate action to deserve it.

Taking responsibility and choosing your actions deliberately are examples of self service and self-respect. If you minimize the things in life you don't want and maximise the things in life you do, then you are serving yourself. Serving is the basis of deserving and when you serve yourself, happiness is always the end result. After all: YOU DESERVE IT.

10 things to remember

1. To un-deserve, you must first admit that you deserve.
2. Inaction is a form of action.
3. The only true failure is not trying.
4. "No" is sometimes more important than "yes".
5. "No" protects you from deserving things you don't want.
6. You deserve what you settle for.
7. Play to win, don't play to not lose.
8. You can deserve things you don't want.
9. Serving yourself is about respecting yourself and adding value to yourself.
10. You are always in control – it just may not feel like it sometimes.

youdeservethisbook.com

Exercise – Undeserve

Okay, yes, well spotted, we did just illustrate this exercise in the chapter, but how likely were you to actually do it? If you're like I used to be, then it would probably never leave the page. These end of chapter activities, in particular this one, are designed to move you to act even if you are skim reading the book.

Don't skip this exercise, give it a go – what's the worst that could happen?

To know how to un-deserve something is as important, if not more important than to know how to deserve something.

There will be many things you deserve currently which you simply may not want, here we look to identify at least one of them and set about eradicating it.

Once you eliminate negative things you deserve you not only leave more room for positive things, you feel more in control and are serving yourself.

Step 1.
Choose something you don't feel you deserve. It's best to start with something small and manageable rather than heading straight for trying to un-deserve something complex.

Step 2.
Whether you believe you deserve it or not, the fact that it's in your life and that you can influence it means you do deserve it. Own that fact. Embrace the reality that you can attract unwanted things into your life.

Step 3.
If you were able to influence this situation, how could you change this influence and thus un-deserve? Essentially what is the opposite approach required to achieve the opposite outcome?

Step 4.
There are likely a myriad of possible causes for you to deserve the current situation. By simply selecting one of the possible causes,

ideally the one you believe is most likely to cause the outcome, you can ensure the highest chance of success from the get-go.

Step 5.
The final step is to take action. Select the most likely possible cause from Step 4 and eliminate it.

Tip
If you find admitting you deserve it tough, view this exercise as a scientific experiment where the outcomes are not necessarily right or wrong. We are merely exploring a theory and seeking factual evidence to prove or disprove. Try not to get caught up in emotion, try to stick to the facts.

Duration
20 minutes – 1 hour depending on complexity.

When completed, ask yourself:
Once you took ownership for the situation, how much easier was it for you to look objectively at how to resolve it?

What else could you eliminate with this process?

youdeservethisbook.com

20 – Confusion

Desire vs. Deserve.

- Do you really deserve it, or do you just really want it?
- Can you deserve without desire?

In this chapter, we'll look at the difference between desire and deserve. We'll acknowledge what a great divide there can be between desire and deserve, and how you need to stay focussed on facts, reality and the here and now.

Desire and deserve are two very different things.
One can work without the other, but they work best together.

desire
/dɪˈzaɪə/

noun

1. a strong feeling of wanting to have something or wishing for something to happen.
   "he resisted public desires for choice in education"
   synonyms: wish, want, More

verb

1. strongly wish for or want (something).
   "he never achieved the status he so desired"
   synonyms: wish for, want, long for, yearn for, crave, set one's heart on, hanker after/for, pine for/after, thirst for, itch for, be desperate for, be bent on, have a need for, covet, aspire to; More

Let me explain.
To desire is to "strongly wish for or want something"; it's that feeling you get when you see a jumper or a person that you really like and you want them for yourself.

Desire is easy.

youdeservethisbook.com

We can all desire; it takes no action (other than thinking) and is a purely selfish act of thinking about what we like and what we want. It's unlimited. Desire is all "me, me, me".

deserve
/dɪˈzɜːv/

verb

do something or have or show qualities worthy of (a reaction which rewards or punishes as appropriate).

To deserve is to "do something or have or show qualities worthy of a reaction". In lay terms this means to earn something or be entitled to something through your own efforts.

Deserving is more difficult.

It requires action and often considered thought or planning. Deserving is largely based on serving others and adding value to them, it's a more selfless act (see "Selfmore" Chapter 3). Deserve is more "you, you, you".

- There is no limit on what you can desire; by definition it's based on thought and as such it's limitless.
- There is a limit on what you can deserve as it's based on your abilities and actions.

This disparity is where the trouble begins. It explains why so many of us desire so much and yet deserve so little of it.

If it's so easy to want things, then why is deserving so much more complex? It's this confusion, not aided by the similarity in how both words are spelt, that can make us expect deserve to be as easy as desire.

We may feel that we deserve more than we currently have, but the reality is that we don't. If we did, we'd have it already.

That's not to say you can't deserve more and it certainly doesn't mean you don't deserve what you already have. The point is that feeling you deserve more is simply desire in disguise.

youdeservethisbook.com

You don't deserve more. You want more.

I realise now that I used to subconsciously feel that the longer I wanted something, the more I felt I deserved it. It was almost as though I expected the thinking to make a difference. This is the Hope Bias.

An excess of desire doesn't create deserve.

If you feel you deserve something, but don't get it, you can feel resentful. I wanted to be happy and to leave my job, but I didn't deserve to achieve it at that point. As such I concluded my job was terrible and I was trapped; where actually the job was comfortable and I was choosing to stay there.

Feeling resentful means you are less likely to take positive action and adapt from such a negative headspace. You will be in a victim mentality and victims are not response-able.

In order to deserve, it helps to be in a positive frame of mind; open to opportunities and generous to the thought of helping (serving) others.

By desiring alone, you place yourself in a negative spiral which can ultimately take you further from where you want to be and you get your hopes up. This is what happened to me.

When it comes to deserve – there are no sob stories or extenuating circumstances. If you're having a tough time at the moment, you don't deserve a "lucky break" (not that luck exists but that's another story; Chapter 13), you don't deserve any special treatment. You desire it.

Just as if things are going well, you don't deserve a "lucky break" or something negative to happen just because things are going well. This is a common misconception; that the world exists in balance and will "restore balance" when bad things have happened.

Desire and deserve are an issue of perception. You see the world in a certain way based on your thoughts, feelings, experiences and more besides…

If you've had some bad news or something bad happens to you, then you don't deserve something good to counterbalance it – it's just not the way YOU DESERVE IT works. It's not the way life works.

You want something good to happen, we all want good things.

If you consider why you feel you deserve something good to happen, you will find your answer to be along the lines of "because I deserve a break" or "I've been having a tough time". It's based on emotion rather than fact. If I asked you for factual evidence to prove you deserved it, I suspect you would struggle.

YOU DESERVE IT doesn't work like this.

Making the distinction between desire and deserve can save you years of potential disappointment and heartache. I wanted material success for a long time and latterly I desired to become a coach / speaker / author. I thought about it long and hard for years (about 10 years to be exact). But that was all I did – I just thought about it, I took no appropriate action.

I didn't deserve it. I desired it.

With my personal history, I felt somewhat "owed" by life; 10 years on it turns out this was a considerable error in judgement to make and one that has kept me well away from the life I desired so much.

I'd suffered living in a broken home, witnessing failed suicide attempts, verbal abuse, running away from home at 14 with my mum and brother, the suicide of a parent, the 2004 tsunami; there were a large number of items in my "because I deserve a break" thinking which drove me to believe the world owed me a favour and I would not have to try as hard as others to achieve the same outcomes. This was an illusion – I deserved nothing.

Far from requiring less effort, having experienced so many traumas, I had to dig deep and put in more effort just to get by, let alone excel. Hundreds of hours of counselling, countless rounds of medication and endless days of depression and suicidal thoughts had to be conquered before I could even consider making some solid progress and to be approaching "normal life".

I realise now that victim mentality kills your ability to achieve. For the years I felt a victim and "owed" in some way, my achievements were limited versus what I felt I was truly capable of.

I realise now, victims don't deserve it.

There was always a seemingly invisible wall stopping me from moving forward. It was frustrating, unpleasant and self-perpetuating. I felt I deserved so much more than I had.

The truth was I didn't deserve anything more than I had. It hurt to realise it, but this was reality.

Deserve is based on causality, action, reward and fact. It's not based on sob stories and feeling sorry for yourself. I felt I deserved so many good things but none of them materialised.

After years of this I began to question why I seemed to be getting nowhere.

I was confusing desire with deserve.

In doing so, I had an excuse for any potential failure (I was taking no action and thus no risk) and I had more fuel for my "sob story"; it was a subconscious win-win but a real life lose-lose.

Perception was the key; my biased thinking was holding me back and I didn't realise it until years later.

The slow realisation that I was wasting my time wanting things but not pursuing them was the genesis of this book and of my journey.

I began to ask why if I believed I deserved so much, that I had so little of it. How could I feel so strongly about something and to be so wrong? What was missing? What was I missing?

I had infused deserve with emotion, special circumstances and a sob story. "Deserving things might work like that for other people, but I'm special and I'm owed and so things will fall into place" was the kind of skewed thought process that perpetuated my stagnation. This was my victim mentality.

If there are things in your life now which you truly believe you deserve but don't have, then I'm glad you're reading not only this book, but this chapter.

You need to ask yourself:

"If I believe I deserve XYZ, why don't I actually have it?"

Better yet, try listing the facts which prove you do deserve it.

If you are working on something to reach your goal, then it may only be a matter of time; perhaps you haven't yet done everything you need to deserve the end result. You're on your way, taking appropriate action – that's vital.

More likely, this question will force you to realise you have taken minimal or zero appropriate action toward your goal; you've simply thought about it a lot and have a desire for it. You may have even taken action, such as reading books, but what *appropriate* action have you taken to move forward?

YOU DESERVE IT isn't paint by numbers; it takes trial and error to get it right – as well as time.

After that first question, "If I believe I deserve XYZ, why don't I have it?", you may conclude you've either done nothing to directly deserve your goal, not done enough or perhaps you feel you've done all you can and are still unsure as to why you don't have what you believe you deserve.

Let's flip the question over to help shed a little more light onto the situation and eradicate any emotion or biased thinking.

Now ask yourself:

"Why do I believe I deserve it?"

This question moves you from potential victim mentality of focussing on why you don't have what you think you deserve and why the world is such a cruel and unforgiving place, to the positive reasons you do deserve it.

Past experiences, "bad luck", feeling hard done by or special in some way are not suitable answers here. Only tangible, factual evidence will suffice. I would suspect that you will flounder here, as I did. That's okay, that's the point. I believed I deserved so much because I'd had a hard time and was thus "special" – not because I had taken action. Thinking I was "owed" in this way actually kept me from action.

Deserve without action is desire.

Whatever your situation, this is universally true. With no action, you deserve nothing. If you think you deserve something but have taken no action, then it's simply desire in disguise.

Don't let desire fool you.

Desire is easy, instant and it feels good, for a while. Desire only becomes deserve when it's acted upon.

On reflection I realise that if I'd already had everything I desired, then life would be dull. If you could deserve everything you ever imagined through thought alone, the world would be an unfulfilling, empty place.

youdeservethisbook.com

This book, my own journey has been a fulfilling, trying and eye-opening experience.

If on day one I deserved everything, if I typed out the book perfectly first time in an afternoon, got speaking and coaching clients without really trying, then it would be a hollow victory.

Wherever my YOU DESERVE IT journey takes me will be all the sweeter because I do deserve it, not because I was "owed" some "good luck" or other nonsense.

You need desire to deserve.

The reality is that deserve can take time, planning and a whole lot of appropriate action. Sustained effort to reach a goal, the effort and tenacity to take on certain things in life (such as writing a book) can take everything you have to give. That's a reason to pursue them, not a reason to avoid them.

It can be a hard journey to YOU DESERVE IT. You know the destination will be worthwhile, but the real magic is in the journey.

To deserve the very best things in life takes first a desire. This desire fuels everything and keeps you motivated until you reach your goal.

youdeservethisbook.com

10 things to remember

1. Desire and Deserve are often confused.
2. You can't deserve without desire.
3. When you feel you deserve more, it's more likely that you want more.
4. When you know the difference between desire and deserve, everything changes.
5. Ask yourself – "Why do I think I deserve it?"
6. Deserve without action is desire.
7. Don't let desire fool you and keep you from what you can deserve.
8. It all starts with desire.
9. Desire is all "me me me" deserve is all "you you you" – being Selfmore helps transition from desire to deserve.
10. Desire is easy, deserve takes effort.

youdeservethisbook.com

Exercise – 100 Smiles Program

This activity focusses on making other people smile. Starting today your goal is to collect 100 smiles from those around you. Be nice, let in traffic, surprise a loved one, do a favour, impress your boss – what can you do to bring a smile to someone else's face and get you nearer the goal of 100 smiles?

Example
When I first started this, I counted 36 smiles for the day. Not quite 100, but the way those 36 smiles made me feel had me hooked. My daily focus is to get 100 smiles from those around me – I may not ever hit the magic hundred, but I'm having a lot of fun trying.

Examples include:

- Surprise gifts.
- Letting people out in traffic.
- Compliments.
- Opening doors.
- Remembering special occasions.
- Offering to help.
- Being courteous.
- Being polite.

Guidance
The world is full of genuinely nice kind-hearted people. We spend too much time on serious things, complaining, frowning, and working. Take a moment to make someone smile and you will encourage them to make others smile – and you will feel great. The small things in life, the trivial and the beautiful – they are often the source of the most happiness.

Tip
Try to get to 100 as quickly as possible to keep the momentum.

What you'll need
Notebook and pen.

youdeservethisbook.com

Duration
7 days

When completed, ask yourself:
Why stop at 100? When you set out to make people smile it's enjoyable for both parties, it invites more opportunities into your life, encourages reciprocity and just feels great!

Conclusion

We've come a long way, baby.

It's no coincidence that this book goes from confusion to conclusion. This was always the plan. Until this point there was no book dedicated to deserve. No exploration in what it means to truly deserve something. It has been covered in a psychological and academic sense, but I wanted a book which demystified the concept – something useful and accessible for everyone.

As a reader of hundreds of personal development books I wanted something that you could use in everyday life – not a hypothetical book which, although pleasing to read, would soon be discarded and forgotten about.

We all have opinions about what we deserve and don't – but that's the point. YOU DESERVE IT cares little for opinions – it's causality and fact which decide. It may seem "harsh" or "unfair" but it's the way it all works – whatever happens, life goes on.

YOU DESERVE IT has been the convergence of my life experience, my own struggles to get what I felt I deserved in life and to eradicate the things I didn't feel I deserved. This book offers the tools and the example of my own life to explain how to deserve everything you want in your life.

Twenty chapters, hundreds of hours of work; it all comes down to these simple truths (not exhaustive, and in no particular order):

You deserve everything you have in your life right now. (Chapter 1)
When you accept that the quality of your life reflects the quality of your decisions, everything changes.

You don't deserve bad things which happen to you and aren't your fault, but you are responsible for how you respond.
Whilst you deserve your life, you don't deserve cancer, tsunamis or any other incidents which occur without your input. Although these things can be major setbacks and make

life harder, there is always a choice to be made – and that choice is always yours.

Only you can limit yourself.
It's clichéd but it's true. If you set your sights on a goal, you decide what you deem "reasonable" and you decide how dedicated you are to the cause.

"I want doesn't get", but it's a great starting point. (Chapter 15)
"I want" without action gets nothing, but having a clear image of what you do want is the vital first step in pursuing your goals and being a planner rather than a settler.

You don't deserve any more – if you did, you'd have it already. (Chapter 2)
You may feel you deserve more than you have, but until you do what is necessary you won't achieve it. It's this feeling of deserving more which drives us all to improve and to move forwards.

It's not what happens to you, it's what you do about it.
This is my personal mantra. The tsunami, the suicide or my depression could have literally killed me. We all have obstacles to face in life – it's up to you whether they are challenges to be overcome or problems which will impede you.

There are no special circumstances or sob stories – you can't negotiate with YOU DESERVE IT.
When you consider what you deserve it's an entirely subjective and, of course, biased thought. What you deserve is determined by your actions and the value you add – no amount of sob stories or self-pity will change that. This is true however "unfair" or terrible your life may seem.

To deserve you must serve. (Chapter 3)
The pinnacle of YOU DESERVE IT is an outward focus on what you can do for others, not what you are entitled to. When you understand it's give THEN receive, you are streets ahead of most people.

youdeservethisbook.com

Action is important, appropriate action is vital.
Taking action is key; too much analysis and research can waste time and leave you stuck. Your actions must be relevant to your goals otherwise you are wasting your time.

Desire is not deserve. (Chapter 20)
However much you want something, dream about it and wish for it – it will never "manifest" without a plan – the law of attraction requires ACTION.

Your biases and perception may be holding you back – focus on facts and evidence.
Become a detective. Seek the facts. Seek proof. Ignore opinions, thoughts and preconceptions which have no basis in fact.

Inaction is a form of action. (Chapter 5)
Hidden Choices were one of the key discoveries I made in writing this book. Everything is a choice, everything has a consequence. When you understand the repercussions of your actions and own it, you can make better decisions.

The Hope Bias. (Chapter 5)
This is very similar to relying on the law of attraction. The Hope Bias can mislead you to think you are "working towards" something when you aren't.

Victims don't deserve it.
Being a victim is a matter of opinion. We can choose to be victims, to seize our power and let our decisions shape our worlds or we can succumb to victim mentality, release our power and become a settler. It's a cruel world.

The Procrastination Illusion. (Chapter 2)
Spending too much time being theoretical and planning, without acting, gets you nowhere. You never move from preparation to real world and thus never deserve what you seek.

youdeservethisbook.com

> **Luck is the opposite of deserve. (Chapter 13)**
> Luck doesn't exist. Luck is a man-made concept to explain random events. If you can't control it, rely upon it or replicate it then it serves no purpose in your quest to deserve.

The concepts I discuss in this book are meant to be *actionable*; they are there to help you in your own life and not to remain simply theoretical. They come from my experiences and the setbacks and successes I have experienced in my own life. I have read far too many books and skipped over the exercises, not practised the techniques and thus stayed stuck firmly in the procrastination illusion. Life is about living, it's about taking action, taking risk, making mistakes and being human.

> **No book in the world, this one included,
> can change anything about you
> if you don't adopt some of the thinking
> and put into practice some of the ideas.**

While writing this conclusion I watched a speech about innovation by Guy Kawasaki who encouraged his audience with this phrase "don't worry – be crappy". What he means is that it's best to start and to iterate than to not start as you are waiting for everything to be perfect. Nothing will ever be perfect and you will spend your life dreaming of the day when you will finally be "ready" to begin.

> **Take it from me – you are ready right now.**

Thank you for taking the opportunity to read this book, it's no small investment of your time and I hope you have found the impetus you need to forge ahead and pursue what you feel you deserve.

Remember that whatever happens, it's decisions, not conditions, which shape our lives – it's not what happens to you, it's what you do about it. Keep moving forward, never give in, it's all on you. The time is NOW.

youdeservethisbook.com

Wishing you the very best.

James.

PS. I love to hear inspiring stories and how YOU DESERVE IT has helped readers change their lives and follow their goals. I also love comments, feedback and suggestions.

Please feel free to email me **james@jamesnewell.co**

youdeservethisbook.com

Your questions answered

This is potentially the most important part of the book. It helps to answer the most common questions I have been asked and have asked myself throughout my YOU DESERVE IT journey.

I had lots of questions when I started out about what I did and didn't deserve; this book was my attempt at finding the answers. As I conclude the book I have revisited some of the most obvious and pressing questions you are trying to answer yourself.

In the preceding chapters I go into more detail, but this is a quick reference guide which allows you to navigate the content and answer the common questions.

What do I deserve in my life?
Everything you have in your life (everything which you can influence). This does not include accidents, illness and other situations over which you have no influence or control. (Chapter 1)

Why don't I have what I think I deserve?
What you think you deserve and what you actually deserve are every different. What you think you deserve is based on perception and emotion, what you actually deserve is based on fact. (Chapter 19)

How do I deserve more?
To deserve more, you have to serve more – this means adding value, being genuine, following your passion and leaving the world in a better condition for you having been here. (Chapter 3)

Can I deserve less?
You can deserve less but something has to change. You either have to cease taking action or take different action. You may wish to "un-deserve" something you don't want. (Chapter 19)

youdeservethisbook.com

How do I un-deserve things that I don't want?

To un-deserve something you have but don't want, you need to first admit you deserve it, determine possible causes and eliminate those causes one at a time. (Chapter 19)

I have a terminal illness / have lost a loved one / am disabled / was in an accident – are you really saying I deserve this?

No. Absolutely not. This is an important point to understand.

I didn't deserve the tsunami, I don't deserve depression, anxiety or to have lost a parent to suicide – I have not influenced any of those situations.

What you do deserve is the result of how you respond to these situations. YOU DESERVE IT is about action more than circumstance – it's not what happens to you, it's what you do about it. If you let terrible things overtake you and turn to drink or drugs to cope and ruin your life then your actions have deserved the outcome. It's a cold hard truth, it's not nice to hear but it's the reality, it's the way YOU DESERVE IT works. Life can be a cruel hard place. (Chapter 6)

I don't feel like I deserve my life – why do I have it?

Your actions have brought you to where you are, you have taken appropriate action to reach a goal (Chapter 15).

This has either been intentional or circumstances have led you here, but what you deserve always reflects what you have acted upon. I was a successful salesperson but never planned to be one. I took the appropriate action to achieve the outcome but there was no master plan. Chapter 9 covers the YOU DESERVE IT disconnect which looks at the difference between what you deserve and what you think you should deserve.

youdeservethisbook.com

Glossary

I use a number of concepts in the book which I have either created, or are uncommon and may require explanation – here I have collated them for reference.

The Hedonic Treadmill (Chapter 2)

The concept of adapting to new circumstances, of always seeking more and never finding "enough". The Hedonic Treadmill is a form of "homeostasis" which is a biological term describing how equilibriums tend to be achieved when different elements interact. In other words, it's the reason you dream about having that new car / watch / house for years and when you do finally get it, you find yourself dreaming about something else – you're not happier or more satisfied as you thought you might be, so are back to seeking the next "thing" to make you happier.

"The Planning" and "The Settling" (Chapter 1)

Planning is considering what you want and then working out how to get there, adjusting course en route to your destination. Settling is letting circumstances dictate the destination.

- Planning leads you to deserve what you want.
- Settling leads you to deserve what you get.

Gewüsst Wie (Chapter 11)

German for "know-how", Gewüsst Wie is a combination of your experience, knowledge and skill. Gewüsst Wie comprises of the following five elements, with Desire to improve being the most important as it's the driver for growth and change.

- **Experience** Gaining experience from actually doing a task repeatedly.
- **Knowledge** The knowledge gained from previous successes and failures.
- **Skills** The skills developed as a result of repetition.

youdeservethisbook.com

- **Personality** How you utilise your Experience, Knowledge and Skills is vitally important. Do you harness it or do you neglect it?
- **Desire to improve** Gewüsst Wie is strongest when it's created from a desire to improve and to serve others (kaizen).

Kaizen (Chapter 11)
Kaizen is a Japanese business philosophy of continuous improvement of working practices and personal efficiency.

Appropriate action (Chapter 5)
Action that will help advance you towards your goal rather than indiscriminate or vague action which keeps you busy but gets you nowhere.

To check if your action is appropriate, ask yourself:

- "Will this honestly help me towards my ultimate goal?"
- "Can I prove this will move me towards my goal?"

Or:

- "If I haven't achieved what I want is this action honestly helping me?"

The Hope Bias (Chapter 5)
The Hope Bias is the erroneous belief that by thinking about something for a long time, you will eventually deserve it as you've "invested so much time in it". This is despite taking minimal or no appropriate action towards truly deserving it. Hope is important to keep you motivated but hope alone will not help YOU DESERVE IT.

Responsible / Response-able
The word responsible breaks into response-able, able to choose your response. It's not what happens to you, it's what you do about it.

youdeservethisbook.com

Selfmore (Chapter 3)

Different to selfless, Selfmore is the act of helping others to achieve their goals but with an eye kept firmly upon achieving your own goals. Selfless is concerned with others and having no concern for oneself.

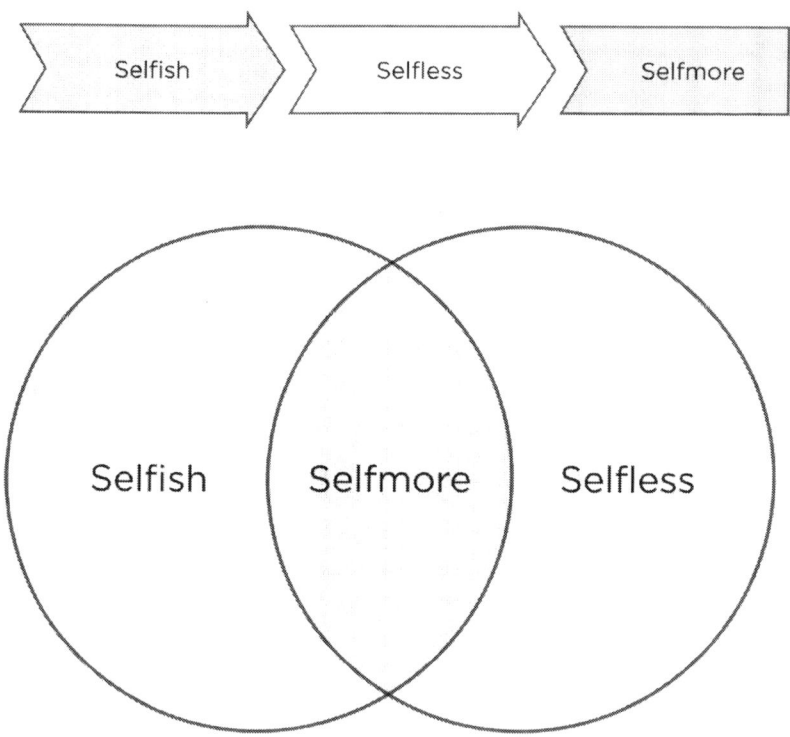

YOU DESERVE IT blueprint (Chapter 14)

A collection of boundaries and preconceived notions we feel confined within when it comes to deserving things. The sense of what you do or don't deserve and of what you could possibly deserve are defined by your blueprint. Your YOU DESERVE IT blueprint can be limiting or empowering – many factors combine to the overall picture.

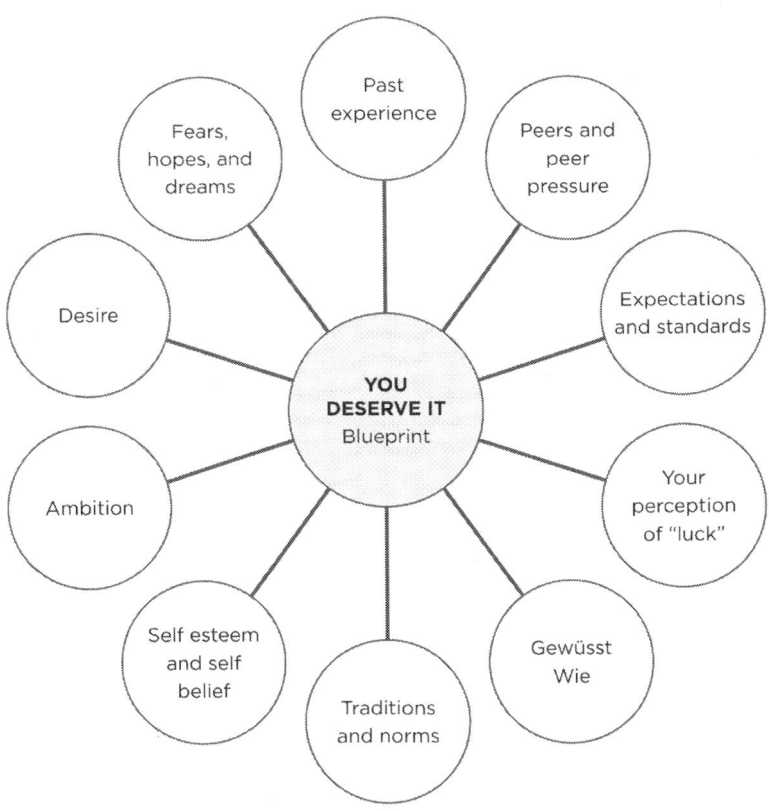

youdeservethisbook.com

Circles of truth (Chapter 15)
The interplay between what we want, what we focus on, what we act upon and the importance of adding value.

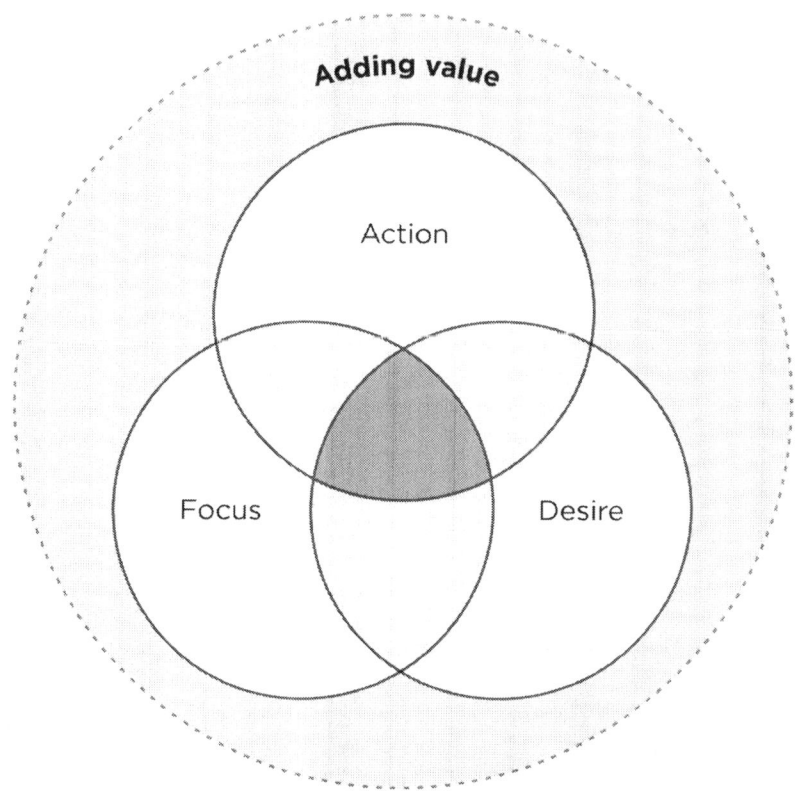

- **Desire** – This is what you want; this can be anything, from a private island to fame and fortune – your thoughts about what you want are not limited in any way as they never need to be justified or made "realistic".
- **Focus** – This is what you think you deserve. If you think you deserve something you begin to focus on it – as I did with becoming a speaker. I focussed on other speakers, authors

and talks seeking to learn more about it. What you focus on and what you think you deserve are limited by your YOU DESERVE IT blueprint.
- **Action** – Appropriate Action is the key. Appropriate Action comes from knowing what you want and understanding how to get it. Action alone is no good – it must be appropriate.
- **Adding value** – The secret ingredient to YOU DESERVE IT is to look at life through the lens of adding value to others whilst getting what you want (also known as Selfmore). If you can add value to others whilst achieving your goals then YOU DESERVE IT.

YOU DESERVE IT Paradox (Chapter 18)

Focussing on what you want to deserve with no regard for other consequences can be counter-productive. An example would be to focus exclusively on making profit in business, at the cost of the quality of your product or service. A poor quality product or service will not sell as well, which leads to less profit. Such "unintended consequences" are explored in "The Cobra Effect" in Chapter 9.

It's best to focus on serving others first and then on what you want. By ignoring adding value or serving others, you massively limit your potential success.

To deserve within your means (Chapter 5)

The notion that you must serve before you deserve. You must add value before you can receive value.

By deserving outside of your means you obtain something you don't deserve and cause issues such as financial debt or contempt of others. To deserve outside your means is to put yourself and your wants first (selfish), which goes against the principles of YOU DESERVE IT (Selfmore).

The YOU DESERVE IT Mindset (Chapter 10)

Taking responsibility for not only the things you can influence and thus deserve, but also the things outside of your control (such as the tsunami for me).

Being responsible for how you deal with truly undeserved events is how you turn tragedy to triumph.

youdeservethisbook.com

Reticular Activating System (Chapter 7)

There is a part of the brain known as the RAS (Reticular Activating System) and its function is primarily to regulate the sleep–wake transition. It also controls what you focus on.

With so many stimuli, light, sound, taste, touch and so many distractions – TV, Internet, news, books etc., the RAS helps us to filter out what we do and don't want to see.

It's because of your RAS for example that if you bought a new car in blue, then you suddenly notice just how many blue cars there are on the roads. The number of blue cars hasn't necessarily changed, but your awareness of them has.

The Circle of YOU DESERVE IT (Chapter 3)

Not to be confused with the Circles of Truth, the Circle of YOU DESERVE IT illustrates how adding value and serving others creates a self-perpetuating cycle of improvement.

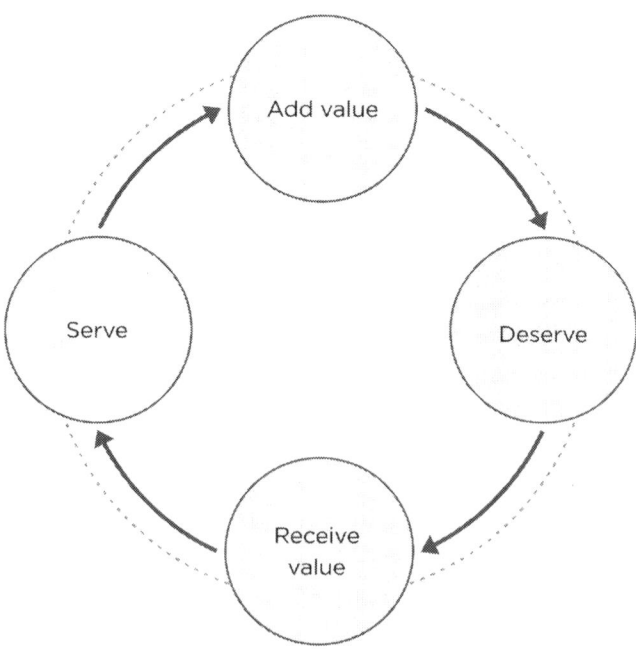

youdeservethisbook.com

Playing to not lose (Chapter 5)

When you play to not lose, instead of playing to win, you are naturally conservative in your actions and your outlook. By seeking to not lose, you limit your potential gains dramatically and focus more on protecting what you have than what you may be able to obtain. You deserve more when you play to win rather than playing to not lose.

Return on Time (Chapter 6)

We are familiar with Return on Investment (ROI) in a monetary sense. We measure how much we receive back versus how much we put in. Return on Time applies this logic to time. If you invest X hours in an activity what do you expect the reward to be? As time is infinitely more valuable than money, such analysis can help you correct your priorities and behaviours when it comes to time management.

Learned Helplessness (Chapter 7)

A condition in which a person suffers from a sense of powerlessness, arising from a traumatic event or persistent failure to succeed. It is thought to be one of the underlying causes of depression.

Methodology Bias (Chapter 8)

By having certain thoughts and opinions about the world around me – I look for things which affirm my beliefs rather than challenge them.

The Confirmation Bias (Chapter 13)

Confirmation bias, also called my side bias, is the tendency to search for, interpret, or recall information in a way that confirms one's beliefs or hypotheses.

The Procrastination Illusion (Chapter 2)

The Procrastination Illusion occurs when you think, plan, want, dream and research the things you want but take no appropriate action towards them. You remain theoretical in your approach, or take small inappropriate action which is unlikely to advance you.

youdeservethisbook.com

YOU DESERVE IT Disconnect (Chapter 9)

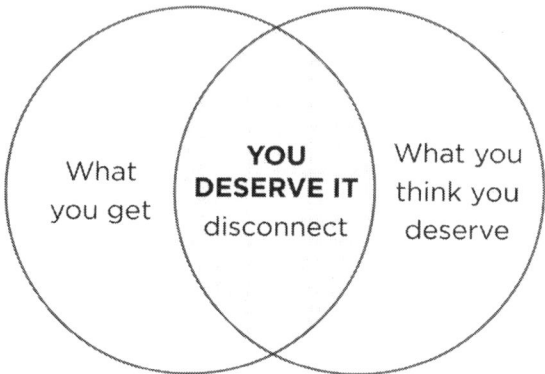

Anything you think you deserve, but don't get and anything which you get which you don't think you deserve fall into the YOU DESERVE IT disconnect.

Establishing the reason for the disconnect is crucial to moving forward.

Parkinson's Law (Chapter 17)

The notion that work expands so as to fill the time available for its completion. An example would be if you have one week to write an essay it will take you a week, if you have 48 hours you will be able to complete it in 48 hours.

The Law of Unintended Consequences (Chapter 9)

Unintended consequences are "Outcomes that are not the ones intended by purposeful action".

With the best plan, focussed action and the best intentions, you can never control 100% of the outcome – there are just too many factors at play.

Unintended consequences are grouped into three types:

1. A positive, often called luck or serendipity.
2. A negative, often called bad luck or misfortune.

3. A perverse effect, you achieve the exact opposite of what you aimed for – also known as the "Cobra Effect".

Imposter Syndrome (Chapter 9)
Imposter syndrome is a psychological phenomenon in which people are unable to internalize their accomplishments.

Despite external evidence of their competence, those with the syndrome remain convinced that they are frauds and do not deserve the success they have achieved. Proof of success is dismissed as luck, timing, or as a result of deceiving others into thinking they are more intelligent and competent than they believe themselves to be.

Serving yourself
Having respect for yourself, looking after yourself. Serving yourself is recognising that we all deserve a certain level of respect, love, attention and care no matter what we do or don't do.

Abundance Mindset (Chapter 14)
Steven Covey coined the idea of abundance mentality or abundance mindset, a concept in which a person believes there are enough resources and successes to share with others. He contrasts it with the scarcity mindset (i.e. destructive and unnecessary competition), which is founded on the idea that, if someone else wins or is successful in a situation, that means you lose. Individuals with an abundance mentality reject the notion of zero-sum games and are able to celebrate the success of others rather than feel threatened by it.

The Hidden Choice (Chapter 5)
When you take no action or make no decision. Your inaction or indecision is actually a choice toward the outcome that the inaction and indecision brings. You may not seek or want this result, but you have "chosen" it and thus it's a "Hidden Choice".

Examples:

- Not choosing to eat healthily is a "Hidden Choice" to eat unhealthily.

youdeservethisbook.com

- Spending beyond your means is a "Hidden Choice" to accumulate debt.

The Five Principles

This is a book filled with strategies, techniques, exercises and real world examples of deserving the life you want and eradicating the rest.

The YOU DESERVE IT concept can be reduced to five key principles which can help navigate any situation and whatever life throws at you.

1. You deserve your current situation.

The most important part of YOU DESERVE IT, and arguably the hardest, is the ability to take ownership for your current situation.

Your life is a result of choices you have made and action you have taken (or not taken).

You deserve your current situation because you are responsible for the things you cause to happen and your response to the things which happen to you.

If something has happened to you that you can't influence then you don't deserve it – and that's an important point.

Being responsible in this context means taking responsibility for a situation rather than taking responsibility for "causing" it. In this same context, responsible means your ability to choose your response.

If you don't like something, change it, if you can't change it then change the way you think about it.

It's all on you.

2. You don't deserve more than you have (yet)

You don't deserve more than you have because if you did, you'd have it already.

Recognise that you can think and feel you deserve something right now, but not actually have it. It's quite normal.

You don't have it because it is not deserved (which is tough to confront) and you feel you deserve it as you are naturally biased.

You can absolutely go on to deserve more, but if you don't have something now, then you don't deserve it now (however you feel about it).

Accept this is the case and establish what you need to do to deserve what you want.

youdeservethisbook.com

To deserve more, you have to serve more, take appropriate action and add more value.

It's all on you.

3. To deserve is to serve.
You must deposit before you can withdraw and give before you receive.

Your impact on others and the value you add to them determines what you deserve.

To deserve more than you have, you must add more value than you currently do.

You don't decide what you deserve, your actions do.

4. Be a planner. Not a settler.
To deserve what you want, you need a plan.

You need to decide upon a destination, how to get there, and you must adjust along the way.

With no plan you will react to life as it happens, you will be unlikely to reach your goals and deserve what you want.

Planners deserve what they want. Settlers deserve what they get.

5. It's all on you.
It's decisions, not conditions, which shape our lives.

We can all face tough situations we have not caused such as accident or illness.

It's your decision about how you respond to a situation which dictates what you will deserve.

Forget luck, forget fairness, focus on what you can do.

It's not what happens to you, it's what you do about it.

youdeservethisbook.com

Acknowledgements

It takes support from countless people to write a book, less still to pursue your dreams. Although I have countless people to thank for supporting me along the way – two people in particular deserve my deepest gratitude.

Firstly, my wife.

Alice has supported me and cheered me on from the very beginning. Through the years of simply not knowing what I wanted to do with my life, my anxiety and depression, to dealing with my difficult past and more.

Alice has provided the solid, steady bedrock on which our family, our home, our happiness are firmly rooted. I may have come from a broken home – but I am now part of a family, my family – and I love her more than she will ever know.

Tim.

Our journey has been amazing – your kindness, your intelligence, your willingness to challenge me has provided the catalyst to my happiness and reassured me that life can be wonderful – whatever terrible things may happen.

I can't express how thankful I am to have you in my life and the ways in which you have inspired and changed me. Without you, there would be no YOU DESERVE IT. The future is even brighter and with your help I am now living my life with purpose – I am "Amazing Every Day".

Thank you.

youdeservethisbook.com

About the Author

"To find and share inspiring ideas with those who need them, because Every Day Should Be Fun."

James Newell is a successful coach, speaker and author. Having lost a parent to suicide, survived the 2004 Asian tsunami and experienced depression and anxiety in his own life, James is no stranger to challenge and adversity.

James has been able to overcome these setbacks to become a successful sales professional and ultimately to find and follow his passion of becoming a coach, speaker and author.

The journey from broken home to coach, speaker and author has been long and challenging. The challenges and lessons learned along the way form the basis of James' message:

You can deserve whatever you want in life if you're willing to go for it. It's decisions, not conditions, which shape our lives.

Dedicating his time to helping and inspiring others, James is living his purpose and has found happiness despite the many setbacks he has faced. His goal is to inspire others to do the same and to remind them that:

It's not what happens to you, it's what you do about it.

James lives in London with his wife Alice and their children.

Find out more about James here:

www.jamesnewell.co

Find out more and access hundreds of inspiring resources:

youdeservethisbook.com

About the Author

www.everydayshouldbefun.com

youdeservethisbook.com

Made in the USA
Lexington, KY
02 May 2018